GLOBALIZATION AND ITS DISCONTENTS

Also by Saskia Sassen

The Global City

The Mobility of Labor and Capital

Losing Control

ERRATA

Page	For	Read
6, line 3	chap. 8	chap. 10
16, line 17	chap. 3	chap. 4
36, line 32	superscript 5	superscript 6
40, line 37	chap. 5	chap. 6
42, line 10	chap. 5	chap. 6
45, line 34	chapters 6 and 7	chapters 7 and 8
48, line 23	chap. 7	chap. 8
48, line 28	superscript 22	superscript 23
70, line 24	chap. 2	chap. 3
71, line 17	chap. 6	chap. 7
84, line 11	chap. 5	chap. 6
88, line 16	chapters 6 and 7	chapters 7 and 8
115, line 15	chap. 7	chap. 8
122, line 4	Table 5.1	Table 1
124, line 35	Table 5.2	Table 2
128, line 37	Table 5.5	Table 5
140, line 21	chap. 8	chap. 10

The New Press regrets the errors.

SASKIA SASSEN

GLOBALIZATION AND ITS DISCONTENTS

THE NEW PRESS
NEW YORK

ISBN 1-56584-395-9

Published in the United States by The New Press, New York
Distributed by W.W. Norton & Company, Inc., New York

The New Press was established in 1990 as a not-for-profit alternative to the large, commercial publishing houses currently dominating the book publishing industry. The New Press operates in the public interest rather than for private gain, and is committed to publishing, in innovative ways, works of educational, cultural, and community value that might not be considered sufficiently profitable. The New Press's editorial offices are located at the City University of New York.

Printed in the United States of America

9 8 7 6 5 4 3 2 1

CONTENTS

Foreword

K. Anthony Appiah

Throughout recorded history, men and women have traveled great distances – in pursuit of trade, of empire, of converts, of slaves – shaping the material and spiritual culture of many places with objects and ideas from far away. Alexander's empire molded not only the politics but the sculpture of Egypt and North India; the Mughals and the Mongols shaped great swathes of Asia; the Bantu migrations populated half the African continent. Islamic states stretch from Morocco to Indonesia; Christianity is strong on every continent; Buddhism, which long ago migrated from India into much of East and Southeast Asia, can now be found in Europe and Africa and the Americas as well. Jews, Gujaratis, Sikhs, and Chinese live in global diasporas. The traders of the Silk Road changed the style of elite dress in Italy; someone brought Chinese pottery for burial in Swahili graves. Think of the Mande merchants of the Sahel, the English, Dutch, Italian, and Iberian sailors of the Age of Adventure, or the Polynesian navigators who first populated the Pacific: we are a traveling species as much as a settled one.

We should recognize, then, the antiquity of the interpenetration of cultures and forms of life. But we must also accept that, in our century, the balance has shifted. The ratio of what is settled to what has traveled has changed everywhere. Ideas, objects, and people from "outside" are now more – and more obviously – *present* than they have ever been. Calling this process "globalization," as we often do, is all very well, but tells us little about what is novel in it or about its significance.

Saskia Sassen has deepened our understanding of the present by focusing on a range of crucial and often misunderstood political, economic, and cultural dimensions of globalization. We have learned from her work, for example, to recognize a new system of global cities (not just New York and London, but Bombay, São Paulo, and Hong Kong) and new kinds of economic regions (not only Silicon valley, but the industrial zones that sit at Mexico's border with the United States.

The essays in this volume build on her work on global cities, but they also contain thoughtful analyses of many other aspects of the new global political economy.

The global cities are important in part as points of control and centers of finance of the great transnational economic empires; but they are also localities, with particular social and material preconditions for their global role. They are not, like the cities of the past, at the hearts of geographically bounded regions whose economies they center: rather, they connect remote points of production, consumption, and finance. Indeed, as the politics of New York State regularly reminds those of us who live here, the global city can become increasingly isolated from—indeed, actively antagonistic to—a regional culture and economy.

Globilization and Its Discontents asks an important question: Why does a transnational system that is so diffuse need to have its management and finance so concentrated? Why, after all, if "knowledge workers" can "telecommute" so easily, are so many of the world's computer screens to be found crowded on desktops in a few square miles of Manhattan, Tokyo, and London? Professor Sassen teaches us to see the material and social matrices that explain, for example, New York's continuing preeminence: how that city's network of fiber optic cable, its large supply of (very cheap) domestic and other service workers, and its concentration of (very expensive) legal, accounting, and financial professionals, together explain why it is worthwhile for companies to keep certain parts of their far-flung system of production, consumption, and finance in a single locus. Others have no doubt noticed each of these elements, but Saskia Sassen limns the intricate relationships among them, deftly exploring connections between concentrations of poverty and wealth in the new global city and between the distant loci of physical production and social reproduction, where the computer chips and the migrants have their origins. Above all, she shows that the globalization of labor flows is part of the same process as the development of global finance and the global circulation of capital.

This approach leads one to think in new ways about the political challenges that the new world system faces. It is now conventional to think of the freeing of movements of finance and of trade from national regulation as one of the sources of the dynamism of a globalized economy, while at the same time insisting, in a different discourse, on the importance of maintaining nationalized systems for the regulation of migration. But if we recognize that the large supply of low-wage labor is an essential part of the economy of New York or Frankfurt and that the available supply of that labor is not to be found among citizens of the United States or Germany, then a "postnational" regulation of migration might come to seem as central a political project as the "postnational" regulation of trade and finance. (And, indeed, those who deal with the real political economy of the city already know this: the rhetoric of the law-and-order Republican mayor here in New York City is surprisingly friendly to illegal immigrants.)

Sassen's work reveals, however, that the notion that the old state system is irrelevant to the multinational corporation is a mistake. The whole framework of international commercial law depends on the courts of national systems and on systems of arbitration, both national and international, that exist at the will of states and require national systems for the execution of their decisions. As a result, it is wrong to say that the new global corporations simply elude the forms of regulation that the nation-state developed in the two preceding centuries.

Nevertheless, if the global corporation is still often within the control of the nation-state, it has many more means for evading regulation than did older forms of capitalism; and the only effective means of regulation will require transnational action. If we care about democratic values, we must explore ways of constructing a political basis for democratic action across national boundaries. The politics that regulates the democratic nation-state depends on the public discourse of print and radio and television, a discourse that is part of the nation's conversation with itself, which is rooted in the everyday interactions of families, churches, schools, universities, unions, and the like. If there is to be a new transnational politics, where are the discourses across nations within which it will be embedded? Sassen suggests that we examine the worlds of those – like the immigrants of color in the global cities of the North – who, as she says, "lack power, but now have 'presence'" (p. xxi). "A central assumption in much of my work," Sassen says, "has been that we learn something about power through its absence and by moving through or negotiating the borders and terrains that connect powerlessness to power" (p. 86).

The powerless, of course, are, in large measure, the poor. Sassen's work draws much-needed attention to the new forms of inequality that the new economy is creating. Her essays describe how the "massive investments in real estate and telecommunications" in "the downtowns of global cities and metropolitan business centers" are correlative to the lack of expenditures on the low-income inner city; how the highly educated workers in leading sections, such as finance, see their incomes rise enormously just as the wages of those who clean their offices or do their photocopying stagnate or sink. Just as Professor Sassen wants to bring together a discourse about global capital and the discourse of migration (reconceived as the globalization of labor), so she wants us to see together the business center and the impoverished inner city. These are phenomena that are occurring all over the world in the global cities, from London to Bombay, outside the North as well as in it. If there is to be a politics that addresses these problems of inequality, it will need to consider the worlds of difference represented in the global city. We must develop a transnational system of alliances if we are to deal with a political economy that, while it is rooted in national regimes, increasingly escapes national regulation.

One crucial form of cross-national affiliation that has grown up in the present is a system of feminist nongovernmental organizations and agendas. In one of the most exciting essays in this book, "Toward a Feminist Analytics of the Global Economy," Professor Sassen explores the centrality of gender in shaping migration, the transnationalization of production, and the new dynamics of inequality. She makes the surprising but (as it turns out) extraordinarily rewarding decision here to focus on what she calls the "unbundling of sovereignty," the process by which regulatory functions that used to be managed by the nation-state are transferred to "supranational, nongovernmental, or private institutions" (p. 92). The work of some of the feminist NGOs shows that this unbundling can provide new opportunities for women and women's organizations as "subjects of international law and the formation of cross-border feminist solidarities" (p. 93). Feminist analysis – and feminist practice – provide a model, then, for the kind of international civil society that will be required if a transnational politics that responds to our new situation is to develop.

I have focused so far on politics and economy; but one learns a great deal, too, from Professor Sassen's work on the diffusion of cultural forms, which many who think about the globalization of culture have neglected. The new literature on cosmopolitanism often focuses either on high culture (Salman Rushdie) or on mass or popular culture (Michael Jackson); the literature on migrants has often attended to everyday experiences of marginality among undocumented workers in North America and Europe. But Sassen's work reminds us that there are globalizing forms of elite culture (like accounting and financial practices) that are nevertheless quite everyday; and migrants (accountants, international lawyers, and bankers) who are far from the experience of marginality.

In short, this book brings together insights important to many fields: from cultural to literary studies, from feminist theory to political economy, from sociology to political science to law. It provides us with a powerful analysis of our situation and should, in my judgment, play an important part in shaping our normative responses to globalization, with its many challenges to an older political philosophy rooted in the nation-state. Professor Sassen shows us the shifting balance between the local and global and the surprising contours of the new international culture, political and material forms that are the matrix of a global economy; and in doing so she enriches our understanding of some of the most fundamental processes of our postmodernity.

PREFACE

I want to thank André Schiffrin for asking me to do this collection of essays with The New Press, and Joe Wood for all the help and good advice in executing it. It was more of a job than I had imagined. These essays, all previously or about to be published, span fifteen years of my research and bring together all the key themes in my work. Some of the pieces are slightly abridged to avoid repetition. All have been kept in their original form to capture the perspective, the knowledge, the expectations of the particular times when they were written. The updating happens through the inclusion of pieces that were written later.

In preparing this collection I was again struck by how important the support from a number of foundations and research centers has been to my work: the Ford, Tinker, and Revson Foundations, The Mexico-U.S. Center for Research (University of California, San Diego), New York University's Center for Latin American and Caribbean Studies, the Russell Sage Foundation, the Center for Advanced Study in the Behavioral Sciences (Stanford University), the Woodrow Wilson International Center for Scholars, and a variety of centers in Europe. To all of these I owe a large debt.

Finally, a very special thank you to R. Burbach. When it was too late to do anything about it, we found out that he had published a book with a similar title. In the best spirit of collegiality he said it was all right with him. I recommend his book.

1

INTRODUCTION:
WHOSE CITY IS IT? GLOBALIZATION
AND THE FORMATION OF NEW CLAIMS

Oone of the organizing themes in this collection is that place is central to many of the circuits through which economic globalization is constituted. One strategic type of place for these developments, and the one focused on here, is the city. Including cities in the analysis of economic globalization is not without conceptual consequences. Economic globalization has mostly been represented in terms of the duality of national–global where the global gains power and advantages at the expense of the national. And it has largely been conceptualized in terms of the internationalization of capital and then only the upper circuits of capital, notably finance. Introducing cities into an analysis of economic globalization allows us to reconceptualize processes of economic globalization as concrete economic complexes situated in specific places. Focus on cities decomposes the national economy into a variety of subnational components, some profoundly articulated with the global economy and others not. It also signals the declining significance of the national economy as a unitary category. To some extent it was only a unitary category in political discourse and policy; the modern nation–state has always had economic actors and practices that were transnational. Nonetheless, over the last fifteen years we can see a profoundly different phase, one where national economies are less and less a unitary category in the face of the new forms of globalization.

Why does it matter to recover place in analyses of the global economy, particularly place as constituted in major cities? Because it allows us to see the multiplicity of economies and work cultures in which the global information economy is embedded. It also allows us to recover the concrete, localized processes through which globalization exists and to argue that much of the multiculturalism in large cities is as much a part of globalization as is international finance. Finally, focusing on cities allows us to specify a geography of strategic places at the global scale, places bound to each other by the dynamics of economic globalization. I refer to this as a new geography of centrality, and one of the questions it engenders is whether this new transnational geography also is the space for a new transnational politics.

Insofar as an economic analysis of the global city recovers the broad array of jobs and work cultures that are part of the global economy though typically not marked as such, I can examine the possibility of a new politics of traditionally disadvantaged actors operating in this new transnational economic geography—from factory workers in export-processing zones to cleaners on Wall Street. This is a politics that lies at the intersection of 1) the actual economic participation of many disadvantaged workers in the global economy and 2) political systems and rhetorics that can only represent and valorize corporate actors as participants, in this regard a politics of exclusion.

If place, that is, a certain type of place, is central in the global economy, we can posit a transnational economic and political opening in the formation of new claims and hence in the constitution of entitlements, notably rights to place, and more radically, in the constitution of "citizenship." The city has indeed emerged as a site for new claims: by global capital which uses the city as an "organizational commodity," but also by disadvantaged sectors of the urban population, which in large cities are frequently as internationalized a presence as is capital. The denationalizing of urban space and the formation of new claims by transnational actors and involving contestation, raise the question—whose city is it?

I see this as a type of political opening with unifying capacities across national boundaries and sharpening conflicts within such boundaries. Global capital and the new immigrant workforce are two major instances of transnational categories/actors that have unifying properties across borders and find themselves in contestation with each other inside global cities. Global cities are the sites of the overvalorization of corporate capital and the further devalorization of disadvantaged economic actors, both firms and workers. The leading sectors of corporate capital are now global in their organization and operations. And many of the disadvantaged workers in global cities are women, immigrants, and people of color, whose political sense of self and whose identities are not necessarily embedded in the "nation" or the "national community." Both find in the global city a strategic site for their economic and political operations.

The analysis presented here grounds its interpretation of the new politics made possible by globalization in a detailed understanding of the economics of globalization, and specifically in the centrality of place against a rhetorical and policy context where place is seen as neutralized by global communications and the hypermobility of capital.[1] We need to dissect the economics of globalization to understand whether a new transnational politics can be centered in the new transnational economic geography. Second, I think that dissecting the economics of place in the global economy allows us to recover noncorporate components of economic globalization and to inquire about the possibility of a new type of transnational politics, a politics of those who lack power but now have "presence."

The essays in this book focus on four major subjects in order to develop these themes. Immigration is one major process through which a new transnational political economy is being constituted, one which is largely embedded in major cities insofar as most immigrants, whether in the United States, Japan, or Western Europe, are concentrated in major cities. Immigration is, in my reading, one of the constitutive processes of globalization today, even though not recognized or represented as such in mainstream accounts of the global economy. This is the subject of Section I.

The global city is a strategic site for disempowered actors because it enables them to gain presence, to emerge as subjects, even when they do not gain direct power. Immigrants, women, African Americans in U.S. cities, people of color, oppressed minorities emerge as significant subjects in a way they are unlikely to do in a suburban context or small town. I explore these issues, especially as they coalesce around the condition of women, in Section II of this collection.

One of the links between the new corporate world of power and the disadvantaged in large cities is the labor market, or, more pointedly, the market for labor. Section III examines the new employment regimes we see in global cities and advanced economies generally and the class alignments and inequalities they entail. Chapter 7 shows how these new inequalities in profit-making capacities of economic sectors, earnings capacities of households, and pricing in upscale and downscale markets have contributed to the formation of informal economies in major cities of highly developed countries.

A whole new arena of politics has emerged with the ascendance of subnational units, especially global cities and high-tech industrial districts, as direct actors in the international stage. Digitalization and the growing importance of electronic space for private and public activities have further relocated various components of politics away from national governments. This relocation of politics is examined in Section IV.

In this first introductory chapter, I develop the setting for the arguments presented in subsequent chapters. Here I organize my discussion in terms of questions of contestation, new class alignments, and the possibility of a new transnational politics or a denationalizing of politics.

PLACE AND PRODUCTION IN THE GLOBAL ECONOMY

Alongside the well-documented spatial dispersal of economic activities have appeared new forms of territorial centralization of top-level management and control operations. National and global markets as well as globally integrated operations require central places where the work of globalization gets done. Further, information industries require a vast physical infrastructure containing strategic nodes with hyperconcentrations of facilities. Finally, even the most advanced information industries have a work process – that is, a complex of workers, machines, and buildings that are more placebound than the imagery of the information economy suggests.

Centralized control and management over a geographically dispersed array of economic operations does not come about inevitably as part of a "world system." It requires the production of a vast range of highly specialized services, telecommunications infrastructure, and industrial services. These are crucial for the valorization of what are today leading components of capital. Rather than simply invoking the power of multinational corporations as the explanatory key of economic globalization, a focus on place and production takes us to the range of activities and organizational arrangements necessary for the implementation and maintenance of a global network of factories, service operations, and markets; these are all processes only partly encompassed by the activities of transnational corporations and banks.

One of the central concerns in my work has been to look at cities as production sites for the leading service industries of our time, and hence to uncover the infrastructure of activities, firms, and jobs, that are necessary to run the advanced corporate economy. I want to focus on the *practice* of global control. Global cities are centers for the servicing and financing of international trade, investment, and headquarter operations. That is to say, the multiplicity of specialized activities present in global cities are crucial for the valorization, indeed overvalorization of leading sectors of capital today. And in this sense such cities are strategic production sites for today's leading economic sectors. This function is also reflected in the ascendance of these activities in developed economies.[2]

The extremely high densities evident in the downtown districts of these cities are one spatial expression of this logic; another one is the recentralization of many of these activities in broader metropolitan areas, rather than universal dispersal. The widely accepted notion that agglomeration has become obsolete now that global telecommunication advances are allowing for maximum dispersal, is only partly correct. It is precisely because of the territorial dispersal facilitated by telecommunication advances that agglomeration of centralizing activities has expanded immensely. This is not a mere continuation of old patterns of agglomeration but, one could posit, a new logic for agglomeration. Information technologies are yet another factor contributing to this new logic for agglomeration. The distinct conditions under which such facilities are available have promoted centralization of the most advanced users in the most advanced telecommunications centers (Castells 1989).

A focus on the work behind command functions, on the actual production process in the finance and services complex, and on global market*places* has the effect of incorporating the material facilities underlying globalization and the whole infrastructure of jobs typically not marked as belonging to the corporate sector of the economy. An economic configuration emerges that is very different from that suggested by the concept of information economy. We recover the material conditions, production sites, and placeboundedness that are also part of globalization and the information economy (*Competition and Change* 1995).

That is to say, we recover a broad range of types of firms, types of workers, types of work cultures, types of residential milieux, never marked, recognized, or represented as being part of globalization processes. Nor are they valorized as such. In this regard, the new urban economy is highly problematic, a fact particularly evident in global cities and their regional counterparts. It sets in motion a whole series of new dynamics of inequality (Sassen 1994, Chap. 5; King 1996). The new growth sectors – specialized services and finance – contain profit-making capabilities vastly superior to those of more traditional economic sectors. While the latter may be essential to the operation of the urban economy and the daily needs of residents, their survival is threatened in a situation where finance and specialized services can earn superprofits. Going informal or subcontracting to informal enterprises is often one solution.[3]

Unequal profit-making capabilities among different economic sectors and firms have long been a basic feature of market economies. But what we see today takes place on another order of magnitude and is engendering massive distortions in the operations of various markets, from housing to labor. For example, we can see this effect in the unusually sharp increase in the starting salaries of business and law school graduates who succeed in entering the top firms, and in the precipitous fall in the wages of low-skilled manual workers and clerical workers. We can see the same effect in the retreat of many real estate developers from the low- and medium-income housing market in the wake of the rapidly expanding housing demand by the new highly paid professionals and the possibility for vast overpricing of this housing supply.

These developments are associated with a dynamic of valorization which has sharply increased the disparity between the valorized, indeed overvalorized, sectors of the economy and devalorized sectors even when the latter are part of leading global industries. This devalorization of growing sectors of the economy has been embedded in a massive demographic transition toward a growing presence of women, African Americans, and Third World immigrants in the urban workforce.

We see here an interesting correspondence between great concentrations of corporate power and large concentrations of "others." Major cities in the highly developed world are the terrain where a multiplicity of globalization processes assume concrete, localized forms. These localized forms are, in good part, what globalization is about. We can then think of cities also as one of the sites for the contradictions of the internationalization of capital, and, more generally, as a strategic terrain for a whole series of conflicts and contradictions.

A NEW GEOGRAPHY OF CENTRALITY AND MARGINALITY

The global economy materializes in a worldwide grid of strategic places, from export-processing zones to major international business and financial centers. We can think of this global grid as constituting a new economic geography of centrality, one that cuts across national boundaries and across the old North–South divide. It signals the emergence of a parallel political geography of power, a transnational space for the formation of new claims by global capital (See Sassen 1996, Chap. 2). This new economic geography of centrality partly reproduces existing inequalities but also is the outcome of a dynamic specific to current types of economic growth. It assumes many forms and operates in many terrains, from the distribution of telecommunications facilities to the structure of the economy and of employment.

The most powerful of these new geographies of centrality at the interurban level binds the major international financial and business centers: New York, London, Tokyo, Paris, Frankfurt, Zurich, Amsterdam, Los Angeles, Sydney, Hong Kong, among others. But this geography now also includes cities such as São Paulo, Buenos Aires, Bangkok, Taipei, Bombay, and Mexico City. The intensity of transactions among these cities, particularly through the financial markets, trade in services, and investment, has increased sharply, and so have the orders of magnitude involved. At the same time, there has been a sharpening inequality in the concentration of strategic resources and activities between each of these cities and others in the same country. Global cities are sites for immense concentrations of economic power and command centers in a global economy, while traditional manufacturing centers have suffered inordinate declines.

One might have expected that the growing number of financial centers now integrated into the global markets would have reduced the extent of concentration of financial activity in the top centers. But it has not.[4] One would also expect this given the immense increases in the global volume of transactions.[5] Yet the levels of concentration remain unchanged in the face of massive transformations in the financial industry and in the technological infrastructure this industry depends on.[6]

The growth of global markets for finance and specialized services, the need for transnational servicing networks because of sharp increases in international investment, the reduced role of the government in the regulation of international economic activity and the corresponding ascendance of other institutional arenas, notably global markets and corporate headquarters – all these point to the existence of a series of economic processes, each characterized by locations in more than one country and in this regard transnational. We can see here the formation, at least incipient, of a transnational urban system (Sassen 1991, chap. 7; 1994, chap. 3; Knox and Taylor 1995).

The pronounced orientation to the world markets evident in such cities raises questions about the articulation with their nation – states, their regions, and the larger economic and social structure in such cities. Cities have typically been deeply embedded in the economies of their region, indeed often reflecting the characteristics of the latter; and generally they still do. But cities that are strategic sites in the global economy tend, in part, to become disconnected from their region and even nation. This conflicts with a key proposition in conventional scholarship about urban systems, namely, that these systems promote the territorial integration of regional and national economies.

Alongside these new global and regional hierarchies of cities and high-tech industrial districts lies a vast territory that has become increasingly peripheral, increasingly excluded from the major economic processes that fuel economic growth in the new global economy. A multiplicity of formerly important manufacturing centers and port cities have lost functions and are in decline, not only in the less developed countries but also in the most advanced economies. This is yet another meaning of economic globalization.

But also inside global cities we see a new geography of centrality and marginality. The downtowns of global cities and metropolitan business centers receive massive investments in real estate and telecommunications while low-income city areas are starved for resources. Highly educated workers employed in leading sectors see their incomes rise to unusually high levels while low- or medium-skilled workers in those same sectors see theirs sink. Financial services produce superprofits while industrial services barely survive. These trends are evident, with different levels of intensity, in a growing number of major cities in the developed world and increasingly in major cities of some of the developing countries that have been integrated into the global economy.

THE RIGHTS OF CAPITAL IN THE NEW GLOBAL GRID

A basic proposition in discussions about the global economy concerns the declining sovereignty of states over their economies. Economic globalization does indeed extend the economy beyond the boundaries of the nation–state. This is particularly evident in the leading economic sectors. Existing systems of governance and accountability for transnational activities and actors leave much ungoverned when it comes to these industries. Global markets in finance and advanced services partly operate through a "regulatory" umbrella that is not state centered but market centered. More generally, the new geography of centrality is transnational and operates in good part in electronic spaces that override all jurisdiction.

Yet, this proposition fails to underline a key component in the transformation of the last fifteen years: the formation of new claims on national states to guarantee the domestic and global rights of capital. What matters for our purposes here is that global capital made these claims and that national states responded through the production of new forms of legality. The new geography of centrality had to be produced, both in terms of the practices of corporate actors and in terms of the work of the state in producing new legal regimes. Representations that characterize the national state as simply losing significance fail to capture this very important dimension, and reduce what is happening to a function of the global/national duality–what one wins, the other loses.

There are two distinct issues here. One is the ascendance of this new legal regime that negotiates between national sovereignty and the transnational practices of corporate economic actors. The second issue concerns the particular content of this new regime, which strengthens the advantages of certain types of economic actors and weakens those of others. The hegemony of neoliberal concepts of economic relations with its strong emphasis on markets, deregulation, and free international trade has influenced policy in the 1980s in the United States and Great Britain and now increasingly also in continental Europe. This has contributed to the formation of transnational legal regimes that are centered in Western economic concepts of contract and property rights.[7] Through the International Monetary Fund (IMF) and the International Bank for Reconstruction and Development (IBRD), as well as the General Agreement on Tariffs and Trade (GATT) (the World Trade Organization since January 1995), this regime has spread to the developing world (Mittelman 1996). It is a regime associated with increased levels of concentrated wealth, poverty, and inequality worldwide. This occurs under specific modalities in the case of global cities, as discussed earlier.

Deregulation has been a crucial mechanism to negotiate the juxtaposition of the global and the national. Rather than simply seeing it as freeing up markets and reducing the sovereignty of the state, we might underline a much less noted aspect of deregulation: it has had the effect, particularly in the case of the leading economic sectors, of partly denationalizing national territory (see Sassen 1996). In other words, it is not simply a matter of a space economy extending beyond a national realm. It is also that globalization – as illustrated by the space economy of advanced information industries – denationalizes national territory. This denationalization, which to a large extent materializes in global cities, has become legitimate for capital and has indeed been imbued with positive value by many government elites and their economic advisers. It is the opposite when it comes to people, as is perhaps most sharply illustrated in the rise of anti-immigrant feeling and the renationalizing of politics.

The emphasis on the transnational and hypermobile character of capital has contributed to a sense of powerlessness among local actors, a sense of the futility of resistance. But the analysis in the preceding sections, with its emphasis on place, suggest that the new global grid of strategic sites is a terrain for politics and engagement. Further, the state, both national and local, can be engaged. Although certain agencies within the state have contributed to the formation and strengthening of global capital, the state is far from being a unitary institution. The state itself has been transformed by its role in implementing the global economic system, a transformation captured in the ascendance of agencies linked to the domestic and international financial markets in most governments of highly developed countries and many governments of developing countries, and the loss of power and prestige of agencies associated with issues of domestic equity. These different agencies are now at times in open conflict.

The focus on place helps us elaborate and specify the meaning of key concepts in the discourse about globalization, notably the loss of sovereignty. It brings to the fore that important components of globalization are embedded in particular institutional locations within national territories. A strategic subnational unit such as the global city is emblematic of these conditions – conditions not well captured in the more conventional duality of national/global.

A focus on the leading industries in global cities introduces into the discussion of governance the possibility of capacities for local governmental regulation derived from the concentration of significant resources in strategic places. These resources include fixed capital and are essential for participation in the global economy. The considerable placeboundedness of many of these resources contrasts with the hypermobility of the outputs of many of these same industries, particularly finance. The regulatory capacity of the state stands in a different relation to hypermobile outputs than to the infrastructure of facilities, from office buildings equipped with fiber optic cables to specialized workforces.

The specific issues raised by focusing on the placeboundedness of key components of economic globalization are quite distinct from those typically raised in the context of the national/global duality. A focus on this duality leads to rather straightforward propositions about the declining significance of the state vis-à-vis global economic actors. The overarching tendency in economic analyses of globalization and of the leading information industries has been to emphasize certain aspects: industry outputs rather than the production process involved; the capacity for instantaneous transmission around the world rather than the infrastructure necessary for this capacity; the impossibility for the state to regulate those outputs and that capacity insofar as they extend beyond the nation – state. And the emphasis is by itself quite correct; but it is a partial account about the implications of globalization for governance.

The transformation in the composition of the world economy, especially the rise of finance and advanced services as leading industries, is contributing to a new international economic order, one dominated by financial centers, global markets, and transnational firms. Cities that function as international business and financial centers are sites for direct transactions with world markets that take place without government inspection, as for instance the euro-markets or New York City's international financial zone (i.e., International Banking Facilities). These cities and the globally oriented markets and firms they contain mediate in the relation of the world economy to nation–states and in the relations among nation–states. Correspondingly, we may see a growing significance of sub- and supranational political categories and actors.

UNMOORING IDENTITIES
AND A NEW TRANSNATIONAL POLITICS

The preceding section argues that the production of new forms of legality and of a new transnational legal regime privilege the reconstitution of capital as a global actor and the denationalized spaces necessary for its operation. At the same time there is a lack of new legal forms and regimes to encompass another crucial element of this transnationalization, one that some, including myself, see as the counterpart to that of capital: the transnationalization of labor. However, we are still using the language of immigration to describe the process.[8] Nor are there new forms and regimes to encompass the transnationalization in the formation of identities and loyalties among various population segments which do not regard the nation as the sole or principal source of identification, and the associated new solidarities and notions of membership. Major cities have emerged as a strategic site not only for global capital but also for the transnationalization of labor and the formation of transnational identities. In this regard they are a site for new types of political operations.

Cities are the terrain where people from many different countries are most likely to meet and a multiplicity of cultures come together. The international character of major cities lies not only in their telecommunication infrastructure and international firms, but also in the many different cultural environments they contain. One can no longer think of centers for international business and finance simply in terms of the corporate towers and corporate culture at their center. Today's global cities are in part the spaces of postcolonialism and indeed contain conditions for the formation of a postcolonialist discourse (Hall 1991; King 1996).

The large Western city of today concentrates diversity. Its spaces are inscribed with the dominant corporate culture but also with a multiplicity of other cultures and identities. The slippage is evident: the dominant culture can encompass only part of the city.[9] And while corporate power inscribes these cultures and identifies them with "otherness" thereby devaluing them, they are present everywhere. For instance, through immigration a proliferation of originally highly localized cultures now have become presences in many large cities, cities whose elites think of themselves as cosmopolitan, as transcending any locality. Members of these "localized" cultures can in fact come from places with great cultural diversity and be as cosmopolitan as elites. An immense array of cultures from around the world, each rooted in a particular country, town, or village, now are reterritorialized in a few single places, places such as New York, Los Angeles, Paris, London, and most recently Tokyo.[10]

I think that there are representations of globality which have not been recognized as such or are contested representations. Such representations include immigration and its associated multiplicty of cultural environments, often subsumed under the notion of ethnicity. What we still narrate in the language of immigration and ethnicity, I would argue, is actually a series of processes having to do with the globalization of economic activity, of cultural activity, of identity formation. Too often immigration and ethnicity are constituted as otherness. Understanding them as a set of processes whereby global elements are localized, international labor markets are constituted, and cultures from all over the world are de- and reterritorialized, puts them right there at the center along with the internationalization of capital as a fundamental aspect of globalization.[11] This way of narrating the large migrations of the post-war era captures the ongoing weight of colonialism and postcolonial forms of empire on major processes of globalization today, and specifically those processes binding countries of emigration and immigration.[12] Although the specific genesis and contents of their responsibility will vary from case to case and period to period, none of the major immigration countries are passive bystanders in their immigration histories.

MAKING CLAIMS ON THE CITY

These processes signal that there has been a change in the linkages that bind people and places and in the corresponding formation of claims on the city. It is true that throughout history people have moved and through these movements constituted places. But today the articulation of territory and people is being constituted in a radically different way at least in one regard, and that is the speed with which that articulation can change. Martinotti (1993) notes that one consequence of this speed is the expansion of the space within which actual and possible linkages can occur. The shrinking of distance and the speed of movement that characterize the current era find one of its most extreme forms in electronically based communities of individuals or organizations from all around the globe interacting in real time and simultaneously, as is possible through the Internet and kindred electronic networks.

I would argue that another radical form assumed today by the linkage of people to territory is the unmooring of identities from what have been traditional sources of identity, such as the nation or the village. This unmooring in the process of identity formation engenders new notions of community, of membership, and of entitlement.

The space constituted by the global grid of cities, a space with new economic and political potentialities, is perhaps one of the most strategic spaces for the formation of transnational identities and communities. This is a space that is both place centered in that it is embedded in particular and strategic locations; and it is transterritorial because it connects sites that are not geographically proximate yet are intensely connected to each other. As I argued earlier, it is not only the transmigration of capital that takes place in this global grid, but also that of people, both rich (i.e., the new transnational professional workforce) and poor (i.e., most migrant workers) and it is a space for the transmigration of cultural forms, for the reterritorialization of "local" subcultures. An important question is whether it is also a space for a new politics, one going beyond the politics of culture and identity, though at least partly likely to be embedded in it.

Yet another way of thinking about the political implications of this strategic transnational space anchored in cities is the formation of new claims on that space. As was discussed earlier, there are indeed new major actors making claims on these cities over the last decade, notably foreign firms that have been increasingly entitled through the deregulation of national economies, and the increasing number of international businesspeople. These are among the new "city users." They have profoundly marked the urban landscape. Their claim to the city is not contested, even though the costs and benefits to cities have barely been examined.

The new city users have made an often immense claim on the city and have reconstituted strategic spaces of the city in their image: their claim is rarely examined or challenged. They contribute to changing the social morphology of the city and to constituting what Martinotti (1993) calls the metropolis of second generation, the city of late modernism. The new city of these city users is a fragile one, whose survival and successes are centered on an economy of high productivity, advanced technologies, and intensified exchanges.

On the one hand, this raises a question of what the city is for international businesspeople: it is a city whose space consists of airports, top-level business districts, top of the line hotels and restaurants – a sort of urban glamour zone, the new hyperspace of international business. On the other hand, there is the difficult task of establishing whether a city that functions as an international business center does in fact recover the costs for being such a center: the costs involved in maintaining a state-of-the-art business district, and all it requires, from advanced communications facilities to top-level security and "world-class culture."

Perhaps at the other extreme of legitimacy are those who use urban political violence to make their claims on the city, claims that lack the de facto legitimacy enjoyed by the new business city users. These are claims made by actors struggling for recognition and entitlement, claiming their rights to the city (Body-Gendrot 1993).[13] These claims have, of course, a long history; every new epoch brings specific conditions to the manner in which the claims are made. The growing weight of "delinquency," for example, smashing cars and shop windows, robbing and burning stores, in some of these uprisings during the last decade in major cities of the developed world, is perhaps an indication of the sharpened inequality. The disparities, as seen and as lived, between the urban glamour zone and the urban war zone have become enormous. The extreme visibility of the difference is likely to contribute to further brutalization of the conflict: the indifference and greed of the new elites versus the hopelessness and rage of the poor.

There are then two aspects of this formation of new claims that have implications for transnational politics. One is these sharp and perhaps intensifying differences in the representation of claims by different sectors, notably international business and the vast population of low-income "others"–African Americans, immigrants, and women. The second aspect is the increasingly transnational element in both types of claims and claimants. It signals a politics of contestation embedded in specific places but transnational in character.

Globalization is a process that generates contradictory spaces, characterized by contestation, internal differentiation, continuous border crossings. The global city is emblematic of this condition. Global cities concentrate a disproportionate share of global corporate power and are one of the key sites for its valorization. But they also concentrate a disproportionate share of the disadvantaged and are one of the key sites for their devalorization. This joint presence happens in a context where the globalization of the economy has grown sharply and cities have become increasingly strategic for global capital; and marginalized people have found their voice and are making claims on the city. This joint presence is further brought into focus by the increasing disparities between the two. The center now concentrates immense economic and political power, power that rests on the capability for global control and the capability to produce superprofits. And actors with little economic and traditional political power have become an increasingly strong presence through the new politics of culture and identity, and an emergent transnational politics embedded in the new geography of economic globalization. Both actors, increasingly transnational and in contestation, find in the city the strategic terrain for their operations. But it is hardly the terrain of a balanced playing field.

NOTES

1   The analysis presented here is grounded in a detailed study of what I think of as strategic components of today's global economy. It is impossible to include this level of detail here and I refer the interested reader, the sceptic, and the critic to some of my other publications which have the necessary theoretical and empirical materials and extended bibliographies. In addition to those referred to here, see *The Mobility of Labor and Capital* (Cambridge: Cambridge University Press, 1988), and *Immigration Policy in a World Economy* (under preparation for the Twentieth Century Fund).

2   Elsewhere (1991, chap. 5) I have posited that what is specific about the shift to services is not merely the growth in service jobs but, most importantly, the increasing importance of services

in the organization of advanced economies: firms in all industries from mining to wholesaling buy more accounting, legal, advertising, financial, and economic forecasting services today than twenty years ago. Whether at the global or regional level, cities are adequate and often the best production sites for such specialized services. The rapid growth and disproportionate concentration of such services in cities signals that the latter have reemerged as significant production sites after losing this role in the period when mass manufacturing was the dominant sector of the economy.

3   Such informal arrangements can be interpreted as a negotiation between 1) these new economic trends, and 2) existing regulatory frameworks that were developed in response to older economic conditions.

4   Furthermore, this unchanged level of concentration has happened at a time when financial services are more mobile than ever before: globalization, deregulation (an essential ingredient for globalization), and securitization have been the key to this mobility – in the context of massive advances in telecommunications and electronic networks. (Securitization is the transformation of hitherto "unliquid capital" into tradeable instruments, a process that took off dramatically in the 1980s). One result is growing competition among centers for hypermobile financial activity. In my view there has been an overemphasis on competition in general and in specialized accounts on this subject. As I have argued elsewhere (Sassen 1991, chap. 7), there is also a functional division of labor among various major financial centers. In this sense we can think of a transnational system with multiple locations.

5   For example, international bank lending grew from US$1.89 trillion in 1980 to US$6.24 trillion in 1991 – a fivefold increase in a mere ten years. Three cities (New York, London, and Tokyo) account for forty-two percent of all such international lending in 1980 and for forty-one percent in 1991 according to data from the Bank of International Settlements, the leading institution worldwide in charge of overseeing banking activity. There were compositional changes: Japan's share rose from 7.2 percent to 15.1 percent and Britain's fell from 26.2 percent to 16.3 percent; the U.S. share remained constant. All increased in absolute terms. Beyond these three, Switzerland, France, Germany, and Luxembourg bring the total share of the top centers to sixty-four percent in 1991, which is just about the same share these countries had in 1980. One city, Chicago, dominates the world's trading in futures, accounting for 60 percent of worldwide contracts in options and futures in 1991.

6   In this context it is worth noting that the discussion around the formation of a single European market and financial system has raised the possibility, and even the need if it is to be competitive, of centralizing financial functions and capital in a limited number of cities rather than maintaining the current structure in which each country has a city that aspires to become a major international financial center.

7   An issue that is emerging as significant in view of the spread of Western legal concepts is the critical examination of the philosophical premises about authorship and property that define the legal arena in the West. See Coombe 1993.

8   This language is increasingly constructing immigration as a devalued process insofar as it describes the entry of people from generally poorer, disadvantaged countries, in search of the better lives that the receiving country can offer; it contains an implicit valorization of the receiving country and a devalorization of the sending country. And it lacks some of the positive connotations historically associated with immigrants.

9   There are many different forms such contestation and "slippage" can assume. See King 1996; Dunn 1994; *Social Justice* 1993. Global mass culture homogenizes and is capable of absorbing an immense variety of local cultural elements. But this process is never complete. I have found the opposite dynamic in the manufacturing of electronic components which shows that employment in lead sectors no longer inevitably absorbs workers into a labor aristocracy. Thus, Third

World women working in export processing zones are not empowered: capitalism can work through difference. Yet another case is that of illegal immigrants; here we see that national boundaries have the effect of creating and criminalizing difference. These kinds of differentiations are central to the formation of a world economic system (Wallerstein 1990).

10 Tokyo now has several, mostly working-class concentrations of legal and unauthorized immigrants coming from China, Bangladesh, Pakistan, and the Philippines, among others. This is quite remarkable in view of Japan's legal and cultural closure to immigrants. Is this simply a function of poverty in those countries? By itself it is not enough of an explanation, because they have long had poverty. I posit that the internationalization of the Japanese economy, including specific forms of investment in those countries, and Japan's growing cultural influence there, have created bridges between those countries and Japan that have reduced the subjective distance with Japan. See Sassen 1991, 307–415; Shank 1994; see also chapter 3 here.

11 There has been growing recognition of the formation of an international professional class of workers and of highly internationalized environments due to the presence of foreign firms and personnel, the formation of global markets in the arts, and the international circulation of high culture. What has not been recognized is the possibility that we are seeing an international labor market for low-wage manual and service workers. This process continues to be couched in terms of the "immigration story," a narrative rooted in an earlier historical period.

12 The specific forms of the internationalization of capital over the last twenty years have contributed to mobilizing people into migration streams. They have done so principally through the implantation of Western development strategies, from the replacement of small-holder agriculture with export-oriented commercial agriculture and export manufacturing, to the Westernization of education systems. At the same time the administrative, commercial, and development networks of the former European empires and the newer forms these networks assumed under the Pax Americana (international direct foreign investment, export-processing zones, wars for democracy) have not only created bridges for the flow of capital, information, and high-level personnel from the center to the periphery but, I argue, also for the flow of migrants from the periphery to the center.

13 Body-Gendrot (1993) shows how the city remains a terrain for contest, characterized by the emergence of new actors, often younger and younger. It is a terrain where the constraints placed upon, and the institutional limitations of governments to address the demands of equity, engenders social disorders. She argues that urban political violence should not be interpreted as a coherent ideology but rather as an element of temporary political tactics, which permits vulnerable actors to enter in interaction with the holders of power on terms that will be somewhat more favorable to the weak.

SECTION I

PEOPLE ON THE RUN

2

THE DE FACTO TRANSNATIONALIZING OF IMMIGRATION POLICY[1]

W hile the state continues to play the most important role in immigration policy making and implementation, the state itself has been transformed by the growth of a global economic system and other transnational processes. These have brought on conditions that bear on the state's regulatory role and capacity. Two particular aspects of this development are of significance to the role of the state in immigration policy making and implementation. One is the relocation of various components of state authority to supranational organizations such as the institutions of the European Union (EU), the newly formed World Trade Organization (WTD), or international human rights codes. A second is the emergence of a new privatized transnational legal regime for cross-border business transactions which now also includes certain components of cross-border labor mobility, notably service workers.

The major implication for immigration policy is that these developments have had an impact on the sovereignty and territoriality of the state and that insofar as the state has participated in the implementation of many of these new arrangements, the state itself has been transformed and so has the inter-state system. Thus, insofar as immigration policy is deeply embedded in the question of state sovereignty and the interstate system, it is no longer sufficient simply to assert the sovereign role of the state in immigration policy design and implementation. It is also necessary to examine the transformation of the state itself and what that can entail for migration policy and the regulation of migration flows and settlements.

Nor is it sufficient simply to assert that globalization has brought with it a declining significance of the state in economic regulation (see chap. 8 here). The state is the strategic institution for the legislative changes and innovations necessary for economic globalization as we know it today (e.g., Panitch 1996; Cox 1987). Some of these issues may seem far removed from the question of immigration policy. But we need to expand the analytic terrain within which we examine the options in immigration policy making in the highly developed countries.

Here I focus on how this reconfiguration has brought with it a de facto transnationalism in the handling of a growing number of immigration issues. This can take many forms: the shift of certain elements of immigration policy onto supranational institutions in the European Union; the sharp increase in the extent and content of collaboration in the U.S.-Mexico Binational Immigration Commission; the rapid increase in the use of international human rights instruments by judges adjudicating on immigration and refugee questions in both Europe and the United States; the formation of a privatized regime for the circulation of service workers as part of efforts in the major free-trade agreements to liberalize international trade and investment in services.

I consider these and other developments a *de facto* transnationalism because they are fragmented, incipient, and have not been fully captured at the most formal levels of international public law and conventions, nor in national representations of the sovereign state. My argument is, then, that there is more on-the-ground transnationalism than hits the formal eye.

The first section briefly examines two of the cornerstones of current immigration policy in highly developed countries: the border and the individual as sites for regulatory enforcement. Ensuing sections focus on the constraints faced by the state in highly developed countries in the making of immigration policy today.

THE BORDER AND THE INDIVIDUAL
AS REGULATORY SITES

While the new conditions for transnational economies are being produced and implemented by governments and economic actors in highly developed countries, immigration policy in those same countries remains centered in older conceptions about control and regulation.[2]

In my reading there is a fundamental framework that roots all the country-specific immigration policies of the developed world in a common set of conceptions about the role of the state and of national borders. The purpose here is not to minimize the many differences in national policies, but to underline the growing convergence in various aspects of immigration policy and practice.[3]

First, the sovereignty of the state and border control, whether land borders, airports, or consulates in sending countries, lie at the heart of the regulatory effort. Second, immigration policy is shaped by an understanding of immigration as the consequence of the individual actions of emigrants; the receiving country is taken as a passive agent, one not implicated in the process of emigration. In refugee policy, in contrast, there is a recognition of other factors, beyond the control of individuals, as leading to outflows.[4] Two fundamental traits of immigration policy are, then, that it singles out the border and the individual as the sites for regulatory enforcement.

The sovereignty of the state when it comes to power over entry is well established by treaty law and constitutionally. The Convention of the Hague of 1930 asserted the right of the state to grant citizenship; the 1952 Convention of Refugees which asserted that the right to leave is a universal right, remained silent on the right to entry – better silence than evident contradiction. (As is well known, the status of refugees and their right not to be forcibly returned are established in international law, but there is no corresponding right of asylum; such right is at the discretion of a receiving state.) There are various human rights declarations and conventions that urge states to grant asylum on humanitarian grounds, but they all recognize the absolute discretion of states in this matter.[5] A few states, notably Austria and Germany, until recently gave those formally recognized as refugees a legal right to asylum – but this was revised in the early 1990s. More recently, the various agreements toward the formation of the European Union keep asserting the right of the state to control who can enter. This is quite a contrast with the assertions in the GATT, North American Free Trade Agreement (NAFTA), and the EU about the need to lift state controls over borders when it comes to the flow of capital, information, services, and domestic financial markets.

Second, on the matter of the individual as a site for enforcement, two different operational logics are becoming evident. One of these logics – the one embedded in immigration policy – places exclusive responsibility for the immigration process on the individual, and hence makes of the individual the site for the exercise of the state's authority. There is a strong tendency in immigration policy in developed countries to reduce the process to the actions of individuals: The individual is the site for accountability and for enforcement. Yet, it can be argued that international migrations are embedded in larger geopolitical and transnational economic dynamics (Sassen 1988). The worldwide evidence shows rather clearly that there is considerable patterning in the geography of migrations, and that the major receiving countries tend to get immigrants from their zones of influence. This holds for countries as diverse as the United States, France, or Japan. Immigration is at least partly an outcome of the actions of the governments and major private economic actors in receiving countries. Economic internationalization and the geopolitics resulting from older colonial patterns suggest that the responsibility for immigration may not be exclusively the immigrant's (Sassen 1988; 1996). Analytically these conditions can only enter into theorizations about the state and immigration when we suspend the proposition, implicit in much immigration analysis, that immigration is the result of individual action.

In the other logic, that embedded in human rights agreements, the individual emerges as a site for contesting the authority (sovereignty) of the state because she is the site for human rights.

BEYOND SOVEREIGNTY: CONSTRAINTS ON STATES' POLICY MAKING

When it comes to immigration policy, states under the rule of law increasingly confront a range of rights and obligations, pressures from both inside and outside, from universal human rights to not so universal ethnic lobbies. The overall effect is to constrain the authority of the state and to undermine key notions about immigration control.

First, we see emerging a de facto regime, centered in international agreements and conventions as well as in various rights gained by immigrants, that (in principle) could condition the state's role in controlling immigration. (See, e.g., Hollifield 1992; Baubock 1994; Sassen

1996, Part Three.) An example of such an agreement is the International Convention adopted by the General Assembly of the United Nations on December 18, 1990, on the protection of the rights of all migrant workers and members of their families (Resolution 45/158). Further, there is a set of rights of resident immigrants widely upheld by legal authorities. We have also seen the gradual expansion over the last three decades of civil and social rights to populations legally marginalized, whether women, ethnic minorities, or immigrants and refugees.

The extension of rights, which has taken place mostly through the judiciary, has confronted states with a number of constraints internal to the state. For instance, there have been attempts by the legislature in France and Germany to limit family reunification which were blocked by administrative and constitutional courts on the grounds that such restrictions would violate international agreements. The courts have also regularly supported a combination of rights of resident immigrants which have the effect of limiting the government's power over resident immigrants. Similarly, such courts have limited the ability of governments to restrict or stop asylum seekers from entering the country.[6]

Finally, the numbers and kinds of political actors involved in immigration policy debates and policy making in Western Europe, North America, and Japan are far greater than they were two decades ago: the EU, anti-immigrant parties; vast networks of organizations in both Europe and North America that often represent immigrants (or claim to do so) and fight for immigrant rights; immigrant associations and immigrant politicians, mostly in the second generation; and, especially in the United States, so-called ethnic lobbies.[7] The policy process for immigration is no longer confined to a narrow governmental arena of ministerial and administrative interaction. Public opinion and public political debate have become part of the arena wherein immigration policy is shaped.[8] Whole parties position themselves politically in terms of their stand on immigration, especially in some of the European countries. Although this has happened before, both in this and the previous century, it is also the case that we are seeing a sharper version of it than we have in the prior two or three decades.

These developments are particularly evident in the case of the EU.[9] Europe's single-market program has had a powerful impact in raising the prominence of various issues associated with the free circulation of people as an essential element in creating a frontier-free community; the earlier EC institutions lacked the legal competence to deal with many of these issues but had to begin to address them. Gradually EU institutions have wound up more deeply involved with visa policy, family reunification, and migration policy – all formerly exclusively in the domain of the individual national states. National governments resisted and continue to resist EU involvement in these once exclusively national domains. But now both legal and practical issues have made such involvement acceptable and inevitable notwithstanding many public pronouncements to the contrary.

It is becoming evident that many aspects of immigration and refugee policy intersect with EU legal competence. A key nexus here is the free movement of persons and attendant social rights as part of the formation of a single market. In practice the EU is assuming an increasingly important role and the fact that these are immigration countries is slowly being acknowledged. The monetary and economic union would require greater flexibility in movement of workers and their families and thereby pose increasing problems for national immigration laws regarding non-EU nationals in EU member states.

There is now growing recognition for the need of an EU-wide immigration policy, something denied for a long time by individual states. This became an urgent matter with the collapse of the socialist bloc and the rapid increase in refugee flows. (These have now largely subsided.) Though very slowly, the general direction has been toward a closer union of member states' immigration policies.

In the case of the United States, the combination of forces at the governmental level is quite different yet has similar general implications about the state's constraints in immigration policy making. Immigration policy in the United States is largely debated and shaped by Congress, and hence is highly public and subject to a vast multiplicity of local interests, notably ethnic lobbies.[10] This has made it a very public process, quite different from other processes of policy making.[11] Immigration has been attacked as part of a broader renationalizing of politics in the United States – a process that can be seen as partly a reaction to economic globalization, and in that regard not unlike the ascendance of regionalism in Western Europe in the context of a strengthened European Union.

Thus, after two decades of rights-based liberalism, Congress and public opinion are now pushing for pronounced curtailments of the rights and entitlements of legal immigrants, not to mention undocumented immigrants. Immigration policy and other types of legislation have expanded the rights of immigrants, including those of undocumented immigrants.[12] Even as the 1990 immigration act was passed in a great hurry and without much public debate, public opinion was already turning against immigration. And the recently approved immigration reform of 1996 tightens the rules regulating legal entries and sets stricter limits on the ability of immigrants who are U.S. citizens and permanent residents to bring in other family members into the United States. These developments are happening in a broader context of a drive to fiscal cost cutting, and radical devolution to the states.[13]

The fact that immigration in the United States has historically been the preserve of the federal government assumes new meaning in today's context of devolution – the return of powers to the states.[14] Alford Aman Jr. (1995) has noted that although political and constitutional arguments for reallocating federal power to the states are not new, the recent re-emergence of the Tenth Amendment as a politically viable and popular guideline is a major political shift since the New Deal in the relations between the federal government and the states. There is now an emerging conflict between several state governments and the federal government around the particular issue of federal mandates concerning immigrants – such as access to public health care and schools – without mandatory federal funding. Thus, states with disproportionate shares of immigrants are asserting that they are disproportionately burdened by the putative costs of immigration. In the United States the costs associated with immigration are an area of great debate and wide-ranging estimates.[15] At the heart of this conflict is the fact that the federal government sets policy but does not assume responsibility, financial or otherwise, for the implementation of many key aspects of immigration policy. The devolution now under way is going to accentuate some of these divisions further.

States are beginning to request reimbursement from the federal government for the cost of benefits and services that they are required to provide, especially to undocumented immigrants (Clark et al. 1994; GAO 1994; 1995a). In 1994, six states (Arizona, California, Florida, New Jersey, New York, and Texas) filed separate suits in federal district courts to recover costs they claim to have sustained because of the

federal government's failure to enforce U.S. immigration policy, protect the nation's borders, and provide adequate resources for immigration emergencies (Dunlap and Morse 1995).[16] The amounts range
from $50.5 million in New Jersey for FY 1993 costs of imprisoning 500
undocumented criminal felons and construction of future facilities, to
33.6 billion in New York for all state and county costs associated with
undocumented immigration between 1988 and 1993. U.S. district court
judges have dismissed all six lawsuits; some of the states are appeal-
ing the decision.

CAUGHT IN A WEB OF OTHER PROCESSES

One of the questions raised by these developments concerns the nature of the control national states have in regulating immigration. The
question here is not so much, how effective is a state's control over its
borders – we know it is never absolute. The question concerns rather
the substantive nature of state control over immigration given international human rights agreements, the extension of various social
and political rights to resident immigrants over the last twenty years,
the multiplication of political actors involved with the immigration
question, and the interaction effects between immigration and other
processes.

There is, first, the matter of the unintended consequences of policies, whether immigration policies as such or other kinds of policies
which have immigration impacts. For instance, the 1965 U.S. Immigration Act had consequences not intended or foreseen by its framers
(Reimers 1983; Briggs 1992); there was a generalized expectation it
would bring in more of the nationalities already present in the country, that is, Europeans, given its emphasis on family reunion (see the
next chapter here). Other kinds of unintended consequences are related to the internationalization of production and foreign aid (Sassen
1988; *Journal für Entwicklungspolitik* 1995; Bonacich et al. 1994). These
often turned out to have an unexpected impact on immigration. Similar unintended consequences have been associated with military aid
and subsequent refugee flows, for example, El Salvador in the decade
of the 1980s (Mahler 1995). Although immigration policy has rarely
been an explicit, formal component of foreign policy in the United
States, the latter has had a significant impact on immigration besides
the well-established fact of refugee flows from Indochina. If one were

to put it discreetly, one would say that foreign aid has rarely deterred emigration.[17]

It is also a fact that domestic U.S. policies with a foreign, overseas impact have contributed to emigration to the United States. There is the notorious sugar price support provision of the early 1980s: tax payers paid $3 billion annually to support the price of sugar for U.S. producers. This kept Caribbean Basin countries out of the competition and resulted in a loss of 400,000 jobs there from 1982 to 1988. The Dominican Republic lost three quarters of its sugar export quota in less than a decade. The 1980s was also an era of large increases in U.S. immigration from that region.

A second type of condition that illuminates the issue of the substantive nature of the control by states over immigration is a twist on the zero-sum argument. If a government closes one kind of entry category, recent history shows that another one will have a rise in numbers. A variant on this dynamic is that if a government has, for instance, a very liberal policy on asylum, public opinion may turn against all asylum seekers and close up the country totally; this in turn is likely to promote an increase in irregular entries.[18]

There is a third set of conditions that can be seen as reducing the autonomy of the state in controlling immigration. Large-scale international migrations are embedded in rather complex economic, social, and ethnic networks. They are highly conditioned and structured flows. States may insist in treating immigration as the aggregate outcome of individual actions and as distinct and autonomous from other major geopolitical and transnational processes. But they cannot escape the consequences of those larger dynamics and of their own insistence on isolating the immigration policy question.

These constraints on the state's capacity to control immigration should not be seen as a control crisis. Rather, my effort here is to open up the immigration policy question beyond the familiar range of the border and the individual as the sites for regulatory enforcement. These constraints signal that international migrations are partly embedded in conditions produced by economic internationalization both in sending and in receiving areas. While a national state may have the power to write the text of an immigration policy, it is likely to be dealing with a complex, deeply embedded and transnational process that it can only partly address or regulate through immigration policy as conventionally understood.[19]

WHEN DIFFERENT REGIMES INTERSECT

Immigration policy continues to be characterized by its formal isolation from other major processes, as if it were possible to handle migration as a bounded, closed event. There are, one could say, two major epistemic communities – one concerning the flow of capital and information; the other, immigration. Both of these epistemic communities are international, and both enjoy widespread consensus in the community of states.

The coexistence of such different regimes for capital and for immigrants has not been seen as an issue in the United States. The case of the EU is of interest here because it represents an advanced stage of formalization, and in this effort European states are discovering the difficulties if not impossibility of maintaining two such diverse regimes. The EU and the national governments of member states have found the juxtaposition of the divergent regimes for immigration flows and for other types of flows rather difficult to handle. The discussion, design, and implementation of policy aimed at forming a European Union make it evident that immigration policy has to account the facts of rapid economic internationalization. The EU shows us with great clarity the moment when states need to confront this contradiction in their design of formal policy frameworks. Other major free-trade systems in the world are far from that moment and may never reach it. Yet they contain less formalized versions of the juxtaposition between border-free economies and border controls to keep immigrants out. NAFTA is one such instance, as are, in a more diffuse way, various initiatives for greater economic integration in the Western hemisphere.

Though less clearly than in Western Europe and free-trade systems, these issues are present in other regions with cross-border migrations. They are regional systems constituted as zones of influence of major economic or geopolitical powers (e.g., the long-term dominance of the United States over the Caribbean Basin). What matters here is that to a good extent major international migration flows have been embedded in some or another variant of these regional systems. The quasi-transnational economic integration characterizing such regional systems produces its own variety of contradictions between drives for border-free economic spaces and border controls to keep immigrants and refugees out.

There are strategic sites where it becomes clear that the existence of two very different regimes for the circulation of capital and the circulation of immigrants poses problems that cannot be solved through the old rules of the game, where the facts of transnationalization weigh in on the state's decisions regarding immigration. For instance, the need to create special regimes for the circulation of service workers both within GATT and NAFTA as part of the further internationalization of trade and investment in services (see Sassen, in progress). This regime for the circulation of service workers has been uncoupled from any notion of migration; but it represents in fact a version of temporary labor migration. It is a regime for labor mobility which is in good part under the oversight of entities that are quite autonomous from the government. This points to an institutional reshuffling of some of the components of sovereign power over entry and can be seen as an extension of the general set of processes whereby state sovereignty is partly being decentered onto other non- or quasi-governmental entities for the governance of the global economy.[20]

For example, NAFTA's chapters on services, financial services, telecommunications, and "business persons" contain considerable detail on the various aspects relating to people operating in a country that is not their country of citizenship. Chapter Twelve, "Cross-Border Trade in Services," of the NAFTA (White House document, September 29, 1993) includes among its five types of measures those covering "the presence in its territory of a service provider of another Party" under Article 1201, including both provisions for firms and for individual workers. Under that same article there are also clear affirmations that nothing in the agreement on cross-border trade in services imposes any obligation regarding a non-national seeking access to the employment market of the other country, or to expect any right with respect to employment. Article 1202 contains explicit conditions of treatment of non-national service providers, so do Articles 1203, 1205, 1210 (especially Annex 1210.5), and 1213.2a and b. Similarly, Chapter Thirteen on telecommunications and Chapter Fourteen on financial services contain specific provisions for service providers, including detailed regulations applying to workers. Chapter Sixteen on "Temporary Entry for Business Persons" covers provisions for those "engaged in trade in goods, the provision of services or the conduct of investment activities" (Article 1608).

The development of provisions for workers and business persons signals the difficulty of *not* dealing with the circulation of people in the implementation of free-trade and investment frameworks. In their own specific ways, each of these efforts – NAFTA, GATT, and the European Union – has had to address cross-border labor circulation.

One instantiation of the impact of globalization on governmental policy making can be seen in Japan's new immigration law passed in 1990. Although this is quite different from how the issue plays in the context of free-trade agreements, it nonetheless illustrates one way of handling the need for cross-border circulation of professional workers in a context of resistance to the notion of open borders. This legislation opened the country to several categories of highly specialized professionals with a Western background (e.g., experts in international finance, in Western-style accounting, in Western medicine, etc.) in recognition of the growing internationalization of the professional world in Japan; it made illegal the entry of what is referred to as "simple labor" (see chap. 3 here). This can be read as importing "Western human capital" and closing borders to "immigrants."

Further, the need to address cross-border circulation of people has also become evident in free-trade agreements in the less-developed world, notably in Latin America. There has been a sharp increase in activity around the international circulation of people in each of the major regional trading blocks: Mercosur, the Grupo Andino, and the Mercado Comun de Centroamerica. Each one has launched a variety of initiatives in the early 1990s on international labor migration among their member countries. This is in many ways a new development. Some of the founding treaties precede the flurry of meetings on labor migrations and the circulation of people. But it is clear that conditions in the early 1990s forced this issue on the agenda. When one examines what actually happened it becomes evident that the common markets for investment and commerce in each of these regions themselves became activated in the late 1980s. It is the increased circulation of capital, goods, and information under the impact of globalization, deregulation, and privatization that has forced the question of the circulation of people onto the agenda.

In the case of the Pacto Andino, an agreement on labor migration was set up in the early stages of the trade agreement. The Simon Bolivar Agreement on Social and Labour Integration was created in 1973, which resulted in an operational agreement, the 1977 Andean

Labour Migration Statement. Parallel administrative agencies were created in each country's ministry of labor to implement and enforce it. But it, along with the general agreement on the Andean common market became basically inactive. It was not until the 1989 agreement of an Andean strategy signed by the presidents of the member countries that they became reactivated. Furthermore, the outlook itself of the Grupo Andino has changed from its earlier period, reflecting the sharp changes in the overall global and regional context.[21] (For more detailed accounts, including the original treaty documents, see *Acuerdo de Cartagena* 1991a, b, c; Banco Interamericano de Desarrollo/JUNAC 1993; JUNAC-OIM. 1993; Leon and Kratochwil 1993; OIM 1993; Marmora 1985a, b.)

Mercosur, created in 1991, represents a new generation of regional agreements (Kratochwil 1995). The founding treaty was signed by the presidents of Argentina, Brazil, Paraguay, and Uruguay in Asunción only in 1991; but this agreement actually absorbed earlier cross-border agreements in the region that had been semi- (or fully) dormant for years (Torales 1993). It acquired legal status in international law with the 1994 Ouro Preto Protocol which puts the Customs Union into effect. Not long after the founding, migration and labor officials of member countries set up two working groups, one of which included a commission on migration control and border-control simplification. Various additional committees and working groups have been set up that are concerned with general border and social and labor questions. Labor migration is on several agendas and is the subject of various agreements. (For detailed accounts see OIM 1991b; CEPAL 1994; Torales 1993; Marmora 1994.)

ODECA, the Organization of Central American States was created in 1951 and the Central American Common Market thirty years ago. It was not until 1991 that a Central American Migration Organization (OCAM) was set up. In 1991 a Central American Parliament (PARLACEN) was set up and a new System for Regional Integration (SICA); neither of these institutions has the full participation of all the countries of the region but the aim is to achieve this. The OCAM has been very active over the last few years. But it must be emphasized that the conditions in this region are radically different from those in the other two Latin American regional blocks: the devastating civil war has created large refugee flows all over the region and the cessation of many of the worst military conflicts has brought with it complicated return flows. But while this dominates it is also the case that the 1990s has seen an enormous interest in regional economic integration and a framework for the circulation of persons linked to it. This is an effort that lies outside the region's refugee and return migration crisis and is clearly linked to the new economics of the 1990s. (For more detailed accounts, see Directores Generales de Migraciones, 1992; CEPAL 1992; Stein 1993; SIECA 1991; OIM 1991a, d; see also Fagen and Eldridge 1991.)

In the case of the United States and its major immigration source country, Mexico, it appears that the signing of NAFTA has also had the effect of activating a series of new initiatives regarding migration—a sort of de facto bilateralism which represents possibly a radically new phase in the handling of migration between these two countries. It is worth providing some detail on these.

U.S.–Mexico: Toward De Facto Bilateralism?

Not unlike what was the case in Latin America, we are seeing a reactivation of older instruments and a flurry of new activity around the question of international migration. To provide better coordination between the two countries, Presidents Carter and Lopez Portillo established the U.S.–Mexico Consultative Mechanism. This eventually led to the formation of the U.S.–Mexico Binational Commission in 1981 to serve as a forum for meetings between cabinet-level officials from both countries. It was conceived as a flexible mechanism that would meet once or twice a year. One of the early working groups was the border relations action group, formed in 1981.

What is different over the last two years is the frequency, focus, and actual work that is getting done in the meetings of the working groups, though the 1996 immigration law changes in the United States have had a chilling effect to say the least. NAFTA has further contributed to strengthening the contacts and collaboration in the working groups. Particularly active is the working group on migration and consular affairs.[22] It became an effective means of resolving serious border problems of mutual interest. In their joint communique of May 16, 1995 they discussed progress made on the agreements reached at their prior meeting, in Zacatecas in February 1995. Of particular concern is ensuring the safe operation of borders, to prevent and eliminate criminality and violence affecting both migrants in transit and border communities. They also reaffirmed their commitment to protect the human and civil rights of all Mexican migrants in the United States regardless of their legal status. Many of the members of the working group for both countries seem convinced that this is a new phase of collaboration and communication that is unprecedented. It is also the first time that the Mexican government has gotten so involved with international migration issues; it is generally acknowledged that in the past it had a laissez faire position and did not develop policy.

There are also disagreements between the two delegations, which are discussed openly. Notably, the Mexican delegation is deeply concerned about the growing anti-immigrant feeling and measures in the United States. The United States delegation has agreed to collaborate to combat these developments. The Mexican delegation also expressed concern at the U.S. proposal to expand and strengthen border fences to improve security in various locations. They emphasized the negative effects of such a measure on the border communities and Mexican efforts to resolve the problems in the most troubled locations. Notwithstanding these serious disagreements, and perhaps precisely because of them, both delegations are convinced of the importance to continue the collaboration and communication that has developed over the last two years.

The February 1995 meeting in Zacatecas was extremely important in advancing the effort toward closer collaboration and open communications.[23] One of the agreements reached at the Zacatecas meeting was for the Mexican government to create groups to combat violence in border locations. One effort has been to expand the activities of the human rights nongovernmental organization group called BETA. On the U.S. side, there now is a citizens advisory panel that has as one of its first purposes reviewing procedures dealing with reports of abuse at the border. The border liaison mechanisms have turned out to be a very effective and useful way of handling border problems and new ones are being set up at additional border locations.

Another major effort coming out of the Zacatecas meeting is to facilitate documented migration and the return of undocumented migrants in full compliance with human rights codes. Acting upon this agreement, the U.S. delegation affirmed in the joint communiqué of May 16, 1995, that all backlogs for border crossing cards had been eliminated at major ports of entry by April 1, 1995. Finally, both delegations are developing criteria, procedures, and legal conditions consistent with international practices for the safe and orderly repatriation of undocumented Mexican migrants to ports of entry within Mexico without intermediate stops, with full respect for their human rights.

Both delegations recognize that having access to the necessary information about migration is essential and continue to support the ongoing Binational Study on Migration, a binational group of experts. The expectation is that this will facilitate the development of new and constructive long-term policies to deal with bilateral migration flows.

There are also non-official indications of a move toward de facto bilateralism regarding international migration. One example is the enormous expansion and strong government support received by the Colegio de la Frontera Norte, headquartered outside Tijuana but with units across the whole border. The goal of this university is to develop a body of research and a cadre of professionals who understand the border as a region that involves both the United States and Mexico. A second example is the formation of the U.S.–Mexico Consultative Group sponsored by the Carnegie Endowment for International Peace in Washington, D.C. It seeks to facilitate cooperation between the United States and Mexico on migration and attendant labor issues by engaging senior policy makers and nongovernmental experts from the two countries in an ongoing unofficial off-the-record dialogue. The first meeting was held in June 1995. Among the top government representatives were the respective ambassadors of the two countries.

*   *   *

All of these developments have the effect of 1) reducing the autonomy of the state in immigration policy making and 2) multiplying the sectors within the state that are addressing immigration policy and therewith multiplying the room for conflicts within the state. The assertion that the state is in charge of immigration policy is too general, and to take it as a given is less and less helpful. Policy making regarding international issues can engage very different parts of the government. The state itself has not only been transformed by its participation in the global economy, but has of course never been a homogeneous actor. It is constituted through multiple agencies and social forces. Indeed it could be said (cf. Mitchell 1989) that although the state has central control over immigration policy, the work of ex-

ercising that claimed power often begins with a limited contest between the state and interested social forces. These interest groups
include agribusiness, manufacturing, humanitarian groups, unions,
ethnic organizations, zero-population-growth advocates. Today we
need to add to this the fact that the hierarchies of power and influence
within the state are being reconfigured by the furthering of economic
globalization.[24]

The conditions within which immigration policy is being made and
implemented today range from the pressures of economic globalization and its implications for the role of the state to international agreements on human rights. And the institutional setting within which
immigration policy is being made and implemented ranges from national states and local states to supranational organizations.

Why does this transformation of the state and the interstate system
matter for immigration? The displacement of governance functions
away from the state to non-state entities affects the state's capacity to
control or keep controlling its borders and to exercise its power inside
its borders. New systems of governance are being created. Increasingly they may create conflicts with the state's capacity to keep on
regulating immigration in the same old ways. Further, the transformation of the state itself through its role in the implementation of
global processes, may well contribute to new constraints and vested
interests, but also options. The ascendance of agencies linked to furthering globalization and the decline of those linked to domestic equity questions is quite likely eventually to have an effect on the
immigration agenda.

HUMAN RIGHTS AND IMMIGRATION POLICY

Beyond the new conditions brought about by economic globalization,
immigration policy and practice are also increasingly affected by the
new international human rights regime.[25] The invocation of international covenants to make national policy signals yet another type of
displacement of government functions: a displacement in the legitimation process. This is a move away from statism – the absolute right
of states to represent their people in international law and international relations – toward a conceptual and operational opening for the
emergence of other subjects of, and actors in, international law. The
international human rights regime has been a key mechanism for

making subjects out of those hitherto invisible in international law—first nation people, immigrants and refugees, women. This has brought about a growing number of instances where one sector of the state is in disagreement with another. It is perhaps most evident in the strategic role that the judiciary has assumed in the highly developed countries when it comes to defending the rights of immigrants, refugees, and asylum seekers.

Human rights are not dependent on nationality. This is unlike political, social, and civil rights, which are predicated on the distinction between national and alien. Human rights override such distinctions. Even where rooted in the founding documents of nation–states, as is the case with the United States and France, we need to understand the specific development of these rights over the last few years. Human rights are today a force that can undermine the exclusive authority of the state over its nationals and thereby contribute to transform the interstate system and international legal order.[26] Membership in territorially exclusive nation–states ceases to be the only ground for the realization of rights. All residents, whether citizens or not can claim their human rights (Jacobson 1996; Henkin 1990). They strengthen concepts of personhood. Human rights codes can erode some of the legitimacy of the state if it fails to respect such human rights. It is no longer just a question of national self-determination as the condition for legitimacy, but of respect for international human rights codes (see Franck 1992). This is a very significant shift in that it posits that legitimacy no longer automatically attaches to invocations of self-determination. At the same time it is important to emphasize that human rights depend on the state for their implementation.

The growing influence of human rights law is particularly evident in Europe. It was not until the 1980s that the same began in the United States, though it still lags behind.[27] This has been seen partly as a result of American definitions of personhood which have led courts in some cases to address the matter of, for instance, undocumented immigrants within the domain of American constitutionalism, notably the idea of inalienable and natural rights of people and persons, without territorial confines. The emphasis on persons makes possible interpretations about undocumented immigrants in a way it would not if the emphasis were on citizens. It was not until the mid-1970s and the early 1980s that domestic courts began to consider human rights codes as normative instruments in their own right. The rapid growth of undocumented immigration and the sense of the state's incapacity to control the flow and to regulate the various categories in its population was a factor leading courts to consider the international human rights regime; it allows courts to rule on basic protections of individuals not formally accounted in the national territory and legal system, notably undocumented aliens and unauthorized refugees.[28]

The growing accountability of states under the rule of law to international human rights codes and institutions, together with the fact that individuals and non-state actors can make claims on those states in terms of those codes, signals a development that goes beyond the expansion of human rights within the framework of nation–states. For theorists who have taken a radical stance on this subject (e.g., Jacobson 1996 and Soysal 1994), it contributes to redefining the bases of legitimacy of states under the rule of law and the notion of nationality. Under human rights regimes states must increasingly take account of persons qua persons, rather than qua citizens. The individual is now an object of law and a site for rights regardless of whether a citizen or an alien.[29]

Immigrants in accumulating social and civil rights and even some political rights in countries of residence have diluted the meaning of citizenship an the specialness of the claims citizens can make on the state (see Bosniack 1992). When it comes to social services (education, health insurance, welfare, unemployment benefits) citizenship status is of minor importance in the 1970s and 1980s. What mattered above all was residence and legal alien status. This began to change in the early 1990s with a sharpening of anti-immigrant sentiment, leading to a considerable shrinking of immigrant rights–as is the case in recent laws passed in the United States in 1996 and in France in 1993. Most countries will pay retirement benefits even if recipients no longer reside there; and some countries have also granted local voting rights, for example, Sweden and the Netherlands. In most countries, permanent residents are guaranteed civil rights either constitutionally or by statute. The little difference between the claims of citizens and immingrants may have contributed to a low propensity to naturalize among certain nationality groups. With the 1996 changes in U.S. immigration law, which increase this difference, came a sharp growth in the applications for citizenship.

Even unauthorized immigrants can make some of these claims.

Schuck and Martin have noted that new "social contracts" are being negotiated in the United States every day between undocumented aliens and U.S. society, contracts that cannot be nullified through claims about nationality and sovereignty. Courts have had to accept the fact of undocumented aliens and to extend to these aliens some form of legal recognition and guarantees of basic rights (see Bosniack 1992; Isbister 1996). Various decisions have conferred important benefits associated with citizenship to undocumented aliens; and even though recent court rulings in the United States begin to chip away at these rights, they remain a significant statement about the rights of personhood.

CONCLUSION

The developments described here point to a number of trends that may become increasingly important for sound immigration policy making. First, where the effort toward the formation of transnational economic spaces has gone the farthest and been most formalized, it has become very clear that existing frameworks for immigration policy are problematic. It is not the case, as is often asserted, that the coexistence of very different regimes for the circulation of capital and for that of people is free of tension and contention. This is most evident in the legislative work necessary for the formation of the EU. Lesser versions of this tension are evident in the need to design special provisions for the circulation of workers in all the major free-trade agreements.

Second, we see the beginning of a displacement of government functions on to nongovernmental or quasi-governmental institutions. This is most evident in the new transnational legal and regulatory regimes created in the context of economic globalization. But it is also intersecting with questions of migration, specifically temporary labor migration, as is evident in the creation of special regimes for the circulation of service workers and business persons within WTO and NAFTA as part of the further internationalization of trade and investment in services. This regime for the circulation of service workers has been separated from any notion of migration; but it represents in fact a version of temporary labor migration. It is a regime for labor mobility which is in good part under the oversight of entities that are quite autonomous from the government. We can see in this displacement the elements of a privatization of certain aspects of the regulation of cross-border labor mobility.

Third, the legitimation process for states under the rule of law calls for respect and enforcement of international human rights codes, regardless of the nationality and legal status of an individual. While enforcement is precarious, it nonetheless signals a major shift in the legitimation process. This is perhaps most evident when the judiciary in the highly developed countries has defended the rights of immigrants, refugees, and asylum seekers against decisions by the legislature.

Finally, the state itself has been transformed by this combination of developments. This is so partly because the state under the rule of law is one of the key institutional arenas for the implementation of these new transnational regimes – whether the global rights of capital or the human rights of all individuals regardless of nationality. And it is partly because the state has incorporated the objective of furthering a global economy, as is evident in the ascendence of certain government agencies, (e.g., Treasury), and the decline of others, such as those linked to the social fund.

Because so many processes are transnational, governments are increasingly not competent to address some of today's major issues unilaterally or even from the exclusive confines of the interstate system narrowly defined. This is not the end of states' sovereignty, but rather that the "exclusivity and scope of their competence" (cf. Rosenau 1992) has changed, that there is a narrowing range within which the state's authority and legitimacy are operative.

There is no doubt that some of the intellectual technology that governments have and allow them to control their population, (i.e., Foucault's governmentality), has now shifted to non-state institutions. This is dramatically illustrated in the new privatized transnational regimes for cross-border business and the growing power of the logic of the global capital market over national economic policy (see Sassen 1996, chap. 2).

These are transformations in the making as we speak. My reading is that they matter. It is easy to argue the opposite: the state is still absolute and nothing much has changed. But it may well be the case that these developments signal the beginning of a new era. Scholarship on mentalities has shown how difficult it is for people to recognize systemic change in their contemporary conditions. Seeing continuity is much simpler and often reassuring.

Official immigration policy today is not part of the new rules of the game. Is this helpful in seeking to have a more effective long-term immigration policy in today's globalizing world?

NOTES

1   This chapter is based on *Immigration Policy in a Global Economy: From National Crisis to Multilateral Management*, a book being prepared for the Twentieth Century Fund. I thank the Fund for its support.

2   One of the key obstacles to even beginning to think along totally different lines about immigration policy is the widespread conviction that any other approach than border control would lead to massive invasions from the Third World. Much general commentary and policy making wittingly or not tends to proceed as if most people in less developed countries want to go to a rich country, as if all immigrants want to become permanent settlers, as if the problem of current immigration has to do basically with gaps or failures in enforcement, as if raising the levels of border control is an effective way of regulating immigration. This type of understanding of immigration clearly leads to a certain type of immigration policy, one centered in the fear of being invaded by people from less developed countries everywhere and hence on border control as the only answer. The evidence on immigration shows that most people do not want to leave their countries, that overal levels of permanent immigration are not very large, that there is considerable circulation and return migration, that most migration flows eventually stabilize if not decline (see Sassen, in progress, for a review of the evidence on these issues). Making these the central facts about the reality of immigration should allow for a broader set of options when it comes to immigration policy than would be the case with mass emigration and invasion. See also Isbister 1996.

3   There is a vast and rich scholarly literature that documents and interprets the specificity and distinctiveness of immigration policy in each of the highly developed countries (e.g., Weil 1991; Cornelius, Martin and Hollifield 1994; Weiner 1995; Soysal 1994; Thrandhardt 1993; Bade 1992, to mention just a few). As a body this literature allows us to see the many differences among these countries.

4   Refugee policy in some countries does lift the burden of immigration from the immigrant's shoulders. U.S. refugee policy, particularly for the case of Indochinese refugees, does acknowledge partial responsibility on the part of the government. Clearly, in the case of economic migrations, such responsibility is far more difficult to establish, and by its nature far more indirect.

5   One important exception is the 1969 Convention on Refugee Problems in Africa adopted by the Organization of African States which includes the right to entry.

6   These efforts, which mix the conventions on universal human rights and national judiciaries, assume many different forms. Some of the instances in the United States are the sanctuary movement in the 1980s, which sought to establish protected areas, typically in churches, for refugees from Central America; judicial battles, such as those around the status of Salvadoreans granted indefinite stays though formally defined as illegal; the fight for the rights of detained Haitians in an earlier wave of boat lifts. It is clear that notwithstanding the lack of an enforcement apparatus, human rights limit the discretion of states in how they treat non-

nationals on their territory. It is also worth noting in this regard that the United Nations High Commissioner on Refugees is the only UN agency with a universally conceded right of access to a country when an emergency crisis is declared.

7   While these developments are well known for the cases of Europe and North America, there is not much general awareness of the fact that we are seeing incipient forms in Japan as well (see, e.g., Shank 1995; and chapter 3 here). For instance, in Japan today we see a strong group of human rights advocates for immigrants; efforts by non-official unions to organize undocumented immigrant workers; organizations working on behalf of immigrants which receive funding from individuals or government institutions in the sending countries. (E.g., the Thai ambassador to Japan announced in October 1995 that his government will give a total of 2.5 million baht, about US$100,000, to five civic groups that assist Thai migrant workers, especially undocumented ones; see *Japan Times, October* 18, 1995.)

8   Further, the growth of immigration, refugee flows, ethnicity, and regionalism raise questions about the accepted notion of citizenship in contemporary nation – states and hence about the formal structures for accountability. My research on the international circulation of capital and labor has raised questions for me on the meaning of such concepts as national economy and national workforce under conditions of growing internationalization of capital and the growing presence of immigrant workers in major industrial countries. Further, the rise of ethnicity in the United States and in Europe among the mobile workforce raises questions about the content of the concept of nation-based citizenship. The portability of national *identity* raises questions about the bonds with other countries, or localities within them; and the resurgence of ethnic regionalism creates barriers to the political incorporation of new immigrants (see, e.g., Soysal 1994; Baubock 1994; Sassen 1996).

9   There is a large and rich literature on the development of immigration policy at the European level; please refer to note 3 for a few citations.

10 Jurisdiction over immigration matters in the U.S. Congress lies with the judiciary committee, not with the foreign affairs committee as might have been the case. Congressional intent on immigration is often at odds with the foreign-affairs priorities of the executive. There is a certain policy making tug of war (Mitchell 1989). It has not always been this way. In the late 1940s and 1950s there was great concern with how immigration policy could be used to advance foreign-policy objectives. The history of what government agency was responsible for immigration is rather interesting. Earlier, when the Department of Labor (DOL) was created in 1914, it got the responsibility for immigration policy. On June 1933, President Roosevelt combined functions into the Immigration and Naturalization Service (INS) within DOL. The advent of World War II brought a shift in the administrative responsibility for the country's immigration policy: in 1940 President Roosevelt recommended it be shifted to the Department of Justice, because of the supposed political threat represented by immigrants from enemy countries. This was meant to last for the war and then INS was to be returned to the DOL. But it never was. It also meant that immigration wound up in Congress in committees traditionally reserved for lawyers, as are the Senate and House Judiciary Committees. It has been said that this is why immigration law is so complicated (and, I would add, so centered in the legalities of entry and so unconcerned with broader issues).

11 There are diverse social forces shaping the role of the state depending on the matter at hand. Thus, in the early 1980s bank crisis, for instance, the players were few and well coordinated; the state basically relinquished the organizing capacity to the banks, the IMF, and a few other actors, all very discreet, indeed so discreet that if you look closely the government was hardly a player in that crisis. This is quite a contrast with the deliberations around the passing of the 1986 Immigration and Reform Control Act – which was a sort of national brawl. In trade liberation discussions there are often multiple players, and the executive may or may not relinquish powers to Congress.

12 This is illustrated by the now famous 1982 U.S. Supreme Court decision in *Player v. Doe* where undocumented immigrant children were guaranteed the right to a K – 12 public school education; deportation hearings, and use of appeal rights for apprehended undocumented immigrants and political asylum applicants.

13 A major new piece of legislation where many of these attempts come together is the welfare reform as it affects immigrants. Under past law, naturalized U.S. citizens had full eligibility on the same terms as native-born individuals and so did lawful permanent residents (with the exception of deeming provisions). But the sharp changes recently approved by Congress will have the effect of curtailing or eliminating completely the eligibility of legal immigrants for most federal means-tested programs.

14 In this light, it is worth noting that in November 1995 a federal judge ruled large sections of California's Proposition 187 (aimed at severely curtailing the rights of undocumented immigrants and their children) unconstitutional, citing individual rights and the fact that the state is powerless to enact its own scheme to regulate immigration.

15 See General Accounting Office 1995. The latest study by the Washington-based Urban Institute found that immigrants contribute US$30 billion more in taxes than they take in services.

16 President Clinton's 1994 crime bill earmarked $1.8 billion in disbursements over six years to help reimburse states for these incarceration costs.

17 Take El Salvador in the 1980s: billions of dollars in aid poured in while hundreds of thousands of Salvadorans poured out as U.S. aid raised the effectiveness of El Salvador's military control and aggression against its own people. Or take the case of the Philippines, a country that received massive aid and has had high emigration. In both cases it was foreign aid dictated by security issues. Emigration resulting from U.S. economic and political interventions is evident in the Dominican emigration in the 1960s and in the emigration from India and Pakistan to the United States – the latter two associated as well with security aid from the United States. (I have long argued as a scholar (1988) that policy makers should attach migration impact statements to various policies.)

18 Increasingly, unilateral policy by a major immigration country is problematic. One of the dramatic examples was that of Germany which began to receive massive numbers of entrants as the other European states gradually tightened their politics and Germany kept its very liberal asylum policy. Another case is the importance for the EU today that the Mediterranean countries – Italy, Spain and Portugal – control their borders regarding non-EU entrants.

19 On a somewhat related matter, it seems to me that the sense of an immigration control crisis that prevails today in many of the highly developed countries is in some ways unwarranted, even though states have less control than they would like because immigration is caught in a web of other dynamics. When we look at the characteristics of immigrations over time and across the world, it is clear that these are highly patterned flows, embedded in other dynamics which contain equilibrating mechanisms, that they have a duration (many immigrations have lasted for fifty years and then come to an end); that there is more return migration than we generally realize (e.g., Soviet engineers and intellectuals who went back to Moscow from Israel; Mexicans who returned after becoming legal residents through the IRCA [Immigration Reform and Control Act of 1986] amnesty program, feeling that now they could circulate between the two countries); we also know from earlier historical periods when there were no controls that most people did not leave poorer areas to go to richer ones, even though there were plenty of such differences in Europe within somewhat reasonable travel distances. (For a full treatment, see Sassen 1996; in progress.)

20 Elsewhere (Sassen 1996; in progress) I have argued that in some ways this can be seen as yet another instance of privatization of that which is profitable and manageable. We are seeing the

privatizing of what was once government policy in several emergent cross-border legal and regulatory regimes for international business, notably the rapid growth of international commercial arbitration and the growing importance of credit-rating agencies. In this case it would be a privatizing through NAFTA of immigration policy components that are characterized by high-value added (persons with high levels of education and/or capital), manageability (they are likely to be temporary and working in leading sectors of the economy and hence are visible migrants, subject to effective regulation), and benefits (given the new ideology of free trade and investment). Governments are left with the supervision of the "difficult" and "low-value added" components of immigration – poor, low-wage workers, refugees, dependents, and potentially controversial brain-drain flows. This can clearly have a strong impact on what comes to be seen as the category "immigrant" with policy and broader political implications.

21   An Andean social charter was created with the active participation of trade unions and the Andean Parliament, as was a basic regulatory framework for regional international migration. In 1992, the member countries set up the Committee of Migration Officers of the Andean Group, which includes migration officials of the member countries, to advise the JUNAC, the technical and administrative body of the Cartagena Agreement.

22   The U.S. delegation for this group is chaired by the assistant secretary of state for consular affairs and the INS commissioner.

23   The meeting of the working group on migration and consular affairs in Zacatecas followed the three meetings held in 1994. The Mexican delegation was headed by the undersecretary for bilateral affairs from the secretariat of foreign affairs, the undersecretary of population and migration services of the National Migration Institute. The U.S. delegation was headed by the INS commissioner, the U.S. ambassador to Mexico, and the deputy assistant secretary for interamerican affairs of the Department of State. These are then fairly high-level government delegations; they are not simply technical personnel.

24   For instance, an item on internal changes in the state which may have impacts on immigration policy is the ascendance of so-called soft security issues. According to some observers, recent government reorganization in the departments of State, Defense, and the CIA reflects an implicit redefinition of national security.

25   This is a complex subject that cannot be developed here, but it is important to include some reference to its impact. (For fuller treatments about the impact on immigration policy in particular, see Jacobson 1996; Heisler 1986; see also Soysal 1994; Baubock 1994; Sassen 1996: chap. 3; in progress.)

26   Already in the early twentieth century there were several legal instruments that promoted human rights and made the individual an object of international law. But it was not until after WWII that we see an elaboration and formalization of such rights; the covenants and conventions that guarantee human rights today are derived from the Universal Declaration of Human Rights adopted by the UN in 1948. And it is not until the late 1970s and 1980s that there is a sufficiently large array of instruments and agreements that judiciaries, particularly in Europe, regularly invoke in their decisions. In the case of the Americas, the system for the protection of human rights is the Inter-American Commission on Human Rights. It is grounded on two distinct legal documents. They are the Charter of the Organization of American States and the American Convention on Human Rights, adopted in 1969 and entered into force in 1978. The human rights regime of the Organization of American States was markedly strengthened in a 1967 protocol that came into force in 1970.

27   And its weight in many of the Latin American countries is dubious. For a very detailed (and harrowing) account of the situation in Mexico, see Reding 1995. See also generally Sikkink 1993.

28 For instance, the Universal Declaration was cited in seventy-six federal cases from 1948 through 1994; over ninety percent of those cases took place since 1980 and of those, forty-nine percent involved immigration issues, and up to fifty-four percent if we add refugees (Jacobson, 1996: 97). Jacobson also found that the term "human rights" was referred to in nineteen federal cases before the twentieth century, 34 cases from 1900 to 1944, 191 from 1945 to 1969, 803 cases in the 1970s, over 2,000 in the 1980s, and an estimated 4,000 cases through the 1990s.

29 There is a whole debate about the notion of citizenship and what it means in the current context (see Soysal 1994; Baubock 1994, Sassen 1996, chap. 2). One trend in this debate is a return to notions of cities and citizenship, particularly in so-called global cities, which are partly denationalized territories and have high concentrations of non-nationals from many different parts of the world (e.g., Holston 1996; Knox and Taylor 1995; *Social Justice* 1993). The ascendance of human rights codes strengthens these tendencies to move away from nationality and national territory as absolute categories.

3

Immigration has traditionally aroused strong passions in the United States. Although Americans like to profess pride in their history as "a nation of immigrants," each group of arrivals, once established, has fought to keep newcomers out. Over the past two centuries, each new wave of immigrants has encountered strenuous opposition from earlier arrivals, who have insisted that the country was already filled to capacity. (The single exception to this was the South's eagerness to import ever more slaves.) Similar efforts to shut out newcomers persist today. But those who would close the door to immigration are mistaken on two counts: not only do they underestimate the country's capacity to absorb more people, but they also fail to appreciate the political and economic forces that give rise to immigration in the first place.

U.S. policy makers and the public alike believe the causes of immigration are self-evident: people who migrate to the United States are driven to do so by poverty, economic stagnation, and overpopulation in their home countries. Because immigration is thought to result from unfavorable socioeconomic conditions in other countries, it is assumed to be unrelated to U.S. economic needs or broader international economic conditions. In this context, the decision becomes a humanitarian matter; we admit immigrants by choice and out of generosity, not because we have any economic motive or political responsibility to do so. An effective immigration policy, by this reasoning, is one that selectively admits immigrants for such purposes as family reunification and refugee resettlement, while perhaps seeking to deter migration by promoting direct foreign investment, foreign aid, and democracy in the migrant-sending countries.

Although there are nuances of position, liberals and conservatives alike accept the prevailing wisdom on the causes of immigration and the best ways to regulate it. The only disagreement, in fact, is over how strictly we should limit immigration. Conservatives generally maintain that if immigration is not severely restricted, we will soon be overrun by impoverished masses from the Third World, although the demand for cheap agricultural labor at times tempers this position. Liberals tend to be more charitable, arguing that the United States, as the richest country in the world, can afford to be generous in offering a haven to the poor and oppressed. Advocates of a less restrictive policy also note the positive effects of immigration, such as the growth of cultural diversity and a renewed spirit of entrepreneurship.

Not surprisingly, U.S. immigration laws have reflected the dominant assumptions about the proper objectives of immigration policy. The last two major immigration reforms, passed in 1965 and 1986, have sought to control immigration through measures aimed at regulating who may enter legally and preventing illegal immigrants from crossing our borders. At the same time, the U.S. government has attempted to promote economic growth in the migrant-sending countries by encouraging direct foreign investment and export-oriented international development assistance, in the belief that raising economic opportunities in the developing world will deter emigration. Yet U.S. policies, no matter how carefully devised, have consistently failed to limit or regulate immigration in the intended way.

The 1965 amendment to the Immigration and Naturalization Act was meant to open up the United States to more immigration, but to do so in a way that would allow the government to control entries and reduce illegal immigration. It sought to eliminate the bias against non-Europeans that was built into earlier immigration law and to regulate the influx of immigrants by setting up a series of preference categories within a rather elaborate system of general quotas.[2] Under this system, preference was given to immediate relatives of U.S. citizens and, to a lesser extent, to immigrants possessing skills in short supply in the United States, such as nurses and nannies.

The 1965 law brought about major changes in immigration patterns, but not necessarily the intended ones. The emphasis on family reunification should have ensured that the bulk of new immigrants would come from countries that had already sent large numbers of immigrants to the United States – that is, primarily from Europe. But the dramatic rise in immigration after 1965 was primarily the result of an entirely new wave of migration from the Caribbean Basin and South and Southeast Asia. The failure of U.S. policy was particularly evident in the rapid rise in the number of undocumented immigrants entering the country. Not only did the level of Mexican undocumented immigration increase sharply, but a whole series of new undocumented flows were initiated, mostly from the same countries that provided the new legal immigration.

The outcry over rising illegal immigration led to a series of congressional proposals that culminated in the 1986 Immigration Reform and Control Act. This law was intended to rationalize immigration policy and, in particular, to address the problem of illegal immigration. It features a limited regularization program that enables undocumented aliens to legalize their status if they can prove continuous residence in the United States since before January 1, 1982, among other eligibility criteria. A second provision of the law seeks to reduce the employment opportunities of undocumented workers through sanctions against employers who knowingly hire them. The third element is an extended guest-worker program designed to ensure a continuing abundant supply of low-wage workers for agriculture.

So far, the law's overall effectiveness has been limited. While some 1.8 million immigrants applied to regularize their status[3] (a fairly significant number, though less than expected), there is growing evidence that the employer-sanctions program is resulting in discrimination against minority workers who are in fact U.S. citizens, as well as various abuses against undocumented workers. Meanwhile, illegal immigration has apparently continued to rise. Congressional efforts to correct the law's shortcomings have already begun. In a relatively promising departure from earlier immigration policy, the Senate recently approved a bill that seeks to give higher priority to applicants who satisfy labor needs in the United States.[4] Though the 54,000 per-year limit placed on such immigrants would still be small, the proposed law would set an important precedent by acknowledging that immigrants, while only about seven percent of the U.S. labor force, have accounted for twenty-two percent of the growth in the workforce since 1970, and by responding to U.S. Department of Labor forecasts of impending labor shortages in a variety of occupations.

Yet even a modified version of the 1986 law has little chance of successfully regulating immigration for one simple reason: like earlier laws, it is based on a faulty understanding of the causes of immigration. By focusing narrowly on immigrants and on the immigration process itself, U.S. policymakers have ignored the broader international forces, many of them generated or at least encouraged by the United States, that have helped give rise to migration flows.

In the 1960s and 1970s, the United States played a crucial role in the development of today's global economic system. It was a key exporter of capital, promoted the development of export-manufacturing enclaves in many Third World countries, and passed legislation aimed at opening its own and other countries' economies to the flow of capital, goods, services, and information. The emergence of a global economy – and the central military, political, and economic role played by the United States in this process – contributed both to the creation abroad of pools of potential emigrants and to the formation of linkages between industrialized and developing countries that subsequently were to serve as bridges for international migration. Paradoxically, the very measures commonly thought to deter immigration – foreign investment and the promotion of export-oriented growth in developing countries – seem to have had precisely the opposite effect. The clearest proof of this is the fact that several of the newly industrializing countries with the highest growth rates in the world are simultaneously becoming the most important suppliers of immigrants to the United States.

At the same time, the transformation of the occupational and income structure of the United States – itself in large part a result of the globalization of production – has expanded the supply of low-wage jobs. The decline of manufacturing and the growth of the service sector have increased the proportion of temporary and part-time jobs, reduced advancement opportunities within firms, and weakened various types of job protection. This "casualization" of the labor market has facilitated the absorption of rising numbers of immigrants during the 1970s and 1980s – a growing Third World immigrant workforce in what is supposedly one of the leading post-industrial economies.[5] Until we better understand the powerful political and economic forces that drive these international migration flows, and our own role in creating them, U.S. immigration policies will continue to be misguided and frustratingly ineffective.

THE NEW IMMIGRATION

Beginning in the late 1960s, immigration patterns to the United States began to change in several different important ways. First, there was a significant rise in overall annual entry levels. From 297,000 in 1965, immigration levels increased to 373,000 in 1970, rose to 531,000 in 1980, and reached 602,000 in 1986. At the same time, there was a dramatic change in the regional composition of migration flows. As recently as 1960, more than two-thirds of all immigrants entering the United States came from Europe. By 1985, Europe's share of annual entries had shrunk to one-ninth, with the actual numbers of European immigrants declining from almost 140,000 in 1960 to 63,000 in 1985. Today, the vast majority of immigrants to the United States originate in Asia, Latin America, and the Caribbean.

Asians make up the fastest-growing group of legally admitted immigrants. From 25,000 entries in 1960, annual levels of Asian immigrants rose to 236,000 in 1980 and to 264,700 in 1985. While these figures were elevated somewhat by the flow of Southeast Asian refugees admitted in the aftermath of the Vietnam war, refugees account for only a small proportion of the overall rise in Asian immigration. In fact, it is the Philippines, South Korea, and Taiwan, not the refugee-sending countries of Vietnam and Cambodia, that have been the largest Asian sources of immigrants. Even in 1982, when total Asian entries reached an all-time high of 313,000, only 72,000 were Vietnamese, a level that declined to 39,000 by 1983. In the 1980s, the Asian immigration began to include new flows from nations such as Singapore, Malaysia, and Indonesia that had not previously been sources of emigration to the United States.

The increase in Hispanic and West Indian immigration, although not quite as dramatic, has nevertheless been significant. Immigration levels from Latin America and the Caribbean rose in the latter half of the 1960s, then showed a decline in the early 1970s before rising sharply again in the 1980s. Total entries of Hispanics (South and Central Americans, excluding Mexico) reached about 170,000 for the period from 1965 to 1969, declined to 149,000 from 1970 to 1974, and rose to 368,000 from 1980 to 1985. Entries of West Indians reached 351,000 during the period from 1965 to 1969, declined to 318,000 from 1970 to 1975, and rose to 445,000 from 1980 to 1985. (By contrast, there was no comparable dip in the numbers of Asian immigrants in the 1970s.)

The top ten immigrant-sending countries by the late 1980s were all in Latin America, the Caribbean Basin, and Asia. Between 1972 and 1979, Mexico, with more than half a million entries annually, was by far the largest source of legally admitted immigrants, followed by the Philippines with 280,000, South Korea with 225,000, China (defined as including both Taiwan and the People's Republic) with 160,400, India with 140,000, and Jamaica with 108,400. With the exception of Italy, all of the countries sending more than 100,000 immigrants each year were either in the Caribbean Basin or in Asia. Other important sources of immigrants outside these regions were the United Kingdom, West Germany, and Canada, sending about 80,000 each during the 1972–1979 period. By 1987, forty-three percent of the 600,000 entries were from Asia, thirty-five percent from Latin America and the Caribbean Basin, and only ten percent from Europe.

It is important to note that the new Asian immigration, often thought to consist predominantly of professional and middle-class individuals, is increasingly becoming a working-class migration. In several cases, what began as middle-class migrations eventually paved the way for the migration of poorer strata as well as undocumented immigrants. This has been true of South Korean migration, for example, which now includes significant numbers of undocumented immigrants and sweatshop employees, as well as of Filipino and Colombian migration.

Another feature of the new immigration is the growing prominence of female immigrants. During the 1970s, women made up sixty percent of all immigrants from the Philippines, sixty-one percent of South Korean immigrants, fifty-three percent of Chinese, fifty-two percent of Dominicans, fifty-two percent of Colombians, fifty-three percent of Haitians, and fifty-two percent of immigrants from Hong Kong. Even in the well-established, traditionally male-dominated migration flow from Mexico, women now make up almost half of all legal immigrants.[5]

Although most female immigrants still enter as dependents of various kinds, a small but growing number now enter classified as workers. This would appear to indicate that an increasing number of women are migrating independently, in some cases leaving their husbands and children behind. Women represented 45.6 percent of all immigrants admitted legally from 1972 to 1979 under the preference category of skilled and unskilled workers in short supply.[7] Moreover, women made up more than half of the 290,000 admitted under the nonpreference immigrant category, which consists of the spaces that become available when the preference quotas are not fully used.[8]

The new immigration is further characterized by the immigrants' tendency to cluster in a few key U.S. regions. This was true as well of earlier immigration waves, of course; in the early 1900s, New York, Pennsylvania, and Illinois attracted the majority of immigrants.[9] Today, however, there are more ports of entry, a better developed transportation system, and a far-flung distribution of jobs–all of which would seem to facilitate the geographical scattering of immigrants. Yet the states of California and New York receive almost half of all new immigrants, while another one-fourth go to New Jersey, Illinois, Florida, and Texas.

Moreover, the new immigrants tend to cluster in the largest metropolitan areas, such as New York, Los Angeles, San Francisco, Chicago, Houston, and Miami. According to the 1980 census, about one-fifth of all foreign-born residents of the United States lived in New York and Los Angeles; by contrast, these cities contained less than one percent of the total U.S.-born population in 1980. About forty percent of immigrants settle in the ten largest U.S. cities, which together account for less than ten percent of the total U.S. population. In these cities, immigrants make up a considerably higher proportion of the population than they do of the U.S. population as a whole. Thus, while immigrants constitute at most ten percent of the U.S. population, by 1987 they made up thirty percent of the population of New York City and fifteen percent of the populations of Los Angeles and Chicago.

THE INADEQUACY OF CLASSICAL EXPLANATIONS

The main features of the new immigration–in particular, the growing prominence of certain Asian and Caribbean Basin countries as sources of immigrants and the rapid rise in the proportion of female immigrants–cannot be adequately explained under the prevailing assumptions of why migration occurs. Even a cursory review of emigration patterns reveals that there is no systematic relationship between emigration and what conventional wisdom holds to be the principal causes of emigration–namely overpopulation, poverty, and economic stagnation.

Population pressures certainly signal the possibility of increased emigration. Yet such pressures—whether measured by population growth or population density—are not in themselves particularly helpful in predicting which countries will have major outflows of emigrants, since some countries with rapidly growing populations experience little emigration (many Central African countries fall into this category), while other countries with much lower population growth rates (such as South Korea), or relatively low density (such as the Dominican Republic), are major sources of migrants.

Nor does poverty in itself seem to be a very reliable explanatory variable. Not all countries with severe poverty experience extensive emigration, and not all migrant-sending countries are poor, as the case of South Korea and Taiwan illustrate. The utility of poverty in explaining migration is further called into question by the fact that large-scale migration flows from most Asian and Caribbean Basin countries started only in the 1960s, despite the fact that many of these countries had long suffered from poverty.

The presumed relationship between economic stagnation and emigration is similarly problematic. It is commonly assumed that the lack of economic opportunities in less developed countries, as measured by slow growth of gross national product (GNP), plays a key role in inducing individuals to emigrate. But the overall increase in emigration levels took place at a time when most countries of origin were enjoying rather rapid economic growth. Annual GNP growth rates during the 1970s ranged from five to eight percent for most of the leading migrant-sending countries. In fact, most of the key emigration countries were growing considerably faster than other countries that did not experience large-scale emigration. South Korea is the most obvious example. With a GNP growth rate that was among the highest in the world during the 1970s, it was also one of the countries with the fastest-growing level of migration to the United States.

This is not to say that overpopulation, poverty, and economic stagnation do not create pressures for migration; by their very logic, they do. But it is clear that the common identification of emigration with these conditions is overly simplistic. The evidence suggests that these conditions are not sufficient by themselves to produce large new migration flows. Other intervening factors need to be taken into account—factors that work to transform these conditions into a migration-inducing situation.

Take, for example, the cases of Haiti and the Dominican Republic.

At first glance, the high levels of emigration from these countries would seem to offer support for the argument that overpopulation, poverty, and economic stagnation cause migration. Yet one is struck by the fact that these conditions were present in both countries long before the massive outflow of emigrants began. What, then, accounted for the sudden upsurge?

In the case of the Dominican Republic, the answer seems to lie in the linkages with the United States that were formed during the occupation of Santo Domingo by U.S. Marines in 1965 in response to the election victory of the left-wing presidential candidate Juan Bosch. The occupation not only resulted in the growth of political and economic ties with the United States but also produced a stream of middle-class political refugees who emigrated to the occupying country. The settlement of Dominican refugees in the United States in turn created personal and family linkages between the two countries. U.S.-Dominican ties were subsequently further consolidated through U.S. investment in Dominican agriculture and manufacturing for export. Migration to the United States began to increase soon thereafter, rising from a total of 4,500 for the period from 1955 to 1959 to 58,000 between 1965 and 1969. Thus, the new developments that appear to have coincided with the initiation of large-scale emigration were the establishment of close military and personal ties with the United States and the introduction of U.S. direct foreign investment.

Haiti, on the other hand, was not subjected to direct U.S. military intervention, but the establishment of linkages with the United States and the introduction of direct foreign investment seem to have played a similarly important role in producing emigration. Although Haiti has long been desperately poor, massive migration to the United States began only in the early 1970s. In this case, the key new development or intervening process appears to have been the adoption of an export-oriented economic growth policy by President Jean-Claude Duvalier in 1972. Haiti's economy was opened to foreign investment in export manufacturing and to large-scale development of commercial agriculture, with the United States serving as the key partner in this new strategy. The necessary labor supply for these new modes of production was obtained through the massive displacement of small landholders and subsistence farmers. This upheaval in Haiti's traditional occupational structure, in conjunction with growing government repression and the emergence of close political and economic links with the United States, coincided with the onset of a major migration flow to the United States.

In both cases, then, the establishment of political, military, and economic linkages with the United States seems to have been instrumental in creating conditions that allowed the emergence of large-scale emigration.[10] Such linkages also played a key role in the migration of Southeast Asians to the United States. In the period following the Korean War, the United States actively sought to promote economic development in Southeast Asia as a way of stabilizing the region politically. In addition, U.S. troops were stationed in Korea, the Philippines, and Indochina. Together, U.S. business and military interests created a vast array of linkages with those Asian countries that were later to experience large migration flows to the United States. The massive increase in foreign investment during the same period, particularly in South Korea, Taiwan, and the Philippines, reinforced these trends.

In other words, in most of the countries experiencing large migration flows to the United States, it is possible to identify a set of conditions and linkages with the United States that, together with overpopulation, poverty, or unemployment, induce emigration. While the nature and extent of these linkages vary from country to country, a common pattern of expanding U.S. political and economic involvement with emigrant-sending countries emerges. (See Sassen 1988 for a full development of these issues.)

A key element in this pattern is the presence of direct foreign investment in production for export. U.S. investment in the less developed countries quintupled between 1965 and 1980, with much of it going to a few key countries in the Caribbean Basin and Southeast Asia and a large proportion channeled into the development of consumer goods such as toys, apparel, textiles, and footwear. Industries producing for export are generally highly labor intensive (this is, of course, a primary rationale for locating factories in low-wage countries). The labor-intensive nature of these industries is one reason why several of the Asian and Caribbean Basin countries that have been major recipients of direct foreign investment have experienced rapid employment growth, especially in the manufacturing sector. (See also chap. 5 here.)

According to traditional understandings of why migrations occur, this combination of economic trends should have helped to deter emigration, or at least to keep it at relatively low levels. The deterrent effect should have been particularly strong in countries with high levels of export-oriented investment, because such investment creates more employment—managerial and clerical as well as production jobs—than other forms of investment. Yet it is precisely such countries, most notably the newly industrializing countries of Southeast Asia, that have been the leading source of new immigrants. How, then, does foreign investment, especially foreign investment in export industries, explain this seeming contradiction? In particular, how is it that foreign investment can produce both rapid economic growth and high emigration levels in a single country?

THE INTERNATIONALIZATION OF PRODUCTION

To understand why large-scale migrations have originated in countries with high levels of job creation due to foreign investment in production for export, it is necessary to examine the impact of such investment on the economic and labor structure of developing countries.

Perhaps the single most important effect of foreign investment in export production is the uprooting of people from traditional modes of existence. It has long been recognized that the development of commercial agriculture tends to displace subsistence farmers, creating a supply of rural wage laborers and giving rise to mass migrations to cities. In recent years, the large-scale development of export-oriented manufacturing in Southeast Asia and the Caribbean Basin has come to have a similar effect (though through different mechanisms); it has uprooted people and created an urban reserve of wage laborers. In both export agriculture and export manufacturing, the disruption of traditional work structures as a result of the introduction of modern modes of production has played a key role in transforming people into migrant workers and, potentially, into emigrants.

In export manufacturing, the catalyst for the disruption of traditional work structures is the massive recruitment of young women into jobs in the new industrial zones. Most of the manufacturing in these zones is of the sort that employs a high proportion of female workers in industrialized countries as well: electronics assembly and the manufacture of textiles, apparel, and toys. The exodus of young women to the industrial zones typically begins when factory representatives recruit young women directly in their villages and rural schools; eventually, the establishment of continuous migration streams reduces or eliminates the need for direct recruitment.[11] The most obvious reason for the intensive recruitment of women is firms' desire to reduce costs, but there are other considerations as well: young women in patriarchal societies are seen by foreign employers as obedient and disciplined workers, willing to do tedious, high-precision work and to submit themselves to work conditions that would not be tolerated in the highly developed countries. (See also chap. 5 here.)

This mobilization of large numbers of women into waged labor has a highly disruptive effect on traditional, often unwaged, work patterns. In rural areas, women fulfill important functions in the production of goods for family consumption or for sale in local markets. Village economies and rural households depend on a variety of economic activities traditionally performed by women, ranging from food preparation to cloth weaving, basket making, and various other types of crafts.[12] All these activities are undermined by the departure of young women for the new industrial zones.

One of the most serious – and ironic – consequences of the feminization of the new proletariat has been to increase the pool of wage laborers and thus contribute to male unemployment. Not only does competition from the increased supply of female workers make it more difficult for men to find work in the new industrial zones, but the massive departure of young women also reduces the opportunities for men to make a living in many rural areas, where women are key partners in the struggle for survival. Moreover, in some of the poorer and less developed regions and countries, export-led production employing primarily women has come to replace more diversified forms of economic growth that are oriented to the internal market and typically employ men as well. The impressive employment growth figures recorded by most of the main emigration countries in recent years have obscured the reality that export-led growth can lead to unemployment for some groups even as it creates jobs for others.[13]

For men and women alike, the disruption of traditional ways of earning a living and the ascendance of export-led development make entry into wage labor increasingly a one-way proposition. With traditional economic opportunities in the rural areas shrinking, it becomes difficult, if not impossible, for workers to return home if they are laid off or unsuccessful in the job search. This is a particularly serious problem for female workers in the new industrial zones, who are often fired after just a short period of employment. After three to five years of assembling components under microscopes, these workers typically suffer from headaches and deteriorating eyesight. In order to keep wage levels low and replace workers whose health begins to fail, firms continually fire their older workers and hire younger, healthier, and more compliant cohorts of women.[14] Moreover, in the late 1970s and early 1980s, many companies began to move their plants out of older export manufacturing zones, where tax concessions from local governments had been exhausted, and into "new" countries such as Sri Lanka and Indonesia, where labor was even cheaper. All these trends have contributed to the formation of a pool of potential migrants in developing countries such as the Philippines, South Korea, Taiwan, and the countries of the Caribbean Basin. People uprooted from their traditional ways of life, then left unemployed and unemployable as export firms hire younger workers or move production to other countries, may see few options but emigration, especially if an export-led growth strategy has weakened the country's domestic market oriented economy.

But the role played by foreign investment in allowing the emergence of large-scale emigration flows does not end there. In addition to eroding traditional work structures and creating a pool of potential migrants, foreign investment in production for export contributes to the development of economic, cultural, and ideological linkages with the industrialized countries. These linkages tend to promote the notion of emigration both directly and indirectly. Workers actually employed in the export sector—whether managers, secretaries, or assemblers—may experience the greatest degree of Westernization and be most closely connected to the country supplying the foreign capital; they are, after all, using their labor power to produce goods and services for people and firms in developed countries. For these workers, already oriented toward Western practices and modes of thought in their daily experience on the job, the distance between a job in the offshore plant or office and a comparable job in the industrialized country itself is subjectively reduced. It is not hard to see how such individuals might come to regard emigration as a serious option. (See also the next chapter on how this may be happening with Japanese off-shore production.)

In addition to the direct impact on workers in the export sector, the linkages created by direct foreign investment also have a generalized Westernizing effect on the less developed country and its people. This "ideological" effect in promoting emigration should not be underestimated; it makes emigration an option not just for those individuals employed in the export sector but for the wider population as well. Thus, a much larger number of people than those directly or indirectly employed by foreign-owned plants and offices become candidates for emigration. In fact, the workers actually employed in foreign plants, offices, and plantations may not be the ones most likely to make use of these linkages and emigrate.

Although foreign investment, along with other political, military, and cultural links, helps to explain how migration becomes an option for large numbers of individuals in some developing countries, it does not fully explain why the United States has been overwhelmingly the main destination for migrants.[15] After all, Japan, West Germany, the Netherlands, and Great Britain all have direct foreign investment in developing countries. The evidence seems to suggest that, given the complex and indirect relationship between foreign investment and migration, the national origin of the foreign capital that enters a country may matter less than the type of production it goes into (i.e., labor-intensive export production) and than the other linkages that recipient countries may have already established with capital-sending countries. Thus, high levels of Japanese foreign investment in export production in the 1970s may well have ultimately promoted migration to the United States, because the United States had a greater number of other linkages with developing countries at the time—a function of its economic and military dominance—and was presumably seen as a more hospitable country for immigration.

It is in this context that the 1965 liberalization of U.S. immigration law and the unfading image of the United States as a land of opportunity acquire significance. The conviction among prospective emigrants that the United States offers unlimited opportunities and plentiful employment prospects, at least relative to other countries, has had the effect of making "emigration" almost identical with "emigration to the United States." This has tended to create a self-reinforcing migration pattern to the United States. As new bridges for migrants are created by foreign investment (in conjunction with political and military activity) and strengthened by the existence of economic opportunities in the United States, the resulting new migrations create additional bridges or linkages between the United States and migrant-sending countries. These, in turn, serve to facilitate future emigration to the United States, regardless of the origin of the foreign investment that created the conditions for emigration in the first place.

Although the United States remains the most important destination for migrants, the recent experience of Japan may offer a glimpse of what the future holds. As Japan has become the leading global economic power and the major foreign investor in Southeast Asia in the 1980s, a familiar combination of migration-facilitating processes appears to have been set in motion: the creation of linkages that eventually come to serve as bridges for potential emigrants, and the emergence of emigration to Japan as something that would-be emigrants see as a real option. (This is discussed further in the next chapter.)

THE NEW LABOR DEMAND IN THE UNITED STATES

At first glance, both the heavy influx of immigrants into the United States over the past two decades and their clustering in urban areas would appear to defy economic logic. Why would an increasing number of immigrants come to this country at a time of high overall unemployment and sharp losses of manufacturing and goods-handling jobs? And why would they settle predominantly in the largest U.S. cities, when many of these were in severe decline as centers of light manufacturing and other industries that traditionally employed immigrants? The liberalization of immigration legislation after 1965 and the prior existence of immigrant communities in major urban centers no doubt played some role in attracting immigrants from the older, primarily European, emigration countries. But the most important reason for the continuation of large inflows among the new migrant groups has been the rapid expansion of the supply of low-wage jobs in the United States and the casualization of the labor market associated with the new growth industries, particularly in the major cities. (These are subjects discussed in detail in chapters 6 and 7.)

Thus, any analysis of the new immigration is incomplete without an examination of the changes in labor demand in the United States. In fact, one might argue that while the internationalization of the economy has contributed to the *initiation* of labor migration flows to the United States, their *continuation* at high and ever-increasing levels is directly related to the economic restructuring in the United States. This restructuring also helps to explain the concentration of most of the new immigrants in large cities.[15]

The increase in low-wage jobs in the United States is in part a result of the same international economic processes that have channeled investment and manufacturing jobs to low-wage countries. As industrial production has moved overseas, the traditional U.S. manufacturing base has eroded and been partly replaced by a downgraded manufacturing sector, which is characterized by a growing supply of poorly paid, semi-skilled or unskilled production jobs. At the same time, the rapid growth of the service sector has created vast numbers of low-wage jobs (in addition to the better-publicized increase in highly paid investment banking and management consulting jobs). Both of these new growth sectors are largely concentrated in major cities. Such cities have seen their economic importance further enhanced as they have become centers for the management and servicing of the global economy; as Detroit has lost jobs to overseas factories, New York and Los Angeles have gained jobs managing and servicing the global network of factories.

These trends have brought about a growing polarization in the U.S. earnings structure since the late 1970s. Along with a sharp decline in the number of middle-income blue- and white-collar jobs, there has been a modest increase in the number of high-wage professional and managerial jobs and a vast expansion in the supply of low-wage jobs. Between 1963 and 1973, nine out of ten new jobs created were in the middle-earnings group, while the number of high-paying jobs was shrinking. Since 1973, by contrast, only one in two new jobs has been in the middle-income category. If one takes into consideration the increase in the number of seasonal and part-time workers, then the growing inequality within the labor force; becomes even more pronounced. The proportion of part-time jobs increased from fifteen percent in 1955 to twenty-two percent in 1977.[16] By 1986, part-time workers made up fully a third of the labor force; about eighty percent of these fifty million workers earn less than $11,000 a year.[17]

These changes have been reflected in a decline in average wages and an increasing polarization of income distribution. Inflation-adjusted average weekly wages, which rose steadily during the post-war period and peaked in 1973, stagnated during the rest of the 1970s and fell into the 1980s. This decline was accompanied by an increase in the degree of inequality in the distribution of earnings, a trend that first emerged in the 1970s and accelerated in the 1980s.[18] A report released recently by the staff of the House Ways and Means Committee found that from 1979 to 1987, the bottom fifth of the population experienced a decline of eight percent in its personal income, while the top fifth saw its income increase by sixteen percent.[19]

As mentioned earlier, one important generator of new low-wage jobs has been the downgraded manufacturing sector. This sector of the U.S. economy was created by the convergence of three trends: the social reorganization of the work process, notably the growing practice of subcontracting out production and service work and the expansion of sweatshops and industrial homework (all of which have the effect of isolating workers and preventing them from joining together to defend their interests); the technological transformation of the work process, which has downgraded the skill levels required for a variety of jobs by incorporating skills into machines and computers; and the rapid growth of high-technology industries that employ large numbers of low-wage production workers. Somewhat surprising, the downgrading of the skill and wage levels of industrial production jobs has taken place across a broad spectrum of industries–from the most backward to the most modern. Thus, while the garment and electronics industries would at first glance appear to have little in common, both have produced large numbers of dead-end, low-wage jobs requiring few skills. Both industries have made use of unconventional production processes such as sweatshops and industrial homework. Moreover, both have contributed to the disenfranchisement of workers, as is evident from the decline in union membership in areas of rapid high technology growth such as Los Angeles and Orange counties in California.[20]

More important than the downgraded manufacturing sector as a source of new low-wage jobs, however, is the growth of the service sector.[21] Unlike traditional manufacturing, which is characterized by a preponderance of middle-income jobs, the majority of service jobs tend to be either extremely well paid or very poorly paid, with relatively few jobs in the middle-income range. The growth industries of the 1980s–finance, insurance, real estate, retail trade, and business services–feature large proportions of low-wage jobs, weak unions, if any, and a high proportion of part time and female workers. Sales clerks, waitresses, secretaries, and janitors are among the growth occupations. The Bureau of Labor Statistics has reported declines in real earnings in these industries since the 1970s.[22] (For an update, see chap. 6 here.)

In addition to employing low-wage workers directly, the expanded service sector also creates low-wage jobs indirectly, through the demand for workers to service the lifestyles and consumption requirements of the growing high-income professional and managerial class. The concentration of these high-income workers in major cities has facilitated rapid residential and commercial gentrification, which in turn has created a need for legions of low-wage service workers— residential building attendants, restaurant workers, preparers of specialty and gourmet foods, dog walkers, errand runners, apartment cleaners, childcare providers, and so on. The fact that many of these jobs are "off the books" has meant the rapid expansion of an informal economy in several major U.S. cities. For a variety of reasons, immigrants are more likely than U.S. citizens to gravitate toward these jobs: these jobs are poorly paid, offer little employment security, generally require few skills and little knowledge of English, and frequently involve undesirable evening or weekend shifts. In addition, the expansion of the informal economy facilitates the entry of undocumented immigrants into these jobs. (See chap. 7 here.)

Whether in the service sector or the downgraded manufacturing sector, the new low-paying jobs attract large numbers of immigrants. Significantly, even immigrants who are highly educated and skilled when they arrive in the United States tend to gravitate toward the low-wage sectors of the economy.[22] The growing absorption of educated immigrants is partly linked to the growth of clerical and technical jobs in the service sector and the increased casualization of the labor market for these jobs.

Thus, while the redeployment of manufacturing to less developed countries has helped promote emigration from these countries, the concentration of servicing and management functions in major U.S. cities has created conditions for the absorption of the immigrant influx in New York, Los Angeles, Miami, Chicago and Houston. The same set of processes that has promoted emigration from several rapidly industrializing countries has simultaneously promoted immigration into the United States.

The fact that it is the major growth sectors such as high technology and services, rather than the declining sectors of the U.S. economy, that are the primary generators of low-wage jobs suggests that the supply of such jobs will probably continue to expand for the foreseeable future. As long as it does so, the influx of immigrant workers to fill these jobs is likely to continue as well.

TOWARD A WORKABLE IMMIGRATION POLICY

The Achilles' heel of U.S. immigration policy has been its insistence on viewing immigration as an autonomous process unrelated to other international processes. It should be clear by now that powerful international forces are at work behind the outflow of emigrants from the developing world and the influx of immigrants into the United States. Yet U.S. officials and the public at large persist in viewing immigration as a problem whose roots lie exclusively in the inadequacy of socioeconomic conditions in the Third World, rather than also being a by-product of U.S. involvement in the global economy. As a result, they fail to recognize that the proposals dominating the debate on immigration policy – sanctions on employers, deportation of illegal immigrants, stepped-up border patrols – are unlikely to stem the flow.

The 1986 immigration law, ostensibly designed to rationalize immigration policy, has not only failed to slow immigration but threatens to do harm both to our own society and to the immigrants themselves. The employer-sanctions program will consolidate a supply of powerless, low-wage workers by further restricting the job opportunities of undocumented immigrants who do not qualify for regularization. The combination of such sanctions and a regularization program that excludes a large number of undocumented workers will contribute to the formation of an immigrant underclass that is legally as well as economically disadvantaged. The expanded guest-worker program is likely to hamper the efforts of domestic agricultural workers to improve their own wages and work conditions. Moreover, this guest-worker program may bring about the development of new linkages with the countries sending agricultural workers, thereby having the unintended effect of facilitating new illegal migration outside the bounds of the program.

A workable U.S. immigration policy would be based on the recognition that the United States, as a major industrial power and supplier of foreign investment, bears a certain amount of responsibility for the existence of international labor migrants. The past policies of the United States toward war refugees might serve as a model for a refashioned immigration policy. Few people would assert that flows of refugees from Indochina after the Vietnam War were caused by overpopulation or economic stagnation, even though the region may in fact have suffered from these problems. Instead, it is widely recognized that U.S. military activities were to some degree responsible for creating the refugee flows. When the United States granted Indochinese refugees special rights to settle here, it was acknowledging this responsibility, at least indirectly. A similar acknowledgment is due in the case of labor migrations.

When drafting laws in most areas of foreign relations, lawmakers generally make an effort to weigh the differing degrees of responsibility of various actors and take into account such complex phenomena as the globalization of production and international flows of capital and information. Why, then, is it not possible to factor in similar considerations in the designing of immigration policy? To be sure, international migration poses special problems in this regard, because the relationship of immigration to other international processes is not readily apparent or easily understood. But the overly simplistic approach most policymakers have adopted until now has greatly hindered the fashioning of a fair and effective immigration policy. The precise features of such a policy will have to be elaborated through further study and debate. But one thing is clear: U.S. immigration policy will continue to be counterproductive as long as it places the responsibility for the formation of international migrations exclusively on the shoulders of the immigrants themselves.

NOTES

1 This chapter is drawn from the author's book *The Mobility of Labor and Capital: A Study in International Investment and Labor Flow* (New York: Cambridge University Press, 1988).

2 Earlier agreements barred Chinese labor immigration (1882), restricted Japanese immigration (1907), and culminated in the 1924 National Origins Act. This act was the first general immigration law in that it brought together the growing number of restrictions and controls that had been established over a period of time: the creation of classes of inadmissible aliens, deportation laws, literacy requirements, etc. The 1965 immigration law ended these restrictions. In this sense it was part of a much broader legislative effort to end various forms of discrimination in the United States, such as discrimination against minorities and women.

3   About 1.8 million aliens applied under the main legalization program; in addition, 1.2 million applied under special legalization programs for agriculture. While the majority applying under the main program are expected to obtain temporary resident status, it is now becoming evident that a growing proportion may not be complying with the second requirement of the procedure, that of applying for permanent residence.

4   Several clauses are attached to the bill, ranging from a doubling of Hong Kong's special visa allowance to the granting of 4,800 visas each year to millionaires prepared to employ at least ten U.S. workers. The bill also expands two existing worker preferences: professionals who are outstanding artists and individuals in occupations that cannot be filled by U.S. workers.

5   Detailed documentation of these issues can be found in Sassen, *The Mobility of Labor and Capital.*

6   A similar trend is taking place in the undocumented Mexican migration. See R. Warren and J. S. Passel, *Estimates of Illegal Aliens from Mexico Counted in the 1980 U.S. Census* (Washington, DC: Bureau of the Census, Population Division, 1983).

7   Marion F. Houstoun, et al., "Female Predominance of Immigration to the United States Since 1930: A First Look," *International Migration Review,* vol. 28, no. 4 (winter 1984), 945.

8   Nonpreference classes result from undersubscription of preference classes. Nonpreference entries ceased to be available in 1978, but recent lawsuits opened up admissions in this class again beginning in 1985.

9   *Abstracts of Reports of the Immigration Commission,* U.S. Senate, 61st Congress (Washington, D.C.: U.S. Government Printing Office, 1911), 105.

10 See also *Labor Migration Under Capitalism: The Puerto Rican Experience,* a study by the history task force of the Centro de Estudios Puertorriqueños (New York: Monthly Review Press, 1979); Alejandro Portes and John Walton, *Labor, Class and the International System* (New York: Academic Press, 1981).

11 See, for example, Norma Diamond, "Women and Industry in Taiwan," *Modern China,* vol. 5, no. 3 (July 1979), 317–40. In her research in Taiwan, one of the most developed of the Asian countries, Diamond found that women were actively sought out by factory representatives who went to the rural sectors to recruit them. About seventy-five percent of the female industrial workforce in Taiwan is between fifteen and twenty-four years of age. See also Helen I. Safa, "Runaway Shops and Female Employment: The Search for Cheap Labor," *Signs,* vol. 7, no. 2 (winter 1981), 418–33.

12 See E. Boserup, *Women's Role in Economic Development* (New York: St. Martin's Press, 1970); also E. Boulding, *Women: The Fifth World,* Foreign Policy Association Headline Series no. 48 (Washington, D.C.: February 1980).

13 In a detailed examination of the employment impact of export-led industrialization, the United Nations Industrial Development Organization (UNIDO) found that, in general, this type of development eliminates more jobs than it creates because of its disruptive effect on the national manufacturing sector, especially in the less developed countries of the Caribbean and Southeast Asia. *World Industry Since 1960: Progress and Prospects* (Vienna: UNIDO, 1979).

14 See June Nash and Maria Patricia Fernandez Kelly, *Women and Men in the International Divisions of Labor* (Albany, N.Y.: SUNY Press, 1983). See also the film *The Global Assembly Line,* by Lorraine Gray.

15 See the next chapter for a discussion of how such tendencies toward casualization are also operating in major cities in Japan. This is an important process facilitating the labor market incorporation of the new illegal immigration to Japan.

16 Paul Blumberg, *Inequality in an Age of Decline* (New York: Oxford University Press, 1980), 67 and 79; W. V. Deutermann, Jr. and S. C. Brown, "Voluntary Part-Time Workers: A Growing Part of the Labor Force," *Monthly Labor Review*, no. 101 (June 1978).

17 Bennett Harrison and Barry Bluestone, *The Great U-Turn* (New York: Basic Books, 1988). Even the U.S. government, in an effort to cut labor costs, has increasingly encouraged the use of part-time and temporary workers in its own hiring. The result has been a growing trend toward subcontracting out such services as food preparation, building maintenance, warehousing, and data processing. U.S. Congressional Budget Office, *Contract Out: Potential for Reducing Federal Costs* (Washington, D.C.: U.S. Government Printing Office, June 1987).

18 It should be noted that notwithstanding an increase in multiple-earner families and an increase in transfer payments, family income distribution in the United States has also become more unequal. Blumberg found that family income adjusted for inflation increased by thirty-three percent from 1948 to 1958 and by forty-two percent from 1958 to 1968, but grew by only nine percent from 1968 to 1978. Median family income kept growing throughout the postwar period but stagnated after 1973. Blumberg op. cit.

19 Linda Bell and Richard Freeman, "The Facts About Rising Industrial Wage Dispersion in the U.S.," Proceedings (Industrial Relations Research Association, May 1987); Organization for Economic Cooperation and Development, *OECD Employment Outlook* (Paris: OECD, 1985), 90–91. Several analysts maintain that the increase in inequality in the earnings distribution is a function of demographic shifts, notably the growing participation of women in the labor force and the large number of young workers of the "baby boom" generation. Both of these categories of workers traditionally earn less than white adult males. See Robert Z. Lawrence, "Sectoral Shifts and the Size of the Middle Class," *Brookings Review*, Fall 1984. However, when Harrison and Bluestone (op. cit.) analyzed the data while controlling for various demographic factors as well as the shift to a service economy (another category with a prevalence of low-wage jobs), they found that these demographic variables did not adequately account for the increased inequality in the earnings distribution. Rather, they found that *within* each group, (e.g., white women, young workers, white adult men, and so on), there has been an increase in earnings inequality. They also found that the growth of the service sector accounted for one-fifth of the increase in inequality, but that most of the rest of the growth in inequality occurred *within* industries. (See their appendix Table A.2 for analysis of eighteen demographic, sectoral, and regional factors.) The authors explain the increased inequality in the earnings distribution in terms of the restructuring of wages and work hours (chaps. 2 and 3).

20 See various articles on this topic in Nash and Fernandez Kelly op. cit.

21 The decline of mass production as the central force in national growth and the shift to services as the leading economic sector have contributed to the demise of a broader set of social and economic arrangements. In the postwar period, the economy functioned according to a dynamic that transmitted the benefits accruing to the core manufacturing industries to more peripheral sectors of the economy. The benefits of price and market stability and increases in productivity were transferred to a secondary set of firms, which included suppliers and subcontractors as well as less directly related industries. Although there were still firms and workers that did not benefit from this "shadow effect," their number was probably small in the postwar period. By the early 1980s, the shadow effect and the wage-setting power of leading industries had eroded significantly. The importance of this combination of processes for the expansion of the middle class and the overall rise in wages can be seen in the comparison of data for the postwar period with the income trends of the past two decades. See Barbara Ehrenreich, *Fear of Falling* (New York: Pantheon, 1989) on the meaning of this process for the middle class in the 1980s.

22 See Robert G. Sheets, Stephen Nord, and John J. Phelps, *The Impact of Service Industries on Underemployment in Metropolitan Economic* (Lexington, Mass: D.C. Health and Co., 1987). An

overall measure of the weight of low-wage jobs in service industries can be found in this study, which is the most detailed analysis of the impact of service growth on the creation of low-wage jobs in major metropolitan areas using census data for 1970 and 1980. The authors found that from 1970 to 1980 certain service industries had a significant effect on the growth of what they define as underemployment, that is, employment paying below poverty-level wages in the 100 largest metropolitan areas. The highest relative contribution resulted from what the authors call "corporate services" (finance, insurance, real estate, business services, legal services, membership organizations, and professional services) such that a one percent increase in employment in these services was found to result in a 0.37 percent increase in full-time, year-round low-wage jobs, while a one percent increase in distributive services resulted in a 0.32 percent increase in such jobs. The retail industry had the highest effect on the creation of *part-time*, year-round, low-wage jobs, such that a one percent increase in retail was found to result in a 0.88 percent increase in such jobs.

23 According to the Immigration and Naturalization Service, twenty-five percent of both male and female immigrants entering between 1985 and 1987 reported managerial and professional occupations, and about forty-eight percent reported being operators (a broad category of jobs ranging from assembly line workers to elevator operators), laborers, or farmworkers.

4

ECONOMIC INTERNATIONALIZATION: THE NEW MIGRATION IN JAPAN AND THE UNITED STATES[1]

The general proposition argued in this chapter is that international migrations are embedded in larger social, economic, and political processes. Although individuals experience migration as the outcome of their personal decisions, the option to migrate is itself socially produced. Because immigration flows tend to share many characteristics, this embeddedness is easily lost in immigration analysis or made so general as to lose explanatory power. An example is the notion that poverty as such is a migration push factor; yet many countries with great poverty lack a significant emigration history. It takes a number of other conditions to activate poverty into a push factor.

This chapter explores whether the concrete processes through which economic internationalization and more specifically globalization bind major immigrant- receiving countries to their emigrant-sending countries are one form of this embeddedness. Elsewhere I have developed such an analysis for the case of the United States (Sassen 1988) and also in more theoretical terms (1993). A new illegal immigration into Japan raises questions concerning the impact of the internationalization of the Japanese economy on the formation of this flow.

Japan has never had immigration, although it has a history, even if at times brief, of forced labor recruitment, colonization and emigration. It lacks belief in the positive contributions made by immigration. The concept of "immigration" did not exist in its law on the entry and exit of aliens. Yet, since the mid-1980s there has been increasing immigration from South Korea, Bangladesh, Thailand, Philippines, Pakistan, Malaysia, and Iran. Japan is now a major foreign-aid donor, investor, and exporter of a wide range of consumer goods in the countries whence originate most of its new immigrants, except Iran. This may have created objective and subjective bridges between these countries and Japan, thus contributing to a reduction in the sociological distance by familiarizing people with Japan. The United States has played a similar role in regions and countries whence come most of its immigrants. Further, regions with emigration traditions – such as some of the Bangladeshi states have added Japan to their possible destinations besides the Middle Eastern OPEC countries.

The first section of the chapter briefly addresses the impact of economic internationalization on the formation of new immigration flows generally. The second section examines both the magnitude and forms of Japan's recent economic presence in South and Southeast Asia. The third and fourth sections briefly review questions of policy in the United States and Japan during the last few years. The policy issue is now of great concern in Japan. Following an intense two-year debate, a new law was passed and became effective in June 1990, but it proved inadequate and is already under review. This is reminiscent of events in the United States: no sooner had the long-debated 1986 Immigration Reform and Control Act been passed than it came under attack and in 1990 a new immigration act was signed. The fifth section conveys evidence of illegal immigration to Japan. The sixth section discusses conditions in receiving countries that make possible the adaptation of immigrants with a view to understanding how illegal immigrants in Japan could become part of the Japanese economy involving Japanese employers deeply steeped in an anti-immigration culture.

ECONOMIC INTERNATIONALIZATION AND IMMIGRATION

Migrations do not just happen; they are produced. And migrations do not involve just any possible combination of countries; they are patterned. Further, immigrant employment is patterned as well; immigrants rarely have the same occupational and industrial distribution as citizens in receiving countries. And while it may seem that migrations are ever present, distinct phases and patterns are clearly discernible during the last two centuries.

Mass migration during the 1800s made an integral contribution to the formation of a trans-Atlantic economic system. Before this period, labor movements across the Atlantic had been largely forced (notably slavery) and mostly from colonized African and Asian territories. Similarly, migration to the United Kingdom during the 1950s originated in what had once been British territories, and migration into Western Europe during the 1960s and 1970s occurred within the context of direct recruitment and European regional dominance over the Mediterranean and some Eastern European countries.

The renewal of mass immigration to the United States during the 1960s took place within the context of expanded U.S. economic and military activity in Asia and the Caribbean Basin. The United States is at the heart of an international system of investment and production that binds these various regions. In the 1960s and 1970s, it played a crucial role in the development of a world economic system. It passed legislation aimed at opening its own and other countries' economies to the flow of capital, goods, services, and information. This central military, political, and economic role contributed to both the creation of conditions that mobilized people into migration, whether local or international, and to the formation of links with the United States that subsequently served as bridges (often unintended) for international migration. (See previous chapter.)

The United Nations' *Demographic Yearbook* (1985) and *World Population Prospects* (1987) show that in the mid-1980s the United States received about nineteen percent of global permanent emigration. A breakdown by region and country of origin shows that it received twenty-seven per cent of total Asian emigration, including 81.5 percent of all Korean emigration and almost 100 per cent of emigration from the Philippines. It received seventy percent of Caribbean emigration, but almost 100 percent of emigration from the Dominican Republic and Jamaica and sixty-two percent from Haiti. It also received 19.5 percent of all emigration from Central America, but fifty-two percent of emigration from El Salvador, the country with the greatest U.S. involvement in the region.

Elsewhere (1988) I have identified three processes as constituting a larger framework within which the new U.S. immigration occurred after 1965: offshore production; internationalization of major cities which emerge as centers for international business and for the coordination and management of a global economic system; and the development of conditions in the United States that make it an attractive location for foreign manufacturers and other types of firms and, at the limit, would make certain areas of the United States competitive with Third World countries as production sites. At least two of these conditions have also emerged in Japan: rapid growth in both off-shore manufacturing and of Tokyo and other major Japanese cities as international business centers. The third development has not occurred in Japan; direct foreign investment in Japan, though increasing in the 1980s, is at very low levels (Sassen 1991).

The implications of these developments for migration in the United States are as follows. Migration has increased as a result of linkages between the United States and several Third World countries through the internationalization of production. In major cities there has been an increase in both high-income and low-income jobs as well as casualization of the labor market, thus creating conditions for the absorption of a large number of immigrant workers. The increased presence of foreign manufacturing and other firms in the United States has contributed to the creation of transnational spaces for economic activity. Immigrant workers in manufacturing have contributed to reduced costs of production.

On a more conceptual level one could posit that immigration occurs within systems which can be specified in a variety of ways. The type of economic specification argued her represents but one of several possibilities. However, in other cases, the system within which immigration occurs cannot be specified in political or ethnic terms. One could ask, for example, if there are systemic linkages underlying current East European and Soviet migrations to Germany and Austria. Rather than simply posit the push factor of poverty, unemployment, and the general failure of socialism, we might inquire as to whether linkages are facilitating bridges. We may also ask whether the large pre-1939 migrations to both Berlin and Vienna produced and reproduced migration systems and whether aggressive campaigns during the Cold War showing economic well being as the norn in the West may have induced many people to migrate westward when a more accurate portrayal of conditions might have deterred some of them, though presumably not those who were determined to come at all costs. These historical and current conditions contain elements for specifying systems within which current Eastern European migration to Germany and Austria is taking place. (This is a subject I have examined more recently. See Sassen 1996b.)

Japan, proud of its homogeneity, has traditionally kept its doors closed to immigration, though not to emigration and forced labor recruitment.[2] It is now facing an influx of illegal immigrants from several Asian countries with which it has strong economic ties. These flows have occurred despite Japan's closed-door policy. Has the internationalization of the Japanese economy created conditions that contribute to building bridges which may eventually facilitate migration? It should also be noted that there has been an increase in the number of legal immigrant workers for low-wage jobs as well as high-level manpower, especially to the financial sector, all under categories of entry that were either introduced or expanded in the new 1990 immigration law discussed below. While high-level manpower flows are clearly related to the internationalization of the Japanese economy, this is far less evident in the case of illegal immigration from Asia.

JAPAN'S GROWING PRESENCE IN ASIA

Japan's role in the post–World War II global economy has moved from trade orientation in the 1970s to foreign investment, foreign aid, and the export of culture in the forms of fashion, architectural styles, and (especially to Asia) new models of success in the 1980s. Together with the export of consumer goods, these flows have contributed to a strong Japanese presence in many Asian countries.

Japan's contribution to global direct foreign investment (DFI) has increased rapidly. By 1982, it had become the leading net exporter of DFI, with a gross outflow of $4.5 billion, surpassing the United Kingdom's $4.4 billion. Although this was well below the $7 billion and the $10 billion gross outflows registered for the UK in 1980 and 1981, respectively, it emphasized Japan's importance as a capital exporting country. In 1983, a year of general contraction in direct foreign investment, Japan's decline was relatively smaller than that of other leading countries. By 1986, Japan's direct foreign investment flow had risen to $14.3 billion, and by 1987 to $19.4 billion, for a cumulated stock of almost $80 billion. In 1990 it reached $46.3 billion compared to $40 billion for the United States and $24 billion for the UK. By then Japan had surpassed most of the leading Western European capital exporters, including Germany, the Netherlands, and France. (For sources see Sassen 1991: Part One.)

Although much of Japan's investment is in the United States, its impact is much greater in South and Southeast Asia where Japan has a strong, complex, and multifaceted past and current presence. In the late 1980s a rapidly rising share of Japan's foreign direct investment went to Asia. By 1986 Japan's FDI stock in South, Southeast and East Asia stood at $22.1 billion compared to $16 billion for the U.S., a striking reversal. Since 1986 Japanese direct investment in Thailand, Malaysia, Singapore, Philippines and Indonesia has grown rapidly. Most of this investment is in export-oriented businesses centering on the auto and electronics industries.[3] Some Japanese companies have also shifted their plants from NIEs to ASEAN countries.

Another important aspect of Japan's internationalization is the rapid growth in overseas development assistance in the 1980s. While Japan's overseas development assistance is a small share of Japan's GNP, in absolute amounts it has made Japan the leading donor in the world, especially in view of U.S. retrenchment.[4] Japan surpassed West Germany in 1983 and France in 1984 becoming the second largest donor country. It became the largest donor in 1988, surpassing the U.S. In the 1980s Japan became the largest single donor of overseas development assistance in Asia. *By the mid*-1980s, Japan's foreign aid to Asia reached US$15 billion, or 70 percent of all Japanese aid compared with U.S. aid of US$1.11 billion for Asia and only $500 million for Southeast Asia. In 1989/90 Japan's foreign aid in Asia was $4.8 billion compared to 1.4 billion by the U.S. Japan accounted for about one fourth of all foreign aid in Asia, but by 1990 it was the single largest donor in China, Thailand, Philippines, Indonesia, Malaysia. Japan provided about 70 percent of foreign aid to Thailand, and about half of all aid to Malaysia and Philippines. While it accounted only for about a fifth of all aid to Pakistan and Bangladesh it was on its way to become the largest single donor.

THE NEW 1990 IMMIGRATION LAW IN JAPAN

The Japanese Parliament recently approved several amendments to the law on the entry of aliens. The Immigration Control and Refugee Recognition Law which was passed by the Diet on December 8, 1989 and became effective June 1, 1990, is a revision of a 1981 revision of an earlier law. On the one hand, the amendments expand the number of job categories for which the country will accept foreign workers typically on three-year stays. These relate mostly to professional occupations such as lawyers, investment bankers, accountants with international expertise, and medical personnel. On the other hand, it seeks to restrict and control the inflow of unskilled and semi-skilled workers. For the first time, sanctions are imposed on those employing and contracting illegal workers, which in many ways replicates efforts made by the United States to control entry.

Morita (1992) points out that there had been a set of regulations and practices covering the granting of residence and work permits to foreigners. But numbers were small and the overall situation was one of stability concerning all types of entries. In 1980, work permits were granted to 30,000 foreigners, mostly business managers, professors, artists, entertainers, foreign instructors, and skilled workers. By 1989, such permits had increased to 72,000 and by 1991, to over 200,000; though this still represents a small proportion of Japan's sixty-five million person workforce.

The 1990 law establishes twenty-eight categories for legal residence and work. It allows a variety of professional workers as well as the descendants of Japanese immigrants abroad (up to the third generation) to work and reside legally in Japan, with specific lengths of allowable stay. There are three classifications for foreigners to work in Japan. The first covers diplomats, artists, religious personnel, and journalists; categories of workers that operate internationally and do not represent the typical migrant worker. The second classification describes rather precise categories of professional and technical occupations, ranging from financial and accounting experts to engineering and highly skilled craftworkers. The third classification describes very specific forms of expertise. Temporary visitors, students, and family visitors are prohibited from work. The law also provides for a foreigner already residing in Japan to apply to the immigration office for a work permit. This is designed to cover the children of foreigners legally residing in Japan when they reach work age, rather than illegal workers in unskilled jobs.

In terms of control of illegal immigration (one of the central aims of the new law), two effects have become evident. First, it had a temporary deterrent effect, as did the 1986 IRCA in the United States. Before the law took effect, about 30,000 Bangladeshis and Pakistanis who had been in the country illegally, left, presumably to avoid arrest. In order to avoid a pattern familiar in other countries, in 1989 Japan canceled its visitor's visa exemption agreement with Bangladesh and Pakistan in order to prevent a rush of visitors intending to work illegally before the new law was implemented. The new visa agreement made it very difficult to obtain a visa and thus contributed to a huge reduction in the number of visitors, whether genuine or persons intending to over-stay and become illegal workers. This policy is not unlike the one which evolved in the United States during the late 1980s with known emigration countries: visa applicants from Colombia, the Dominican Republic, Peru, and Ecuador are required to demonstrate means and ties showing that they are on a tourist, short-term business trip, or similar visit, and plan to return to their country of origin. In 1991, Japan also revoked the visa exemption agreement it had signed with Iran in 1975 and, as with Bangladesh and Pakistan, the effect of the revocation was a sharp decline in entries from Iran.

Second, the new law indirectly allows the entry of individuals to be used in low-wage jobs through such categories as "company trainees," students, and the special allocation for Japanese descendants up to the third generation. This has, to some extent, allowed foreign workers to undertake low-wage, unskilled routine jobs that require little if any training. Further, the new law, which also allows students of post-secondary (but not university) institutions, including language and vocational schools, to work for a limited number of hours per week, has become a device to obtain workers for unskilled, low-paid jobs.

Employers can be fined up to two million yen (about $16,000) if they knowingly hire an illegal immigrant, and be imprisoned for up to three years if they continue to employ illegal workers. These are heavy punishments for employers in view of the acute labor shortage, especially in manufacturing. As for contractors and criminal gangs involved in procuring illegal workers, Morita (1992) considers that the present law is weak in its provisions concerning punishment. The new law also completely leaves out any consideration of the immigrant workers' human rights (Miyajima 1989).[5]

Apprehensions under the new law have increased, but so have the numbers of estimated illegal workers. Apprehensions rose from 22,629 *in* 1989 to 36,264 in 1990 and 35,903 in 1991. In addition, 27,136, mostly Chinese in boats, were denied landing in 1991, compared with 13,934 in 1990 and 10,404 in 1989. Even though immigrants tend to live in known residential concentrations, there has been no large-scale deportation (Sassen 1991, Chap. 9). Only a few hundred employers have received sanctions for knowingly hiring illegals. In a country with millions of enterprises and a large number of labor contractors, there are fewer than 2,000 immigration inspectors authorized to check on employers. With weak enforcement of the new law, there appears to be a pattern of growing abuse of illegal immigrants by labor brokers and by immigration officers and police (Miyajima 1989).[6]

The new law is being criticized because it does not address the shortage of labor for unskilled, low-paying or undesirable jobs and therefore pushes some employers either to risk sanctions for hiring illegal immigrants or to close their factories. These include employers of not only small, technologically backward factories, but also highly mechanized, technologically advanced factories (Morita 1992). One strategy being used by many large firms is to replace illegal workers with the descendants of Japanese in South America (Yamanaka 1991; Komai 1992). By making use of existing international channels, large firms are better positioned for access to these labor markets. I recently spoke with some workers who had returned to Brazil. They complained that the jobs they held were hard and dirty, that they received no respect and were not seen as Japanese. Japanese recruiting agents in Brazil are allowed to hire only Japanese descendants, a procedure which many Brazilians consider to be discriminatory hiring.

In so far as the new law relies on restricting visitors' visas, it must travel a fine line between remaining open to vast numbers of genuine tourists and business people *and* closing entry to potentially illegal immigrants. Two-thirds of Japan's tourists and business visitors come from Asia, as do almost all illegal immigrants. The main nationalities identified in the detected illegal population and in the inferred over-stayers population also comprise a large share of Asian tourists and business visitors. With Japan's increasingly strong presence in many countries, there is likely to be an increase in the number of countries listed as having "potential emigration." For example, in the late 1980s Japan established off shore factories and other types of investment in Malaysia; it now appears from apprehension data that illegal migration of Malaysians is one of the newest flows.

In the late 1980s (before the new law was passed), Japan endured a long debate concerning the nature of immigration (Sassen 1991, 311 –

14).[7] At the heart of the debate were the concerns of the Ministry of Justice with maintenance of public order, and the concerns of the Ministry of Labour with employment conditions of domestic workers and the nature of labor shortages in Japan. Morita (1992) notes that although the debate was conceived originally as a labor market issue, it eventually incorporated broader issues relating to the presence of foreigners. The possibility of ethnic conflict and racism can no longer be overlooked. Morita, one of the leading analysts of immigration in Japan, argues that the demand for immigrant workers is structural, not cyclical, and that the inflow of foreign workers will further rigidify the already segmented labor market, thereby increasing demand for foreign workers. Some analysts have also argued that Japan should view immigration from Asia and Latin America as part of the larger issue of international inequality in social and economic development and make immigration policy part of Japan's development policy (Nanami and Kuwabara 1989).

THE NEW ILLEGAL IMMIGRATION IN JAPAN

The legal foreign workforce in Japan comprises a broad spectrum of categories, from professionals to unskilled company trainees.[8] It is largely of Asian origin, with China, the Philippines, Thailand, and Malaysia the major sending countries. The majority are women who come in as "entertainers," mainly from the Philippines.[9] Recently, the number of entrants classified as company trainees and students in post-secondary nonuniversity institutions (mostly language and vocational schools) has increased. The number of descendants of Japanese persons born abroad up to the third generation (who may work legally in Japan) increased rapidly after 1987. Together with "company trainees" and nonuniversity students, they are seen as a legal supply of foreign workers to fill low-wage, typically unskilled, undesirable jobs. Since the new law was passed in 1990, an estimated 150,000 have entered Japan each year under these provisions (Morita 1992).

Finally, there are Koreans and Chinese whose origins go back to Japanese colonization at the turn of the century. In 1985, before the rapid growth of illegal overstayers, there were 850,000 permanent resident aliens in Japan, of whom 683,000 were of Korean origin, many third generation. By 1990, the estimated 700,000 Koreans and 140,000 Chinese accounted for eighty-five percent of registered alien residents and 0.5 percent of Japan's population. Many have been naturalized through having a Japanese parent (see note 2). The vast majority of Japan's legal foreign population reside in large metropolitan areas, particularly Tokyo, Osaka, and Nagoya. Over twenty percent of Koreans, sixty percent of Chinese, and forty percent of Filipinos reside in the Tokyo region and about thirty percent of Koreans, thirty-five percent of Chinese and less than ten percent of Filipinos reside in the Osaka region.

Fragmentary evidence indicates a rapid increase during the last five years in the numbers of foreigners working illegally in Japan – mostly in the Tokyo metropolitan area, Nagoya and Osaka, although they are also employed in agriculture. Typically, they entered the country on tourist visas and overstayed (see Table 1). Labor contractors, mostly members of organized crime groups, often use illegal documents to bring in foreign workers.

A juxtaposition of entries with departures shows that in recent years there have been significantly more entries than departures. While this may be partly explained by legal multiple-year stays and administrative miscount, among certain nationality groups an increasing number of entrants with short-term visas enter to work illegally. For example, in 1987 there were 360,000 Taiwanese entries but only 314,000 departures; 360,000 Korean entries and 149,300 departures; 85,300 Filipino entries and 57,600 departures. Entries from the Philippines more than doubled from about 48,000 in 1983 to 108,300 in 1990. If United States experience is any guide, a growing number of "tourists" and "visitors" will enter the country not to visit but to find gainful employment.[10] Although not too much should be read into these figures, they do support other evidence that illegal immigration is largely achieved through the overstaying of persons on tourist visas.

Estimates based on apprehensions and on entry and exit figures suggest that by 1991 there were up to 300,000 illegal immigrants working in Japan, mostly in construction, manufacturing, and bar and restaurant work. Almost all were from Asia, the largest groups being from South Korea (estimated 100,000), Bangladesh, the Philippines, Pakistan, and Thailand. Since 1988, when the government fully recognized the problem, numbers have kept increasing, although in early

Table 1

Japan: Estimate of Unauthorized Visa-Overstayers
by Nationality and Sex, 1990–92.

Nationality/Sex		July 1990	May 1991	Nov. 1991	May 1992
Bangladesh	M	7,130	7,429	7,725	8,003
	F	65	69	82	200
China	M	7,655	13,836	16,624	19,266
	F	2,385	3,699	5,025	6,471
Iran	M	645	10,578	21,114	38,898
	F	119	337	605	1,103
Korea, S.	M	8,793	17,799	20,469	22,312
	F	5,083	7,871	10,507	13,375
Malaysia	M	5,023	10,099	18,466	27,832
	F	2,527	4,314	6,913	10,697
Myanmar	M	1,041	1,676	2,712	3,611
	F	193	385	713	1,043
Pakistan	M	7,867	7,731	7,786	7,862
	F	122	133	137	139
Philippines	M	10,761	12,905	13,850	14,935
	F	13,044	14,323	15,770	17,039
Sri Lanka	M	1,594	2,143	2,618	2,932
	F	74	138	219	285
Taiwan	M	2,080	2,356	2,790	3,427
	F	2,695	2,885	3,107	3,302
Thailand	M	4,062	6,767	13,780	20,022
	F	7,461	12,326	18,971	24,332
Others	M	10,200	13,021	17,766	21,846
	F	5,879	5,830	8,650	10,010
Total	M	66,851	106,518	145,700	190,996
	F	39,646	53,310	70,699	87,896
Grand total		106,497	159,828	216,399	278,892

Source: Based on recorded entries and exits, Ministry of Justice. Office
of Immigration, Japan.

1900 there may have been a temporary halt in new entries but not in apprehensions.

Data on apprehensions from the Immigration Office of the Ministry of Justice analysed by Morita (1992) help to establish pre- and post-1988 patterns. In the mid 1980s data for apprehended immigrants show the Philippines as the largest single country of origin followed by Pakistan, Bangladesh, Thailand and Korea (see Table 2). Two-thirds of the Filipinos were women, which was also the proportion for Thai apprehensions. However, women were small minorities in the other groups. The high proportion of females among persons apprehended in the mid-1980s was due to the fact that illegal immigrants were mainly "entertainers" recruited for the sex industry. However, by 1989 and 1990, they accounted for only twenty-five percent of apprehensions. Alongside this shift toward male apprehensions was a shift in nationalities due to the passing of the law making it more difficult to obtain visas. This largely explains the sharp decline in apprehensions of Bangladeshi and Pakistani nationals in 1991, which also coincided with a sharp fall in tourist entries from those countries and a sharp increase in apprehensions of Iranians, who appeared to have replaced Bangladeshi and Pakistani nationals as the most visible illegal population in 1991. Japan later canceled its visa exemption agreement with Iran (signed during the oil crisis of 1973); tourist entries and, by inference, illegal overstays, declined sharply.

Figures on apprehensions from 1980 to 1991 show clearly that visa overstaying is the single largest category. Overall apprehensions rose from 2,536 in 1980 to 10,573 in 1986; 17,854 in 1988; 22,626 in 1989; 36,264 in 1990; 35,903 in 1991. Of the 22,626 illegal immigrants apprehended in 1989, 19,105 had overstayed their visitors' visas; fewer than 200 were apprehended for criminal acts. In 1991, overstayers represented 32,820 of 35,903 apprehensions. Only about 2,000 of those apprehended had entered the country illegally in each of these two years. One category of illegal entry that has increased rapidly is boat landings. Although records of such apprehensions are unavailable before 1982, 2,751 were apprehended in 1986, 11,000 in 1988 and 27,100 in 1991. The number of apprehensions of South Koreans, Thais, and Malaysians has also increased. Except for the Philippines, Taiwan, and Thailand, the majority of apprehensions are of men.

*   *   *

Table 2

Japan: Apprehensions by Nationality and Sex, 1982–1991

	1982	1984	1985	1976	1987
Total*	1,889	4,783	5,629	8,131	11,307
	(1,705)	(4,433)	(4,942)	(5,945)	(7,018)
Bangladesh			1	58	438
			(0)	(0)	(1)
China	775	466	427	356	494
	(691)	(330)	(301)	(195)	(284)
Mainland					
Taiwan					
Hong Kong					
Iran					
Korea, S.	132	61	76	119	208
	(97)	(27)	(41)	(50)	(99)
Malaysia					18
					(3)
Pakistan	7	3	36	196	905
	(0)	(0)	(0)	(0)	(0)
Philippines	409	2,983	3,927	6,297	8,027
	(396)	(2,887)	3,578	(4,797)	(5,774)
Thailand	412	1,132	1,073	990	1,067
	(387)	(1,078)	(953)	(826)	(777)

*Figures in parentheses are for women only.

(continued on next page)

Table 2 (continued)

Japan: Apprehensions by Nationality and Sex.
1982–1992

	1988	1989	1990	1991
Total*	14,314	16,608	29,884	32,908
	(5,385)	(4,817)	(5,708)	(7,558)
Bangladesh	2,942	2,277	5,925	293
	(3)	(2)	(10)	(1)
China	502	588	1,142	1,665
	(272)	(272)	(343)	(423)
Mainland	7	39	481	1,162
	(2)	(13)	(53)	(181)
Taiwan	492	531	639	460
	(269)	(256)	(288)	(235)
Hong Kong	3	18	22	43
	(1)	(3)	(2)	(7)
Iran		15	652	7,700
		(2)	(4)	(89)
Korea, S.	1,033	3,129	5,534	9,782
	(264)	(920)	(1,117)	(1,499)
Malaysia	279	1,865	4,465	4,855
	(14)	(174)	(609)	(963)
Pakistan	2,497	3,170	3,886	793
	(2)	(2)	(6)	(0)
Philippines	5,386	3,740	4,042	2,983
	(3,698)	(2,451)	(2,449)	(1,904)
Thailand	1,388	1,144	1,450	3,249
	(1,019)	(775)	(789)	(2,323)

*Figures in parentheses are for women only.

Source: Ministry of Justice, Office of Immigration, Japan.

If immigration simply reflected the "push" of poverty in sending
countries and the pull of plentiful jobs in Japan, one would have expected a large immigration during Japan's period of rapid industrialization when there was a huge demand for labor and many of Japan's
neighbors had still not become industrialized. During this period of
large-scale public and private construction the huge demand for labor
in Japan was filled mainly by rural migrants to major urban areas.[11]
Yet, even though the large rural labor reserves could not satisfy demand, the prospect of foreign workers entering Japan in the 1950s and
1960s was simply inconceivable. Even today the entry of "simple labor" is forbidden.

And if immigration were simply a matter of policy, then the current
illegal immigration in Japan should not have occurred. In the case of
the United States, the law of 1965 had an immense impact because the
US had a far-flung network of production sites and military operations in several Third World countries. In addition to a pent-up demand for emigration, there was also a broad network of linkages
between those countries and the United States. That the new law as
such could not bring about the new immigration to the United States
is also suggested by the fact that, being based on family reunion, it
was expected to induce the immigration of relatives of persons already in the country, that is, mostly Europeans. Instead, the vast majority of immigrants came from the Caribbean Basin and several
Asian countries. (See chap. 2 here).

In its period of high growth, Japan lacked the networks and linkages with potential immigrant-sending countries that could have facilitated the formation of international migration flows. As Japan
internationalizes its economy and becomes a key investor in East and
Southeast Asia, it is likely to create–wittingly or not–transnational
spaces for the circulation of its goods, capital, and culture which in
turn may create conditions for the circulation of people. We may be
seeing the early stages of an international labor market with roles for
both labor contractors and illegal immigrants.

LABOR DEMAND IN JAPAN: ANY ROOM FOR IMMIGRANTS?

In the case of the United States there was a rapid increase in the
supply of low-wage jobs during the late 1970s and an emerging casu-

alization of the labor market. Both of these were associated with new growth industries and a decline and reorganization of manufacturing. Tendencies toward casualization facilitate the incorporation of illegal immigration into labor markets (Sassen 1988). Casualization opens up the hiring process, lifts restrictions on employers, and typically lowers direct and indirect costs of labor. The increase in low-wage jobs in the United States is in part a result of the same international economic processes that have channelled investment and manufacturing jobs to low-wage countries. As industrial production has moved overseas, or to low-wage areas in the U.S. South, the traditional U.S. manufacturing organization based on high wages has eroded and been partly replaced in many industries by a downgraded manufacturing sector characterized by poorly paid, semiskilled or unskilled production jobs and extensive subcontracting. At the same time, the rapid growth of the service sector has created many low-wage jobs in addition to the more publicized increase in highly paid jobs in investment banking, management, and the professions (see also chap. 6).

Can a growing casualization of labor markets also be detected in Japan? Elsewhere (Sassen 1991, chapters 8 and 9) I have described in detail the growth of service jobs in Japan, the replacement of many full-time male workers with part-time females, the growth of types of subcontracting that weaken the claims of workers on their firms, and the fact that most new jobs created in Tokyo in the 1980s were part-time or temporary.

Since the mid-1980s – the key period in terms of economic restructuring – average real earnings in Japan have declined and the manufacturing sector has been losing its wage-setting influence. According to the Ministry of Labor, real earnings increased by 2.9 percent in 1985 and by 1.4 percent in 1986. While the main components of increased earnings used to be bonuses and overtime, closely linked with full-time employment in manufacturing, this category had declined to one percent of the increase in 1985 and to minus 0.5 percent in 1986. Total cash compensation for full-time employees of establishments with thirty or more employees increased by 5.03 percent in 1985, 4.5 percent in 1986, and 3.2 percent in 1987.[12] Unemployment, though small by Western standards, is increasing. While previously largely frictional, unemployment has distinct new patterns and, by 1986, had reached almost three percent. Further, most of the service industries had lower average earnings than the manufacturing, trans-

port, and communications industries. Increases in the hotel and catering, health services, and retail sectors were among the lowest.
Growing industries such as finance, insurance, and real estate either
pay above-average wages or below-average wages as in other service
sectors, a trend common in many Western cities (Sassen 1991: chapters 8 and 9).

Data from the Labor Force Survey in Japan show that the share of
part-time workers increased from about seven percent of all workers
in 1970 to twelve per cent in 1987. Among female workers, the share
almost doubled from about twelve percent in 1985 and over twenty-
three percent in 1987.[13]

While the vast majority of part-time jobs are in the service sector,
they have also increased in manufacturing. The share of part-time
workers in wholesale, retail, and eating and drinking places has increased from 25.4 percent in 1970 to 35.1 percent in 1985, representing
an increase from 330,000 part-time workers in 1970 to 1.17 million in
1985, or forty-one percent of the total increase in part-time work. The
number of part-time jobs in manufacturing doubled from 400,000 in
1970 to 800,000 in 1985. Female part-time workers increased by 38.2
percent, or 1.5 million, from 1982 to 1987, a far larger increase than for
the labor force generally.

Official counts of legal industrial homeworkers in Japan indicate a
decline during the last decade. There were over one million such
workers, almost all women, in 1987, the largest share (thirty-four percent) being in clothing and related work, followed by 18.6 percent in
electrical/electronic equipment (including assembly of electronic
parts) and almost sixteen percent in textiles. The remaining share
includes a broad range of activities, from toy making and lacquer
ware to printing and related work. It is quite possible that the existing
regulations protecting homeworkers and providing them with fringe
benefits are eroding. Official figures indicate a decline in the fully
entitled share of homeworkers but no absolute increase among un-
protected homeworkers. Yet there is some indication that the latter
category may be increasing (Sassen 1991, chap. 9). We need to ask
whether these conditions facilitate the employment of illegal immigrants. We cannot take for granted that labor shortage *ipso facto* explains the incorporation of illegal immigrants. My research suggests
other mediating conditions must be present in order to facilitate their
incorporation. My fieldwork in a large day-laborer market suggests

that such markets are a key mechanism for the incorporation of illegal immigrants into the Japanese labor market; they also make it possible for immigrants to secure jobs without a labor contractor.

In this context, it is worth noting that evidence on detected illegal immigrants provided by the Ministry of Justice and analyzed by Morita (1992) shows that over eighty percent of men apprehended between 1987 and 1990 held construction and factory jobs. According to a study of illegal immigrant employment in major urban areas in Japan carried out by the Immigration Office of the Ministry of Justice, factories employing illegal immigrants cover a broad range of categories: metal processing, plastic processing, printing and binding, planting, press operating, materials coating. An increasing number of women have been apprehended in factories in metals and plastic processing and in auto-parts manufacturing (Morita 1992). Illegal immigrants were generally found in medium-sized and small factories. Figures for 1991 indicate a continuation of these patterns; almost half the illegals detected by the government were in construction and fourteen percent in manufacturing and certain jobs in the retail industry (especially restaurants).

Estimates of illegal immigration for unskilled jobs point to a growing demand. The Ministry of Labor estimates that Japan's labor shortage will reach half a million by the end of the decade, but Japan's most powerful business organization, Keidaren, puts the shortage at about five million. Others estimate a range of between one and two million by the end of the decade. The largest current shortages are in manufacturing, particularly small and medium-sized firms, but there is considerable agreement that the service sector will become a major source of new shortages. As Japanese employees in low-skill service jobs retire and young highly educated Japanese reject their jobs, there may be a gradual acceptance of immigrant workers.

All highly industrialized countries have resorted to immigrant workers to fill low-wage jobs in manufacturing and services. But not all have experienced the combination of conditions that are evident in Japan today: the lowest fertility rate among developed countries, one of the fastest-growing old-age populations, one of the fastest urbanization rates, rural labor reserves depleted to the point where farmers have resorted to employing immigrant workers (and importing brides, given the shortage of young Japanese women willing to live in rural areas). The high educational level required of young Japanese and the ongoing demand for workers in high-paying jobs further reduces the effective supply of labour to fill low-wage, unskilled jobs. Even if current trends continue beyond the recession, and more Japanese are laid off, it is unlikely that they would take low-wage jobs. As in all advanced economies, the labor market is segmented and shortages coexist with unemployment.

CONCLUSION

Although Japan and the United States are countries with radically different histories, cultures, and, to a lesser extent, economic organization, we are seeing the formation of several similar processes. These are forming at a very specific juncture, identified analytically as the intersection of processes of economic internationalization, labor market developments typical of all advanced economies, and the cultural specificity of each country. Placing immigration flows and their continuation at this juncture allows us to see important parallels as well as significant differences in the migration histories in the two countries. The parallels result from each being a global power with strong economic presence in transnational zones of influence. The differences stem in part from the specifics of each country, and in part from the different stages of immigration history. In Japan we are seeing the beginning of a process that occurred in the United States over two or more centuries. Yet we can also see that the particularities of the current period – globalization of leading economies and labor market segmentation – shape migration flows, be it the first time immigration in Japan or the latest in the United States.

Japan is the leading investor, foreign aid donor, and exporter of consumer goods (including cultural products) in a regional Asian economic system. And although not as open to foreign firms as the United States, there is a growing presence of such firms in Japan. This paper argues that the new immigration reflects the globalization of Japan's economy. This is easy to recognize in the case of foreign high-level manpower for the financial industry in Tokyo, but less clearly so in the case of the new, mostly illegal immigration of manual workers employed in construction, manufacturing and low-wage service jobs. In this latter case, internationalization not only provides a context within which bridges are built with the countries of origin of potential emigrants, but also contributes to the Japanese economy becoming more porous, particularly in the large cities.

Japan now has a growing labor demand for low-wage, unskilled jobs in a context where such jobs are being rejected by Japanese youth. The case of Japan shows patterns that are by now vague and ill shaped in other advanced economies with long immigration histories. Japan shows us that even a country with high levels of mechanization will encounter labor shortages as it evolves into a service economy. In the case of Japan, this will be strengthened by low population growth. While advanced service economies tend to have high average levels of education and a growth in high-income jobs, they also engender a large supply of low-wage, unskilled jobs *and* a devaluing of most manual jobs. In a society that is fairly homogeneous and thinks of itself as one nation, one people, these processes of differentiation will produce relative labor shortages.

NOTES

1   The author acknowledges the general support of the Russell Sage Foundation while a Visiting Scholar in 1992–93, and thanks Vivian Kaufman, most particularly, for her invaluable assistance with this chapter.

2   The notion that Japan is a racially homogeneous country is contested by the resident Korean population, many of whom insist on their right to maintain their Korean ethnicity. It is also contested by the indigenous Ainu people, who consider themselves the oldest ethnic people in Japan and who were conquered by the wajin, the Japanese. They are still a significant group in Hokkaido. Among both Koreans and Ainu there are those who argue that Japan is a multiethnic society.

3   Though less so today than in the past, much of this aid consists of loans tied to specific purposes. These have been viewed as serving the interests of Japanese firms wishing to expand their markets and operations overseas. The 1980s saw a major change in Japan's understanding of the role of foreign aid, with greater emphasis being placed on broader political aims linked to Japan as a global power. This is reflected in the much larger share of grants than loans in overall Japanese aid.

4   For detailed accounts of abuses against illegal immigrants, especially by contractors who are typically part of or working for "yakuza" (organized crime) organizations, see *AMPO, Japan-Asia Quarterly Review* vol. 23, no. 4, 1992.

5   This matter is also discussed in *AMPO, Japan-Asia Quarterly Review* vol. 23, no. 4, 1992.

6   The importance of this issue for the Japanese government is evident from the fact that all the major ministries set up working parties to study and consult on the issue and to develop position papers. A review of their main positions points to the complexity of the issue and to the fact that the employment of illegal foreign workers is generally accepted as a given and as increasing.

7   In 1985, before the new immigration took off, the distribution of aliens was as follows: the alien population lawfully staying in Japan was 2.1 million. About one million were foreign personnel;

the remainder were mainly from Asian countries. The majority of Asians (800,000) were first-time entrants, almost all (727,000) having entered on ninety-day visas, and half gave sightseeing as the reason for their visit. The largest single category of those entering with work and other types of visas was that of entertainer (59,693). Of these, over 41,000 were Asians: 36,000 were from the Philippines; 2,500 from Taiwan; and over 800 from Korea. Most of the 465 persons entering as skilled laborers were from Asia. More than 12,000 of the 13,900 who entered, reportedly to study at Japanese language schools, were from Asia. There is growing evidence that the language academies actually front for facilitating the entry of people in search of work. Taiwan and South Korea continue to send the greatest number of visitors to Japan: 300,272 and 299,602, respectively, in 1986, more than 360,000 from each country in 1987, and up to one million and 600,000, respectively, in 1990.

8   The recruitment of women for the "entertainment industry" was initially confined mostly to the Philippines. It has increased sharply, spread to several other countries, and gone beyond the stipulations of the law (Asian Women's Associations, 1988; *AMPO*, 1988).

9   I spent many hours interviewing illegal immigrants in Tokyo in an attempt to learn why they decided to migrate to Japan despite Japan's reputation as a closed society (Sassen 1991, chap. 9). Many were individuals who, in one way or another, had been mobilized into migrant labor. Japan's growing presence in their home countries, together with the consequent availability of information about Japan, had created linkages and made Japan seem a good option for migration.

10 Between 1955 and 1965, the height of this migration, more than half the nation's forty-six provinces experienced absolute decline in population, and fourteen others experienced annual growth rates of less than one percent. Tokyo, Osaka, and Nagoya, the three largest metropolitan areas, were the main destinations of this massive migration. Between 1960 to 1970, the three districts came to account for forty percent of the national population. The population of Greater Tokyo Metropolitan Area increased by ten million from 1950 to 1970 and, by 1984, reached twenty-six million. In 1950, almost fifty percent of the population was engaged in agriculture; in 1970, only ninetten percent.

11 The annual spring negotiations for wages, or Shunto, have seen the delivery of lower rates of increase. Shunto affect the large companies and are the benchmark for smaller firms – not unlike wage negotiations in the steel or auto industries used to be in the United States. But, in 1987, the increases were only slightly higher (3.56 percent) than the prior year in the iron and shipbuilding industries, which once set the average for the country. Further, unlike earlier years, there were only regular wage raises and no additional increases, another indication of the declining position of the basic manufacturing industries which have been a key source for rapid economic growth in the Japanese economy (Sassen 1991, chapters 8 and 9).

12 These figures exclude persons employed in agriculture and forestry. Of 3.6 million female part-time workers, about 0.8 million were in manufacturing; 1.3 million in wholesale and retail trade; 170,000 in FIRE (finance, insurance, real estate); and almost one million in service industries.

SECTION II

WOMEN UNDER FIRE

5

TOWARD A FEMINIST ANALYTICS OF THE GLOBAL ECONOMY[1]

———————

The current phase of the world economy is characterized by significant discontinuities with the preceding periods and radically new arrangements.[2] This becomes particularly evident when one examines the impact of globalization on the territorial organization of economic activity and on the organization of political power. Economic globalization has reconfigured fundamental properties of the nation–state, notably territoriality and sovereignty. There is an incipient unbundling of the exclusive territoriality we have long associated with the nation–state.[3] The most strategic instantiation of this unbundling is the global city, which operates as a partly denationalized platform for global capital. At a lower order of complexity, the transnational corporation and global finance markets can also be seen as having this effect through their cross-border activities and the new legal regimes that frame these activities. Sovereignty is also being unbundled by these economic practices, other noneconomic practices, and new legal regimes. At the limit this means the state is no longer the only site of sovereignty and the normativity that accompanies it. Further, the state is no longer the exclusive subject for international law. Other actors, from NGOs and first-nation people to supranational organizations are increasingly emerging as subjects of international law and actors in international relations.

Developing a feminist analytics of today's global economy will require us to factor in these transformations if we are to go beyond merely updating the economic conditions of women and men in different countries. Much of the feminist scholarship examining the is-

sue of women and the economy and the issue of women and the law
has taken the nation–state as a given or as the context within which
to examine the issues at hand. This approach is a major and necessary contribution. But now, considering the distinct impact of globalization on key systemic properties of the state–i.e., exclusive
territoriality and sovereignty–it becomes important to subject these
properties to critical examination.

The purpose here is to contribute to a feminist analytics that allows
us to re-read and reconceptualize major features of today's global
economy in a manner that captures strategic instantiations of gendering as well as formal and operational openings that make women
visible and lead to greater presence and participation. This re-reading
differs markedly from mainstream accounts of the global economy.
Such mainstream accounts emphasize only technical and abstract
economic dynamics and proceed as if these dynamics are inevitably
gender neutral yet rarely, if ever, address this matter.

My effort is to expand the analytic terrain within which we need to
understand the global economy in order to render visible what is now
evicted from the account. My starting point is based on my studies of
the global economy over the last twenty years. Through these studies
I have found that the mainstream account of economic globalization
is confined to a very narrow analytic terrain. That account operates
like a "narrative of eviction," because it excludes a whole range of
workers, firms, and sectors that do not fit the prevalent images of
globalization. And, in that sense, the rhetoric of international relations, and its most formal instance, international law, can also be seen
as a narrative of eviction. This rhetoric traces the state as its exclusive
subject and has excluded other actors and subjects. These narratives
are centered in a vast array of micropractices and cultural forms enacted, constituted, and legitimized by men and/or in male-gendered
terms. Further, on the operational level, one could say that notwithstanding the growing number of top-level women professionals in
global economic activities and in international relations, both these
worlds can be specified as male gendered insofar as each in its distinct way has the cultural properties and power dynamics that we
have historically associated with men of power, or at least some
power.

Here, I specify two strategic research sites for an examination of the
organizing dynamics of globalization and begin examining how gen-

dering operates in order to develop a feminist reading. These two sites are derived from two major properties of the modern state, exclusive territoriality and sovereignty, and their unbundling under the impact of globalization. The purpose is not an all-encompassing enumeration of gender inequalities. The purpose is to specify sites for the strategic instantiation of gendering and for new forms of women's presence. This paper is a mere beginning–an analytic stage on which we need to place the details contributed by ethnographic research, cultural critiques, sociological surveys, and legal scholarship on men and women in their many specific conditions and subjectivities.

In the first section, I review some of the literature pertinent to this project. In the second and third sections, I focus on the unbundling of state territoriality through one very specific strategic research site, the global city, and try to lay out the implications for empirical and theoretical work on the question of women in the global economy. In the fourth section, I examine the unbundling of sovereignty in an age of globalization in order to explain the implications of the emergence of other actors in international relations and other subjects of international law. While in many ways each of these represent distinct research and theorization efforts encased in very separate bodies of scholarship, both focus on crucial aspects of the broader globalization process and its impact on the organization of the economy and of political power. We must factor both of these aspects into a feminist analytics of the global economy. Here, I can only touch on many of these issues and hence this paper is inevitably an incomplete account.

STRATEGIC INSTANTIATIONS OF GENDERING IN THE GLOBAL ECONOMY

We can identify two older phases in the study of gendering in the recent history of the world economy, both concerned with longer-standing processes of internationalization, and a third phase focused on very recent transformations, often involving an elaboration of the categories and findings of the previous two phases. The research and theorization effort of the first two phases was largely engaged in recovering the role of women in international economic development research so as to balance the excessive, typically unexplicated, focus on men.

A first phase is the development literature about the implantation of cash crops and wage labor generally, typically by foreign firms, and its partial dependence on a dynamic whereby women subsidized the waged labor of men through their household production and subsistence farming. Boserup, Deere, and many others produced an enormously rich and nuanced literature showing the variants of this dynamic.[4] Far from being unconnected, the subsistence sector and the modern capitalist enterprise were shown to be articulated – but through a gender dynamic that veiled this articulation.

A second phase was the scholarship on the internationalization of manufacturing production and the feminization of the proletariat that came with it (see chap. 5).[5] The key analytic element in this scholarship was that off-shoring manufacturing jobs under pressure of low-cost imports mobilized a disproportionately female workforce in poorer countries which had hitherto largely remained outside the industrial economy. In this regard it is an analysis that also intersected with issues of national economies, such as why women predominate in certain industries, notably garment and electronics assembly, no matter what the level of development of a country.[6]

Together these two analytics have produced an enormous literature, impressive in its detail and its capacity to illuminate.[7] It is impossible here to do justice to these two bodies of scholarship and their contribution to new frameworks for empirical analysis and theorization. The quality of the empirical studies and theoretical formulations these two bodies of scholarship produced helps us understand how much work we need to do in order to theorize the current phase, which contains both of these two longer-standing dynamics and a whole new one – the latter, the focus of this chapter.

A third phase of scholarship on women and the global economy is emerging from recognition of processes that underline transformations in gendering, in women's subjectives, and in women's notions of membership. These represent many different literatures. Among the richest and most promising is the new feminist scholarship on women immigrants that focuses, for example, on how international migration alters gender patterns and how the formation of transnational households can empower women.[8] There is also an important new scholarship that focuses on the household as a key analytic category to understanding global economic processes[9] and on new forms of cross-border solidarity, experiences of membership and identity formation that represent new subjectives, including feminist subjectivities.[10]

There are many studies that contribute much needed empirical detail, even though not focused on international or cross-border issues, or lacking an international perspective. They range from studies on gendered spaces[11] to studies on women and the liberal state.[12] Many studies of the economic conditions of women and men in the current era, of which there are a very large number in all the major social sciences, are essential to advancing my effort here, and I will be referring to some. Finally, particularly useful is the literature that examines the absences in feminist analysis and the differentiations that still need to be developed.[13]

Most of the studies focusing on gendering in contemporary economic and political processes tend to begin with detailed accounts about women, or comparisons between women and men. For me, this inquiry begins with the specification of the strategic dynamics and transformations that mark the current phase. Both approaches are necessary. The position I take is partly predicated on my reading of the contemporary phase of the world economy as one that has been constituted through major transformations and a new set of dynamics that are strategic (i.e., while not accounting for the majority of processes they are regime making). Thus, export-oriented manufacturing is a strategic dynamic, by no means accounting for most manufacturing jobs; gender is a strategic nexus in this development. My approach entails, in a way, constructing "the difference," theoretically and empirically, so as to specify the current period.[14] The purpose is to understand whether there is gendering in these strategic dynamics and transformations, and if so, what a feminist analytics would be. I relate to this inquiry as a mathematical problem, in its certainty of a solution but its lack of self-evidence. It would diminish the theoretical, empirical, and political importance of the question of gendering to assume that we have understood it by noting discrimination in pay for women and the high incidence of gender-typed occupations.

One important methodological question is what are the strategic sites where current processes of globalization can be studied. In export-oriented agriculture it is the nexus between subsistence economies and capitalist enterprise, and in the internationalization of manufacturing production it is the nexus between the dismantling of an established "labor aristocracy," in major industries with shadow effects on an increasing sector of developed economies and the formation of an offshore proletariat.

And what about today's leading processes of globalization? Among these sites, few are as important as global cities – strategic sites for the valorization of leading components of capital and for the coordination of global economic processes. Global cities are also sites for the incorporation of large numbers of women and immigrants in activities that service the strategic sectors.[15] But it is a mode of incorporation that renders these workers invisible, therewith breaking the nexus between being workers in a leading industry and the opportunity to become – as had been historically the case in industrialized economies – a "labor aristocracy" or its contemporary equivalent.[16] In this sense "women and immigrants" emerge as the systemic equivalent of the offshore proletariat.[17]

A second strategic site pivots on the question of sovereignty and its transformation under the impact of globalization, the subject of the third section. International law, a particularly formalized arena where one can capture the impact of this change, has had the nation – state as its main and fundamentally, i.e., foundationally, only subject. It has also been described as basically male.[18] The strategic nexus for my inquiry is the transformation of sovereignty and the openings this has created for women (and other hitherto largely invisible actors) to become visible participants in international relations and subjects of international law. It is no longer simply a matter of the unified state as the exclusive subject of international law and exclusive actor in international relations representing its people and thereby rendering them invisible as individuals and as particular collectives.

VALORIZATION AND DEVALORIZATION PROCESSES: A FIRST STEP TOWARD LOCATING GENDERING

A central assumption in much of my work has been that we learn something about power through its absence and by moving through or negotiating the borders and terrains that connect powerlessness to power. Power is not a silence at the bottom; its absence is present and has consequences.[19] The terms and language of the debate force particular positions and preempt others.

In the day-to-day work of the leading services complex dominated by finance, a large share of the jobs involved are low pay and manual, many held by women and immigrants. Although these types of workers and jobs are never represented as part of the global economy, they are in fact part of the infrastructure of jobs involved in running and implementing the global economic system, including such an advanced form of it as international finance.[20] The top end of the corporate economy – the corporate towers that project engineering expertise, precision, "techne" – is far easier to mark as necessary for an advanced economic system than are truckers and other industrial service workers, even though these are necessary ingredients.[21] We see here a dynamic of valorization that has sharply increased the distance between the devalorized and the valorized, indeed overvalorized, sectors of the economy.

Immigrant work environments in large cities, often subsumed under the notion of the ethnic economy and the informal economy are rarely recognized as possibly part of the global information economy.[22] Much of what we still narrate in the language of immigration and ethnicity is actually a series of processes having to do with: 1) the globalization of economic activity, cultural activity, and of identity formation; and 2) the increasingly marked racialization of labor-market segmentation so that the components of the production process in the advanced global information economy that take place in immigrant work environments are components not recognized as part of the global information economy.[23]

What we see at work here is a series of processes that valorize and overvalorize certain types of outputs, workers, firms and sectors, and devalorize others. Does the fact of gendering, for example, the devaluing of female-typed jobs, facilitate these processes of devalorization? We cannot take devalorization as a given: devalorization is a produced outcome.

The forms of devalorization of certain types of workers and work cultures I have referred to here and described elsewhere (see e.g. chapters 6 and 7 here) are partly embedded in the demographic transformations evident in large cities. The growing presence of women, immigrants, and people of color in large cities along with a declining middle class have facilitated the operation of devalorization processes. This is significant insofar as these cities are strategic sites for the materialization of global processes and for the valorization of corporate capital.[24]

How have these new processes of valorization and devalorization and the inequalities they produce come about? The implantation of global processes and markets in major cities has meant that the internationalized sector of the economy has expanded sharply and has imposed a new set of criteria for valuing or pricing various economic activities and outcomes. This has had devastating effects on large sectors of the urban economy. It is not simply a quantitative transformation; we see here the elements for a new urban regime.[25]

These tendencies toward polarization assume distinct forms in: 1) the spatial organization of the urban economy; 2) the structures for social reproductions; and 3) the organization of the labor process. In these trends toward multiple forms of polarization lie conditions for the creation of employment-centered urban poverty and marginality. In the remainder of this section I briefly describe some forms of this polarization. These are all subjects I return to in greater detail in chapters 6 and 7.

The ascendance of the specialized services-led economy, particularly the new finance and services complex, engenders what may be regarded as a new economic regime because, although this specialized sector may account for only a fraction of a city's economy, it imposes itself on the entire economy. One of these pressures is toward polarization because of the possibility for superprofits in areas such as finance. This, in turn, contributes to devalorize manufacturing and low-value-added services insofar as these sectors cannot generate the superprofits typical in much financial activity. Low-value-added services and urban-based manufacturing are the sectors where women and immigrants predominate. (See chapter 6 for more detailed occupational and earnings information.)

The super profit-making capacity of many leading industries is embedded in a complex combination of new trends: 1) technologies that make possible the hypermobility of capital on a global scale and the deregulation of multiple markets allowing the implementation of that hypermobility; 2) financial innovations, such as securitization, which create liquid capital and allow it to circulate and make additional profits; and 3) the growing demand for increasingly complex and specialized services in all industries, which contributes to these services' valorization and often overvalorization, as illustrated in the unusually high salary increases beginning in the 1980s for top-level professionals and CEOs.[26] Globalization further adds to the complexity of these services, their strategic character, their glamour, and their overvalorization.

The presence of a critical mass of firms with extremely high profit-making capabilities increases the prices of commercial space, industrial services, and other business needs, and thereby makes survival for firms with moderate profit-making capabilities increasingly precarious. And while firms with moderate profits are essential to the operation of the urban economy and for the daily needs of residents, their economic viability is threatened in a situation where finance and specialized services can earn superprofits. High prices and profit levels in the internationalized sector and its ancillary institutions, such as top-of-the-line restaurants and hotels, make it increasingly difficult for other sectors to compete for space and investments. Many of these other sectors have experienced considerable downgrading and/or displacement, for example, the replacement of neighborhood shops tailored to local needs by upscale boutiques and restaurants catering to new high-income urban elites. There are some interesting research questions to pursue here to understand whether this reconfiguration of economic spaces has had differential impacts on women and men, on male- and female-typed work cultures, on male- and female-centered forms of power and empowerment.[27] The remainder of this section is a brief discussion of some of these areas for research.

Inequality in the profit-making capabilities of different sectors of the economy has always existed. But what we see happening today takes place on another order of magnitude and is engendering massive distortions in the operations of various markets, from housing to labor. For instance, the polarization among firms and households and in the spatial organization of the economy results in the informalization of a growing array of economic activities in advanced urban economies. When firms with low or modest profit-making capacities experience an ongoing, and even increasing, demand for their goods and services from households and other firms in a context where a significant sector of the economy makes superprofits, they often cannot compete even though there is an effective demand for what they sell. Operating informally is often one of the few ways in which such firms can survive. This operation may entail using spaces not zoned for commercial or manufacturing uses, such as basements in residential areas, or space that is not up to code in terms of health, fire, and other such standards. Similarly, new firms in low-profit industries entering a strong market for their goods and services may only be able to do so informally. Another option for firms with limited profit-making capabilities is to subcontract part of their work to informal operations. Informalization often reintroduces the community and the household as an important economic space. This question follows: Does the growth of informalization in advanced urban economies reconfigure some types of economic relations between men and women?

More generally, we are seeing the formation of new types of labor-market segmentation. Two characteristics stand out. One is the weakening role of the firm in structuring the employment relation, which leaves more to the market. A second form in this restructuring of the labor market is what could be described as the shift of labor market functions to the household or community. These emerge as sites that should be part of the theorization about particular types of labor market dynamics today.[28] Both of these trends contain a correspondence between a devaluing of jobs (from full- to part-time jobs, from jobs offering upward mobility within firms to dead-end jobs, etc.) and a feminization of employment in these jobs. I return to this in chapter 6.

The recomposition of the sources of growth and of profit making entailed by these transformations also contribute to a reorganization of some components of social reproduction or consumption. Although the middle strata still are the majority in the population, the conditions that contributed to their expansion and politico-economic power in the post-war decades – the centrality of mass production and mass consumption in economic growth and profit realization – have been displaced by new sources of growth. Is the "systemic abandonment," that is, radical economic marginalization, of a growing segment of households – specifically, low-income female-headed households – completely unconnected to this reorganization of consumption and social reproduction? We need research and theorization that examines the possible articulations of these two types of processes, each the subject of separate bodies of scholarship.

The expansion of the high-income workforce in conjunction with the emergence of new cultural forms has led to a process of high-income gentrification that rests, in the last analysis, on the availability of a vast supply of low-wage workers. This has reintroduced – to an extent not seen in a very long time – the whole notion of the "serving classes" in contemporary high-income households. The immigrant woman serving the white middle-class professional woman has re-placed the traditional image of the black female servant serving the white master.

There is, to some extent, a joining of two different dynamics in the condition of women described above. On the one hand, they are con-stituted as an invisible and disempowered class of workers in the service of the strategic sectors constituting the global economy. This invisibility keeps them from emerging as whatever would be the con-temporary equivalent of the "labor aristocracy" of earlier economic organizational forms, when a worker's position in leading sectors had the effect of empowering them–a dynamic articulating the corporate and the labor sector in a manner radically different from today's.[29] On the other hand, the access to wages and salaries (even if low), the growing feminization of the job supply, and the growing feminization of business opportunities brought about with informalization alter the gender hierarchies in which they find themselves.[30]

This is particularly striking in the case of immigrant women. There is a large literature showing that immigrant women's regular wage work and improved access to other public realms have an impact on their gender relations.[31] Women gain greater personal autonomy and independence while men lose ground.[32] Women gain more control over budgeting and other domestic decisions and greater leverage in requesting help from men in domestic chores. Also, their access to public services and other public resources gives them a chance to become incorporated in the mainstream society–they are often the ones in the household who mediate in this process. It is likely that some women benefit more than others from these circumstances; we need more research to establish the impact of class, education, and income on these gendered outcomes.[33]

In addition to the relatively improved empowerment of women in the household associated with waged employment, there is a second important outcome–their greater participation in the public sphere and their possible emergence as public actors. There are two arenas where immigrant women are active: institutions for public and pri-vate assistance and the immigrant/ethnic community. The incorpora-tion of women in the migration process strengthens the settlement likelihood and contributes to greater immigrant participation in their communities and vis-à-vis the state.[34] For instance, Hondagneu-Sotelo found that immigrant women come to assume more active public and social roles which reinforces their status in the household and the settlement process.[35] Women are more active in community building and community activism, and they are positioned differently from men regarding the broader economy and the state. They are the ones that are likely to have to handle the legal vulnerability of their families in the process of seeking public and social services for their families.[36] This greater participation by women suggests the possibility that they may emerge as more forceful and visible actors and may make their role in the labor market more visible as well.[37]

The demographic transition in large cities toward increasing weight of women generally and immigrant men and women has absorbed a good part of these multiple forms of polarization. This demographic embeddedness has broken the nexus between 1) the condition of being workers in leading sectors of the economy, and 2) constituting a "labor aristocracy" as had been the case historically. And it has broken this nexus right at the center of the most advanced economies rather than through the offshoring of these workers.

THE UNBUNDLING OF SOVEREIGNTY: IMPLICATIONS FOR A FEMINIST ANALYSIS

Economic globalization represents a major transformation, not only in the territorial organization of economic activity, but also in the organization of political power, notably sovereignty as we have known it. Today the major dynamics at work in the global economy have the capacity to undo the intersection of sovereignty and territory embedded in the modern state and the modern inter-state system.[38] As with the discussion earlier, the main concern in this section is to capture strategic instantiations, in this case, the transformation of political power.

Along with the unbundling of territoriality, represented in the discussion earlier by the ascendance of global cities, there is an unbundling of sovereignty. We are seeing the relocation of various components of sovereignty onto supranational, nongovernmental, or private institutions. This brings with it a potential strengthening of alternative subjects of international law and actors in international relations, for example, the growing voice of nongovernmental organizations and minorities in international fora.[39] It also carries implications for conceptions of membership.[40] Both can facilitate the ascendance of women, whether individuals or collectives, as subjects of international law and the formation of cross-border feminist solidarities. Notwithstanding these implications for women, most of the critical analyses of sovereignty have not had a particularly feminist perspective,[41] though there is the beginning of a feminist reading of the state in international relations.[42]

There is an emerging feminist scholarship on international law, but it is not focused on the question of sovereignty and its transformation. Central concerns in this feminist critique are the notion that an ethic of care should prevail among states[43] and that the principle of nonintervention in the internal affairs of states leaves women vulnerable to abuse and injustice.[44] Each of these represents a transfer to the relations among states of the critique of liberal democratic norms prescribing, respectively, the relation between the individual and the state and the distinction between private and public spheres.[45] In the classical liberal tradition, the state does not intervene in home and family.[46] Similarly, according to international law, States do not intervene in the internal affairs of other states. One feminist response is that the state should intervene in the home and in the internal affairs of other states if abuse is occurring.[47] "Feminist approaches to international law may be understood as seeking to personalize and personify its normative constructs."[48] Elshtain's sovereign state/ sovereign self–which has the effect of personifying the State–shows us that international law is male.[49]

The particular form that the feminist critique of international law is taking has the effect of avoiding the question of sovereignty, and the implications of its unbundling for the emergence of new actors in cross-border relations and as subjects of international law. In a critical review of the feminist scholarship on international law, Knop notes that personifying the state has the effect of denying the individual and collective identity of women within a state and across states.[50] Women are confined to the realm of the given state and rendered invisible from the perspective of international law insofar as they are subsumed under the state's sovereignty. Her central argument is that we need both a critical examination of sovereignty and of the assumption that it pertains exclusively to the state.[51]

The impact of globalization on sovereignty has been significant in creating operational and conceptual openings for other actors and subjects.[52] Feminist readings that personify the state leave sover-

eignty unexamined; the state remains the exclusive subject for international law. This is not to deny the importance of the types of
critiques evident in this feminist scholarship. But when it comes to a
critique of international law, leaving out the issue of sovereignty and
taking its confinement to the nation–state as a given represents a
fall-back on statism – the legitimacy of the state as the subject of international law regardless of whether it is representative of a possibly
not so unitary people's will, or more fundamentally, rigorous in its
adherence to the precepts of democratic representation which can
account for differences.[53]

Why does it matter that we develop a feminist critique of sovereignty today in the context of globalization? It matters because globalization is creating new operational and formal openings for the
participation of nonstate actors and subjects. Once the sovereign state
is no longer viewed as the exclusive representative of its population in
the international arena, women and other nonstate actors can gain
more representation in international law; contribute to the making of
international law; and give new meaning to older forms of international participation, such as women's long-standing work in international peace efforts.[54] Beyond these issues of participation and
representation is a question about the implications of feminist theory
for alternative conceptions of sovereignty.[55] It seems to me that at this
point a feminist theory of the state would have to factor in the major
transformations of the state brought about by globalization, most particularly, what I think of as the decentralization of sovereignty onto
nonstate actors and the corresponding formation of other sites for
normativity beyond that embedded in the nation–state.

Here I will confine myself to a brief examination of the transformation of sovereignty under the impact of globalization. This effort parallels that of the first part of this paper – to expand the analytic terrain
within which we conceptualize key properties, in this case sovereignty. I see this as one step in the broader agenda of specifying a
feminist analytics for understanding the global economy today. But,
the major task clearly lies ahead and is collective and cross-border in
character.

Two kinds of developments in this new transnational, social, and
economic order matter for my discussion of sovereignty. One is the
emergence of what I will call new sites of normativity, and the other,
at a more operational level, is the formation of new transnational

legal regimes and regulatory institutions that are either private or supranational and have taken over functions until recently located in governmental institutions.[56] I argue that two institutional arenas have emerged as new sites for normativity alongside the more traditional normative order represented by the nation–state: the global capital market and the international human rights regime. The global capital market now concentrates sufficient power *and legitimacy* to command accountability from governments regarding their economic policies, as was illustrated by the recent crisis in Mexico. So does the international human rights regime, as is particularly evident in matters involving immigration and refugees, where courts have invoked international human rights instruments even when this overrides decisions taken by their national legislatures.

What matters for the purpose of the discussion here is that both contain a de facto transnationalizing of state policy which in turn creates practical and formal openings for the participation of nonstate actors. This represents a transformation of sovereignty as we have known and formalized it.[57] I will confine myself to a brief discussion of sovereignty and the impact of, respectively, the new international human rights regime that came into its own in the 1970s, and the privatization of regulatory regimes for global business.

International Human Rights and State Sovereignty

International human rights, while rooted in the founding documents of nation–states, are today a force that can undermine the exclusive authority of the state over its nationals and thereby contribute to transform the interstate system and international legal order. Membership in nation–states ceases to be the only ground for the realization of rights. All residents, whether citizens or not, can claim their human rights.[58] Human rights begin to impinge on the principle of nation-based citizenship and the boundaries of the nation.

In the early twentieth century there were several legal instruments that promoted human rights and made the individual an object of international law. But it was not until after the second world war that we see an elaboration and formalization of such rights.[59] The International Covenant on Civil and Political Rights and the International Covenant on Economic, Social, and Cultural Rights legislated much of what the Universal Declaration called for.[60] In 1976, a Protocol to the

Covenant on Civil and Political Rights was opened for ratification; it enables private parties to file complaints to the U.N. Human Rights Committee if a state that has ratified the protocol is involved. There is a growing number of other U.N. human rights agreements.[61]

Some of the human rights provisions that go the farthest in supporting needs strongly associated with the current condition of women can be seen as marginalized within the human rights regime. Barbara Stark finds that of the two instruments that constitute the International Bill of Rights, it is the International Covenant on Economic, Social, and Cultural Rights that could make the most difference for women. It is also "the marginalized half" of the international human rights law.[62]

From an emphasis on the sovereignty of the people of a nation and the right to self-determination, we see a shift in emphasis to the rights of individuals regardless of nationality. Jacobson (1996) and others have argued that human rights codes can erode the legitimacy of the state if that state fails to respect such human rights. Self-determination is no longer enough to legitimate a state; respect for international human rights codes is also a factor. It is not clear to what extent the pertinent organizations and instruments are likely to be implemented. One possibility is that international law today basically makes the individual and nonstate groups subsidiary to the laws between states. There is a growing body of cases signaling that individuals and nonstate groups are making claims on the state, particularly in Western Europe, where the human rights regime is most developed.[63]

In both Western Europe and the United States it is interesting to note that immigrants and refugees have been key claimants, and in that sense, mechanisms for the expansion of the human rights regime. Several court cases show how undocumented immigration creates legal voids which are increasingly filled by invoking human rights covenants.[64] In many of these cases, we can see the individual or nonstate actors bringing the claims based on international human rights codes as expanding international law. The state, in this case the judiciary, "mediates between these agents and the international legal order."[65] Courts have emerged as central institutions for a whole series of changes.[66]

The fact that individuals and nonstate actors can make claims on states under the rule of law based on international human rights codes, signals a development that goes beyond the expansion of human rights within the framework of nation–states. It can redefine notions of nationality and membership. Under human rights regimes states must increasingly take account of *persons qua persons*, rather than *qua* citizens. The individual is now an object of law and a site for rights regardless of whether a citizen or an alien, a man or a woman where there are gendered legal regimes.[67]

The as yet small but growing ability of nongovernmental organizations and individuals to make claims on the basis of international human rights instruments has implications beyond the boundaries of individual states. It affects the configuration of the international order and strengthens the international civil arena. The concept of nationality is being partly displaced from a principle that reinforces state sovereignty and self-determination (through the state's right/power to define its nationals), to a concept which emphasizes that the state is accountable to all its residents on the basis of international human rights law.[68] The individual emerges as an object of international law and institutions. International law still protects state sovereignty and has in the state its main subject; but it is no longer the case that the state is the only such subject.

The Privatizing of Transnational Legal Regimes

The particular forms of legal innovation that have been produced, and within which much of globalization is encased and framed, have had distinct impacts on the sovereignty of the state. Many of these legal innovations and changes are often summarized under the notion of "deregulation" and taken as somewhat of a given–though not by legal scholars.[69] In much social science, deregulation is another name for the declining significance of the state.[70] There is a more specific process contained in these legal changes, one that along with the reconfiguration of territory may signal a more fundamental transformation.

Firms operating transnationally need to ensure the functions traditionally exercised by the state in the national realm of the economy, such as guaranteeing property rights and contracts.[71] Insofar as economic globalization extends the economy beyond the boundaries of the nation–state, and hence its sovereignty, this guarantee would appear to be threatened. But in fact globalization has been accompanied by the creation of new legal regimes and legal practices, and the expansion and renovation of some older forms that bypass national legal systems. Globalization and governmental deregulation have not meant the absence of regulatory regimes and institutions for the governance of international economic relations. Among the most important ones in the private sector today are international commercial arbitration, and the variety of institutions which fulfill rating and advisory functions that have become essential for the operation of the global economy.

International commercial arbitration, which aims at by-passing national courts, is today the most important mechanism for solving cross-border business disputes. Dezalay and Garth describe it as a delocalized and decentralized market for the administration of international commercial disputes, connected by more or less powerful institutions and individuals who are both competitive and complementary.[72] It is in this regard far from a unitary system of justice, "organized perhaps around one great lex mercatoria – that might have been envisioned by some of the pioneering idealists of law."[73]

The World Trade Organization has the authority to override local and national authority if there is a violation of the terms of the agreement, and hence can discipline sovereign states. International commercial arbitration is basically a private justice system, and credit-rating agencies are private gate-keeping systems. We are also seeing the formation of transnational legal regimes and their penetration into national systems hitherto closed.[74] Further, national legal systems are becoming more internationalized in some of the major developed economies. Some of the old divisions between the national and the global are becoming weaker, and to some extent, neutralized. Along with others, these various institutions have emerged as important governance mechanisms whose authority is not centered in the state. They contribute to the maintenance of order at the top of the economic system.

These and kindred transnational institutions and regimes raise questions about the relation between state sovereignty and the governance of global economic processes. Does the ascendance of such institutions and regimes entail a decline in state sovereignty? We are seeing a relocation of authority that has transformed the capacities of governments and can be thought of as an example of what Rosenau has described as governance without government.[75] In many ways, the state is involved in this emerging transnational governance system.[76] But it is a state that has itself undergone transformation and participated in legitimating a new doctrine about the role of the state in the economy.[77] Central to this new doctrine is a growing consensus among states to further the growth and strength of the global economy.[78]

An important question running through these different developments is whether the new transnational regimes and institutions are creating systems that strengthen the claims of certain actors (corporations, the global capital market, the large multinational legal firms) and correspondingly weaken the position of smaller players and of states.[79] Global capital has made claims on nation–states and these have responded through the production of new forms of legality. The new geography of global economic processes, the strategic territories for economic globalization, had to be produced, both in terms of the practices of corporate actors and the requisite infrastructure, and in terms of the work of the state in producing or legitimizing new legal regimes.[80]

There is a larger theoretico-political question underlying some of these issues that has to do with which actors gain the legitimacy for governance of the global economy and the legitimacy to take over rules and authorities hitherto encased in the nation–state. It also raises a question about the condition of international public law. Do the new systems for governance that are emerging, and the confinement of the role of nation–states in the global economy to furthering deregulations, markets, and privatization, indicate a decline of international public law?[81]

The ascendance of an international human rights regime and of a large variety of nonstate actors in the international arena signals the expansion of an international civil society.[82] This is clearly a contested space, particularly when we consider the logic of the capital market–profitability at all costs–against that of the human rights regime. But it does represent a space where women can gain visibility as individuals and as collective actors, and come out of the invisibility of aggregate membership in a nation–state exclusively represented by the sovereign. The practices and claims enacted by nonstate actors in this international space may well contribute to creating international law, as is most clearly the case with both the international human rights regime and the demands for rights made by firms and markets with global operations.[83] For women, this means at least

partly working outside the state, through nonstate groups and networks. The needs and agendas of women are not necessarily defined
exclusively by state borders,[84] we are seeing the formation of cross-
border solidarities and notions of membership rooted in gender, sexu-
ality, and feminism, as well as in questions of class and country status,
i.e., First versus Third World, which cut across all of these membership notions.[85]

CONCLUSION

There is not much purpose in writing a conclusion since the effort
here was not to gain closure but to open up an analytic field within
which to understand the question of gendering in the global economy
today. I selected for examination two key features of the organization
of economic and political power: exclusive territoriality and sovereignty. I operationalized these in terms of two strategic instantiations
which capture the impact of globalization. These are the global city, as
emblematic of the incipient unbundling of the exclusive territoriality
of the nation–state, and international law (including customary law
and certain international human rights codes), as emblematic of the
emergence of subjects for international law other than the nation–
state. The purpose was to open up an analytic terrain for a feminist
inquiry of issues that are highly abstract–whether it is international
finance or international public law–and have remained inhospitable
to feminist examination.

NOTES

1   This chapter was partially prepared while the author was a Fellow at the Center for Advanced
    Study in the Behavioral Sciences. The author would like to express her gratitude for financial
    support provided by The National Science Foundation, Grant # SBR-9022192.

2   The notion of a global economy is increasingly used to distinguish the particular phase of the
    world economy that began to emerge in the 1970s. It is characterized by a rapid growth of
    transactions and institutions that are outside the framework of interstate relations. See gener-
    ally James H. Mittelman, ed., *Globalization: Critical Reflections* (1996). For a broader historical
    perspective, see generally Giovanni Arrighi, *The Long Twentieth Century: Money, Power, and
    the Origins of our Times* (1994); Eric Hobsbawm, *Nations and Nationalism Since 1780, Myth,
    Reality* (1991).

3   By unbundling I do not mean dissolution, but rather a form of disarticulation. For a more
    detailed discussion, see Saskia Sassen, *Losing Control? Sovereignty in an Age of Globalization*
    (1996) [hereinafter *Losing Control*].

4 See generally E. Boserup, *Woman's Role in Economic Development* (1970). C. D. Deere, "Rural Women's Subsistence Production in the Capitalist Periphery," 8, 9 *Review of Radical Political Economy* (1976).

5 See, e.g., Maria Patricia Fernandez-Kelly, *For We Are Sold, I and My People: Women and Industry in Mexico;s Frontier* (1982); Helen I. Safa, *The Myth of the Male Breadwinner: Women and Industrialization in the Caribbean* (1995); Saskia Sassen, *The Mobility of Labor and Capital: A Study in International Investment and Labor Flow* (1988); Linda Y. C. Lim, "Women Workers in Multinational Corporations: The Case of the Electronics Industry in Malaysia and Singapore," *Transnational Enterprises: Their Impact on Third World Societies and Cultures* 109 (Krishna Kumar, ed., 1980).

6 See generally Ruth Milkman, *Gender at Work* (1987); Lourdes Beneria and Catherine Stimpson, eds., *Women, Households and the Economy* (1987).

7 For some recent collections and lenghty bibliographies, see generally, Irene Tinker, ed., *Persistent Inequalities: Women and World Development* (1990); June Nash and Helen Safa, eds., *Women and Change in Latin America* (1986); Christine E. Bose & Edna Acosta-Belén, eds., *Women in the Latin American Development Process* (1995); Katheryn Ward, ed., *Women Workers and Global Restructuring* (1990).

8 See, e.g., Sherri Grasmuck and Patricia R. Pessar, *Between Two Islands: Dominican International Migration* (1991); Pierrette Hondagneu-Sotelo, *Gendered Transitions: Mexican Experiences of Immigration* (1994); Monica Boyd, "Family and Personal Networks in International Migraion: Recent Developments and New Agendas," 23 *Int'l Migration Rev.* 638; Mary Garcia Castro, "Work Versus Life: Colombian Women in New York," in *Women and Change in Latin America, supra* note 7 at 231; Mirjana Morokvasic, "Birds of Passage Are Also Women," 18 *Int'l Migration Rev.* 886 (special issue on women immigrants).

9 See, e.g., Joan Smith & Immanuel Wallerstein, eds., *Creating and Transforming Households: The Constraints of the World-Economy* (1992).

10 See, e.g., Linda Basch et al., *Nations Unbound: Transnational Projects, Postcolonial Predicaments, and Deteritorialized Nation–States* (1994); Yasemin Nuhoglu Soysal, *Limits of Citizenship: Migrants and Postnational Membership in Europe* (1994); Zillah Eisenstein, "Stop Stomping on the Rest of Us: Retrieving Publicness from the Privitization of the Globe," 4 *Ind. J. Global Leg. Stud.* (1996). But see Aiwha Ong, "Strategic Sisterhood or Sisters in Solidarity? Questions of Communitarianism and Citizenship in Asia," 4 *Ind. J. Global Leg. Stud.* 107 (1996).

11 See e.g., Daphne Spain, *Gendered Spaces* (1992); Corrine Stoewsand, *Women Building Cities* (unpublished Ph.D. diss., Columbia University, 1996).

12 See e.g., Catharine A. MacKinnon, *Toward a Feminist Theory of State* (1989); Jean Bethke Elshtain, "Sovereign God, Sovereign State, Sovereign Self," 66 *Notre Dame L. Rev.* 1355 (1991).

13 See e.g., Martha Minow, *Making All the Difference: Inclusion, Exclusion, and American Law* (1990); Elizabeth Spelman, *Inessential Woman: Problems of Exclusion in Feminist Thought* (1988); Elshtain, *supra* note 12; Joan Williams, "Restructuring Work and Family Entitlements Around Family Values," 19 *Harv. J. L. & Pub. Pol'y* 753 (1996).

14 I have always rather explicitly positioned myself as someone who wants to construct the difference. I do not deny the existence of many continuities, but my effort has been to understand the strategic discontinuities. This is clearly a partial account, and it must be read alongside many other types of accounts. For an example of scholarly efforts to capture differences, see the work by historians to conceptualize "global history." See e.g., Bruce Mazlish and Ralph Buultjens, eds., *Conceptualizing Global History* (1993). For a more theorized effort to re-read an earlier period characterized by massive shifts, see Nathaniel Berman, "Economic Consequences, Na-

tionalist Passions: Keynes, Crisis, Culture, and Policy," 10 *Am. U.J. Int'l L. & Pol'y* 619 (1995). See also Rosemary J. Coombe, "The Cultural Life of Things: Anthropological Approaches to Law and Society in Conditions of Globalization," 10 *Am. U.J. Int'l L. & Pol'y* 791 (1995).

15 Today's global cities are in part the sites of postcolonialism and contain conditions for the formation of a postcolonialist discourse. See generally Anthony D. King, *Urbanism, Colonialism, and the World-Economy: Cultural and Spatial Foundations of the World Urban System* (1990); Stuart Hall, *The Local and the Global: Globalization and Ethnicity*, in *Culture, Globalization and the World-System: Contemporary Conditions for the Representation of Identity*, edited by Anthony D. King (1991). An interesting question concerns the nature of internationalization today in ex-colonial cities. King's analysis about the distinctive historical and unequal conditions in which the notion of the "international" was constructed is extremely important. During the time of empire, some of the major old colonial centers were far more internationalized than the metropolitan centers. Internationalization as used today is assumed to be rooted in the experience of the center. This brings up a parallel contemporary blindspot well captured in Hall's observation that contemporary post-colonial and post-imperialist critiques have emerged in the former centers of empires and are silent about a range of conditions evident today in ex-colonial cities or countries. Hall, id. Similarly, the idea that the international migrations now directed largely to the center from former colonial territories in the case of Europe, and neo-colonial territories in the case of the United States and Japan, might be the correlate of the internationalization of capital that began with colonialism is simply not part of the mainstream interpretation of that past and the present. See, generally, Sassen *supra* note 5.

16 See Professor Garcia Clark's comments on how in my account "women and immigrants" comes to replace "women and children." Gracia Clark, "Implications of Globalization for Feminist Work," 4 *Ind. J. Global Legal Stud.* 43, 46 (1996). It is, in my reading, a new topos which replaces the Fordist-family wage topos of women and children. I return to this subject in the next two sections.

17 See, generally, Sassen, *supra* note 5.

18 See, generally, Elshtain, *supra* note 12; Mackinnon, *supra* note 12.

19 For me as a political economist, addressing these issues has meant working in several systems of representation and constructing spaces of intersection. There are analytic moments when two systems of representation intersect. Such analytic moments are easily experienced as spaces of silence, of absence. One challenge is to see what happens in those spaces, what operations (analytic, of power, of meaning) take place there. One version of these spaces of intersection is what I have called analytic borderlands. Why borderlands? They are spaces that are constituted in terms of discontinuities; in them discontinuities are given a terrain rather than reduced to a dividing line. Much of my work on economic globalization and cities has focused on these discontinuities and has sought to reconstitute them analytically as borderlands rather than dividing lines. This produces a terrain within which these discontinuities can be reconstituted in terms of economic operations whose properties are not merely a function of the spaces on each side (i.e., a reduction to the condition of dividing line), but also, and most centrally, of the discontinuity itself, the argument being that discontinuities are an integral part of the economic system.

20 A methodological tool I find useful for this type of examination is what I call circuits for the distribution and installation of economic operations. These circuits allow me to follow economic activities into terrains that escape the increasingly narrow geography of mainstrain representations of "the advanced economy" and to negotiate the crossing of socio-culturally discontinuous spaces.

21 This is illustrated by the following event. When the acute stock market crisis happened in 1987 after years of enormous growth, there were numerous press reports about the sudden and

massive unemployment crisis among high-income professionals on Wall Street. The other unemployment crises on Wall Street, affecting secretaries and blue-collar workers, were never noticed nor reported. And yet, the stock market crash created a very concentrated unemployment crisis, for instance, in the Dominican immigrant community in northern Manhattan where a lot of the Wall Street cleaners live.

22 For a critical account of these issues see Anthony D. King, ed., *Representing the City: Ethnicity, Capital and Culture in the 21st-Century Metropolis* (1996).

23 More generally immigration has not been connected to other international processes in the research literature. Among exceptions see, e.g., Sarah J. Mahler, *American Dreaming: Immigrant Life on the Margins* (1995); *II Journal für Entwicklungspolitik, Schwerpunkt: Migration* (1995) issue on migration; Douglas S. Massey et al., "Theories of International Migration: A Review and Appraisal," 19 *Population & Dev. Rev.* 431 (1993). Hall describes the post-war influx of people from the commonwealth into Britain and how England and Englishness were so present in his native Jamaica as to make people feel that London was the capital where they were all headed to sooner or later (Hall, *supra* note 15). This way of narrating the migration events of the post-war era captures the ongoing weight of colonialism and postcolonial forms of empire on major processes of globalization today, and specifically those binding emigration and immigration countries. The major immigration countries are not innocent bystanders; the specific genesis and contents of their responsibility will vary from case to case and from period to period.

24 On this specific issue see Introduction and chap. 8 here. See generally Saskia Sassen, *The Informal Economy: Between New Developments and Old Regulations* (chap. 7 here), which explains a parallel dynamic – the combination of necessary work and devalorization – in the case of the growth of informalization in advanced urban economies.

25 See generally id; *World Cities in a World-System*, *supra* note 189; M. Frost & Nigel Spence, "Global City Characteristics and Central London's Employment," 30 *Urb. Stud.* 547 (1993); *Le Debat* special issue entitled "Le Nouveau Paris" summer 1994.

26 The high profit-making capability of the new growth sectors also rests partly on speculative activity. The extent of this dependence on speculation can be seen in the crisis of the early 1990s that followed the unusually high profits in finance and real estate in the 1980s. The real estate and financial crisis, however, seems to have left the basic dynamic of the sector untouched. The crisis can thus be seen as an adjustment to more reasonable, i.e., less speculative profit levels. The overall dynamic of polarization in profit levels in the urban economy remains in place, as do the "distortions" in many markets.

27 See, e.g., Spain, *supra* note 11; Leonie Sandercock & Ann Forsyth, "A Gender Agenda: New Directions for Planning Theory" 58 *J. Am. Plan. Ass'n* 49 (1992); Alma H. Young & Jyaphia Christos-Rodgers, "Resisting Racially Gendered Space: The Women of the St. Thomas Resident Council, New Orleans, in 5 *Comparative Urban and Community Research: Marginal Spaces* p. 95, edited by Michael Peter Smith (1995); see also Roger Waldinger & Greta Gilbertson, "Immigrant's Progress: Ethnic & Gender Differences Among U.S. Immigrants in the 1980s," 37 *Soc. Perp.* p. 431 (1994) (finding that among immigrants with a high level of education, immigrant men did significantly better in the labor market than their co-national women with similar levels of education).

28 See generally Saskia Sassen, "Immigration and Local Labor Markets," in *The Economic Sociology of Immigration*, edited by Alejandro Portes (1995).

29 See generally Sassen, *supra* note 5 (showing how this concept worked in the United States and in the case of the offshoring of leading sectors such as electronics).

30 See generally Heidi Hartmann, "Changes in Women's Economic and Family Roles in Post-World War II United States," in *Women, Households and the Economy, supra* note 6 at 33; Alice Kesslser-Harris & Karen Brodkin Sacks, "The Demise of Domesticity in America," in *Women, Households and the Economy, supra* note 6 at 65.

31 See e.g., Grasmuck & Pessar, *supra* note 8; Hondagneu-Sotelo, *supra* note 8; Louise Lamphere, from Working Daughters to Working Mothers: Immigrant Women in a New England Community (1987); Boyd, *supra* note 8; Castro, *supra* note 8; Nancy Foner, "Sex Roles and Sensibilities: Jamaican Women in New York and London," in *International Migration: The Female Experience,* edited by Rita James Simon and Caroline B. Brettell (1986). But see e.g., Fernandez-Kelly, *supra* note 5; Yolanda Prieto, "Cuban Women in New Jersey: Gender Relations and Change," in *Seeking Common Ground: Multidisciplinary Studies of Immigrant Women in the United States,* edited by Donna Gabaccia (1992).

32 See generally *Women, Households and the Economy, supra* note 6; Hartmann, supra note 30; Kessler-Harris & Sacks, *supra* note 30.

33 See generally Grasmuck & Pessar, *supra* note 8 finding that Dominican women wanted to settle in New York precisely because of these gains, while men wanted to return. They found women spending large shares of earnings on expensive durable consumer goods such as appliances and home furnishings which served to root the family securely in the United States and deplete the funds needed for organizing a successful return, while men preferred to spend as little as possible to save for the return. *id.* Castro had similar results in her study on Colombian women in New York City. Castro, *supra* note 8.

34 See generally Eugenia Georges, *The Making of a Transnational Community: Migration, Development, and Cultural Change in the Dominic Republic* (1990); Castro, *supra* note 8.

35 See generally Hondagneu-Sotelo, *supra* note 8, Nazli Kibria, *Family Tightrope: The Changing Lives of Vietnamese Americans* (1993).

36 See generally Hondagneu-Sotelo, *supra* note 8; Mahler, *supra* note 23; Ida Susser, *Norman Street: Poverty and Politics in An Urban Neighborhood* (1982).

37 Scholarship on immigrant women contributes to the broader agenda for feminist scholarship aimed at recognizing differences among women – in this case, ethnic-, racial-, and national-centered differences between men and women and among women generally. See, e.g., Patricia Pessar, "On the Homefront and in the Workplace: Integrating Immigrant Women into Feminist Discourse," 68 *Anthropological Q.* p. 37 (1995).

38 There is an enormous literature that is of direct and indirect pertinence here. It is impossible to do justice to the variety of foci and perspectives here. See, e.g., Judith Goldstein & Robert O. Keohane, eds., *Ideas and Foreign Policy: Beliefs, Institutions and Political Change* (1993) (on the impact of the international human rights regime on sovereignty); Losing Control *supra* note 2 (on general questions about the state and international/cross-border processes); Jeswald W. Salacuse, *Making Global Deals: Negotiating in the International Marketplace* (1991) (on more specific regulatory and legal issues, and representing very different perspectives); Kenneth W. Abbott, "GATT as a Public Institution: The Uruguay Round and Beyond," 18 *Brook. J. Int'l L.* 31 (1992); Gerald Aksen, "Arbitration and Other Means of Dispute Settlement," in *International Joint Ventures: A Practical Approach to Working with Foreign Investors in the U.S. and Abroad,* edited by David N. Goldsweig & Roger H. Cummings (2d ed. 1990), 287; Yves Dezalay & Bryant Garth, "Merchants of Law as Moral Entrepreuneurs: Constructing International Justice from the Competition for Transnational Business Disputes," 29 *L. & Soc'y Rev.* 27 (1995); Myres S. McDougal & W. Michael Reisman, "International Law in Policy-Oriented Perspectives," in *The Structure and Process of International Law,* edited by R. St. J. MacDonald and Douglas M. Johnston (1983); Joel R. Paul, "Free Trade, Regulatory Competition and the Autonomous Market

Fallacy," *I Colum. J. Eur. L.* 29 (1995); James N. Rosenau, "Governance, Order, and Change in World Politicis," in *Governance Without Government: Order and Change in World Politics,* edited by James N. Rosenau and Ernst-Otto Czempiel (1992); John Gerard Ruggie, "Territoriality and Beyond: Problematizing Modernity in International Relations" 47 *Int'l Org.* 139 (1993); Kathryn Sikkink, "Human Rights, Principled Issue-Networks, and Sovereignty in Latin America" 47 *Int'l Org.* 411 (1993); Joel P. Trachtman, "International Regulatory Competition, Externalization, and Jurisdiction" 34 *Harv. Int'l L. J.* 47 (1993); David M. Trubek et al., *Global Restructuring and the Law: The Internationalization of Legal Fields and Creation of Transnational Arenas* (University of Wisconsin Global Studies Research Program Working Paper Series on the Political Economy of Legal Change No. 1, 1993); Friedrich Kratochwil, "Of Systems, Boundaries and Territoriality: An Inquiry into the Formation of the State System," *World Pol.,* Oct. 1986. I discuss many of these in my 1996 book, *Losing Control, supra* note 2.

39 See generally Louis Henkin, *The Age of Rights* (1990); Soysal, *supra* note 10; Dr. Erica-Irene A. Daes, "Equality of Indigenous Peoples Under the Auspicies of the United Nations – Draft Declaration on the Rights of Indigenous Peoples," 7 *St. Thomas L. Rev.* p. 493 (1995); David Kennedy, "Some Reflections on The Role of Sovereignty in the New International Order," in *State Sovereignty: The Challenge of A Changing World: New Approaches and Thinking on International Law* 237 (1992) (Proceedings of the 21st Annual Conference of the Canadian Council on International Law, Ottawa); Karen Knop, "The Righting of Recognition: Recognition of States in Eastern Europe and the Soviet Union," in *State Sovereignty: The Challenge of a Changing World: New Approaches and Thinking on International Law, supra.*

40 See generally Soysal, *supra* note 10, Rainer Baubock, *Transnational Citizenship: Membership and Rights in International Migration (1994).*

41 See, e.g., Thómas M. Franck, "The Emerging Right to Democratic Governance," 86 *Am. J. of Int'l L.* p. 46 (1992); McDougal & Reisman, *supra* note 38; Rosenau, *supra* note 38; Ruggie, *supra* note 38.

42 See, e.g., V. Spike Peterson, ed., *Gendered States: Feminist (Re)Visions of International Relations Theory* (1992); Dorinda G. Dallmeyer, ed., *Reconceiving Reality: Women and International Law,* (American Society of International Law Series, Studies in Transnational Legal Policy No. 25, 1993), 143 [hereinafter Reconceiving Reality].

43 See, e.g., Williams, *supra* note 13.

44 See, e.g., Hilary Charlesworth, "The Public/Private Distinction and the Right to Development in International Law," 12 *Austl. Y.B. Int'l L.* p. 190 (1992); Elshtain, *supra* note 12; Karen Engle, "After the Collapse of the Public/Private Distinction: Strategizing Women's Rights," in *Reconceiving Reality, supra* note 42.

45 See generally Karen Knop, "Re/Statements: Feminism and State Sovereignty in International Law," 3 *Transnat'l L. & Contmp. Probs.* 293 (1993).

46 See generally Carole Pateman, "Feminist Critiques of the Public/Private Dichotomy," in *Public and Private in Social Life,* edited by S. I. Benn and G. F. Gaus (1983); Williams, *supra* note 13.

47 See generally Charlesworth, *supra* note 44; Christine Chinkin, "A Gendered Perspective to the International Use of Force," 12 *Aust'l Y. B. Int'l L.* p. 279 (1992); Elshtain, *supra* note 12; Judith G. Gardan, "The Law of Armed Conflict: A Feminist Perspective," in *Human Rights in the Twenty-First Century: A Global Challenge* edited by Kathleen E. Mahoney and Paul Mahoney (1993). The notion is that states should intervene in the private sphere because women often are at risk in homes; extending this notion to the relations among states entails a call for greater mutual responsibilities among states, as is illustrated by the advantages of cross-border collaboration in the environmental field. For radical feminists, the dissolution of borders between the public

and the private is not necessarily desirable insofar as any kind of intervention/penetration is a threat to women.

48 Knop, *supra* note 45: Knop finds the analogy between individual and state analytically restricting. It may simply lead the emerging feminist international law scholarship to transport the feminist debate on the nature of the self and the relationship to others *onto* the level of the state. Further, it can easily treat the state as a unified entity.

49 See generally Elshtain, *supra* note 12.

50 See generally Knop, *supra* note 45.

51 See generally id., Elshtain, *supra* note 12 (noting that gender is not part of many recent critical treatments of sovereignty).

52 See generally *Losing Control, supra* note 2.

53 See, e.g., Franck, *supra* note 41.

54 See, e.g., *Gendered States, supra* note 42 (presenting feminist scholarship concerned with equality for women in the participation of international law making and implementation). This focus still entails working through the state, although it may incorporate the notion, developed in the national context, that equality means taking account of the specific needs of women. See generally *Minow, supra* note 13.

55 According to several feminist scholars, there is today no feminist theory of the state. See, e.g., Knop, *supra* note 45; Denise G. Réaume, "The Social Construction of Women and the Possibility of Change: Unmodified Feminism Revisited," 5 *Canadian J. Women & L.* 463 (1992) (reviewing Catherine A. MacKinnon, *Toward a Feminist Theory of the State* (1989). In her critique, Réaume finds that MacKinnon's text does not contain such a theory notwithstanding its title. See generally id.

56 See generally *Losing Control, supra* note 2.

57 The complicating twist, which I examine in my 1996 book, is that both the global capital market and the human rights regime need the state for the enforcement of, respectively, the global rights of capital – guarantees of contract and property – and the human rights of any person regardless of nationality and legal status. See generally *Losing Control, supra* note 2.

58 David Jacobson, *Rights Across Borders: Immigration and the Decline of Citizenship* (1996), 9; see generally W. Michael Reisman, "Sovereignty and Human Rights in Contemporary International Law," 84 *Am. J. Int'l L.* (1990).

59 The covenants and conventions that guarantee human rights today are derived from the Universal Declaration of Human Rights adopted by the United Nations in 1948. See *Universal Declaration of Human Rights*, G. A. Res. 217 (III), U.N. Doc. A810 (1948). The Universal Declaration is not an international treaty, and thus does not have the legally binding character of treaties. But many view the Declaration to have the status of customary international law – an international and general practice that is accepted and observed as law – because it is so often referred to.

60 See *International Covenant on Civil and Political Rights*, G.A. Res. 2200 (XXI), 21 U.N. Gaor Supp. (No. 16) at 49, U.N. Doc. A/6316 (entered into force Mar. 23, 1976); International Covenant on Economic, Social and Cultural Rights, Jan. 3, 1976, 993 U.N.T.S. 3. It took ten years after ratification procedures in 1966 before thirty-six states ratified the covenants, the number required to make them legally binding.

61 See generally Henkin, *supra* note 39; Farooq Hassan, "The Doctrine of Incorporation," 5 *Hum. Rts. Q.* 68; Jacobson, *supra* note 58.

62 Barbara Stark, "The Other Half of the International Bill of Rights as a Postmodern Feminist Text," in *Reality, supra* note 42 (1993). The Economic Covenant demands positive commitment from governments to secure the basic standards of material existence for its citizens. The Civil Covenant, on the other hand, tends to reproduce existing male hierarchies and to address familiar "negative rights," such as the freedom of religion and expression. The United States has ratified the Civil Covenant (in April 1992) but not the Economic Covenant.

63 Provisions in the European Convention and rules in the Court of Human Rights authorize individuals and nonstate actors to petition. Such petitions have increased rapidly in the 1970s and 1980s. Several states have incorporated many of the Convention's provisions into their domestic law – Germany, The Netherlands, France, Spain, and Switzerland. In this case, decisions by the court have a direct effect on domestic judiciaries, which emerge as a key organ for the implementation of human rights provisions. This pattern has grown markedly since the early 1980s with the growth of case law coming out of the court.

64 See Jacobson, *supra* note 58, at 98–100; see generally Hassan, *supra* note 61; Martin Heisler, *Transnational Migration as a Small Window on the Diminished Autonomy of the Modern Democratic State,"* 485 *Annals Am. Acad. Pol. & Soc. Sci.* 153 (May 1986).

65 Jacobson, *supra* note 58, at 100.

66 See generally Martin Shapiro, "The Globalization of Law," 1 *Ind. J. Global Legal Stud.* 37 (1993) (commenting on a range of other concerns that are played in the judiciary).

67 See generally Henry J. Steiner, "Political Participation as a Human Right," *Harv. Hum. Rts. Y.B.* 7, (Spring 1988); *Ideas and Foreign Policy: Beliefs Institutions and Political Change, supra* note 38; Sikkink, *supra* note 38.

68 This is clearly not an irreversible trend, as current events in the former Yugoslavia indicate, but it does create a new set of conditions that our international legal order must take account of. Matters are sufficiently advanced to the point that even strong nationalist or ethnic resistance must confront the existence of the international human rights regime.

69 See e.g., Salacuse, *supra* note 38; Abbott, *supra* note 38; Aksen, *supra* note 38; Dezalay & Garth, *supra* note 38; Paul, *supra* note 38; Trachtman, *supra* note 38.

70 In chapter one of my 1996 book, I examine whether the impact of economic globalization on national territory and state sovereignty is yet another form of extraterritoriality, only larger. My discussion about territory in the global economy posits that much of what we call global, including some of the most strategic functions necessary for globalization, is embedded in national territories. Is this a form of extraterritoriality that leaves the sovereignty of the state fundamentally unaltered? Or is this a development of a different sort, one wherein the sovereignty of the state is engaged, and where territoriality, as distinct from territory, is partially transformed? I conclude that the materialization of global processes in national territories does not represent a mere expansion of older concepts of extraterritoriality to the realm of the economy, but rather a process of incipient denationalization, though of a highly specialized institutional, rather than geographic, sort. See generally *Losing Control, supra* note 2.

71 See generally, Globalization: Critical Reflections, *supra* note 1; Cox, *supra* note 19; Panitch, *supra* note 19.

72 See generally Dezalay & Garth, *supra* note 38; Yves Dezalay, *Marchands de Droit* (1992).

73 Dezalay & Garth, *supra* note 38, at 58; see generally Thomas E. Carbonneau, ed., *Lex Mercatoria and Arbitration: A Discussion of the New Law Merchant* (1990). Anglo American practitioners tend not to support the continental, highly academic notion of a lex mercatoria. See generally id. The so-called lex mercatoria was viewed by many as a return to an international

law of business independent of national laws. See generally id. Insofar as they are "Americanizing" the field, they are moving it further away from academic law and lex mercatoria.

74 These transnational regimes could, in principle, have assumed various forms and contents. But they are, in fact, assuming a specific form, one wherein the states of the highly developed countries play a strategic geopolitical role. The hegemony of neoliberal concepts of economic relations, with its strong emphasis on markets, deregulation, and free international trade, has influenced policy in the 1980s in the United States and United Kingdom and now increasingly also in continental Europe. See generally Coombe, *supra* note 14. This has contributed to the formation of transnational legal regimes that are centered in Western economic concepts. See generally Globalization: Critical Reflections, *supra* note 1.

75 See generally Rosenau, *supra* note 38.

76 See generally Bob Jessop, *State Theory: Putting the Capitalist State in its Place* (1990); *Losing Control, supra* note 2. For a broader historical overview of the state and sharp change see generally Anthony Giddens, *The Nation-State and Violence* (1987); Charles Tilly, *The Formation of National States in Western Europe* (1975). Even if the state is not as autonomous as the sovereignty rhetoric suggests, its consent to nonstate actors being subjects of international law remains foundational. But states may increasingly no longer be the only entities whose consent is essential. See generally McDougal & Reisman, *supra* note 38.

77 There is a growing consensus among states to further the goals of economic globalization, to the point that some see in this a constitutionalizing of this new role of states. See generally *Globalization: Critical Reflections, supra* note 1.

78 This combination of elements is illustrated by some of the aspects of the Mexican crisis of December 1994, defined rather generally in international political and business circles, as well as in much of the press, as the result of a loss of confidence by the global financial markets in the Mexican economy and government leadership of that economy. A "financial" response to this crisis was but one of several potential choices. For instance, there could conceivably have been an emphasis on promoting manufacturing growth and protecting small businesses and small home owners from the bankruptcies now faced by many.

79 Ruggie, *supra* note 38, at 143 (pointing out that the issue is not whether such new institutions and major economic actors will substitute national states, but rather the possibility of major changes in the systems of states: "global markets and transnationalized corporate structures . . . are not in the business of replacing states" even when they can have the potential for producing fundamental change in the system of states).

80 This is another issue here that I cannot develop, but see *Losing Control, supra* note 2, at 6–12. It has to do with the fact that representations that characterize the nation–state as simply losing significance fail to capture this very important dimension, and reduce what is happening to a function of a global-national duality–what one wins, the other loses. I view deregulation not simply as a loss of control by the state, but as a crucial mechanism to negotiate the juxtaposition of the interstate consensus to pursue globalization and the fact that national legal systems remain as the major, or crucial, instantiation through which guarantees of contract and property rights are enforced.

81 But see generally Alfred C. Aman, Jr., "A Global Perspective on Current Regulartory Reform: Rejection, Relocation, or Reinvention?" 2 *Ind. J. Global Legal Stud.* 429 (1995).

82 See generally Richard Falk, "A New Paradigm for International Legal Studies: Prospects and Proposals," in *Revisiting International Law* (1989). See also Elshtain, *supra* note 12.

83 For instance, individuals and groups can become limited subjects of international law; nonstate forums outside the framework of the United Nations can be used to represent their interests.

See generally Douglas M. Johnston, "Functionalism in the Theory of International Law," 26 *Can. Y.B. Intl'l L.* 3 (1988); Chinkin, *supra* note 47.

84 See generally Isabelle R. Gunning, "Modernizing Customary International Law; The Challenge of Human Rights," 31 *Va. J. Int'l L.* 211 (1991); Elshtain *supra* note 12.

85 See generally Knop, *supra* note 45 (noting that if nongovernmental organizations (NGOs) are to be a channel for women's positions to be heard outside the state, then it is important to develop an international legal basis independent of the consent of the state for NGO participation in the making of international law); Hilary Charlesworth et al., "Feminist Approaches to International Law," 85 *Am. J. Int'l L.*, 613 (1991); Chinkin, *supra* note 47 (focusing on giving power to women's, NGOs, generally).

6

The focus is on the growth of export production in Third World countries and on the massive increase in Third World immigration to the United States. Both have taken place over the last fifteen years and both contain as one constitutive trait: the incorporation of Third World women into wage employment on a scale that can be seen as representing a new phase in the history of women. The article posits that there is a systemic relation between this globalization and feminization of wage labor.

Immigration and offshore production have evolved into mechanisms for the massive incorporation of Third World women into wagelabor. While there is excellent scholarship on both the employment of women in offshore production in less developed countries and the employment of immigrant women in developed countries, these two trends have rarely been seen as related. Yet there are a number of systemic links. Immigration and offshore production are ways of securing a low-wage labor force and of fighting the demands of organized workers in developed countries. They also represent a sort of functional equivalence: that is, productive facilities that cannot be shifted offshore and have to be performed where the demand is, for example, restaurants and hospitals, can use immigrant labor while facilities that can be shifted abroad can use low-wage labor in less developed countries. There is yet another, more basic connection, and one more difficult to describe. The same set of processes that have promoted the location of plants and offices abroad also have contributed to a large supply of low wage jobs in the United States for which immigrant workers are a desirable labor supply.

INDUSTRIALIZATION AND FEMALE MIGRATION

The expansion of export manufacturing and export agriculture in LDCs (less developed countries), both of which are inseparably related with direct foreign investment from the highly industrialized countries (Burbach and Flynn 1979; Tinker and Bramsen 1976: UNIDO 1979; 1980), has mobilized new segments of the population into regional and long distance migrations. The mechanisms inducing migration are quite different in the case of export manufacturing from those in commercial agriculture. In the latter there is a direct displacement of small farmers who are left without, or with severely reduced, means of subsistence (George 1977; NACLA 1978; Burbach and Flynn 1980). In export manufacturing, the fragmentary evidence suggests that the disruption of traditional work structures and the corresponding migration inducements are mediated by a massive recruitment of young women into the new industrial zones (see Sassen 1988). What has made this recruitment effect significant is the locational concentration of export manufacturing in a few countries or regions of countries (UNIDO 1980; OECD 1980; ILO 1982; Lim 1980; Grossman 1981; Fernandez-Kelly 1983; Safa 1981).

Women have a distinct place in each of these developments. Export agriculture has led, in certain areas, to male emigration and to what Elsa Chaney (1980) has called the feminization of small-holder farming; in others, to the proletarianization of women who were once independent producers (Boserup 1970; Nelson 1974; Dauber and Cain 1981; Petritsch 1981). The particular socioeconomic and cultural configurations that contribute to these diverse patterns have received considerable attention in the anthropological and general development literature but space limitations make it impossible to cite the numerous case studies. Overall, the data for the 1950s and 1960s show the prevalence of female rural to urban migration in Latin America and of male rural-to-rural and rural-to-urban migration in Asia and Africa (Chaney 1984; Nelson 1974; Herrick 1971; Byerlee 1972; Orlansky and Dubrovsky 1978; Petritsch 1981). This divergent pattern has been explained in part by the lesser role of women in agriculture in Latin America as compared with Africa and Asia (Boserup 1970).

There is disagreement on this aspect. Several recent studies suggest that the contribution of women to agriculture in Latin America has been underestimated because of deficiencies in data gathering (Recchini de Lattes and Wainerman 1979). The absence of opportunities for paid employment in rural areas is probably a key factor inducing the greater female rural-to-urban migration (Orlansky and Dubrovsky 1978).

The large-scale development of export manufacturing in certain regions introduces a new variable into the inquiry. The available evidence strongly documents the overwhelming presence of women among production workers in export manufacturing (Lim 1980; Safa 1981; Gross 1979; Fernandez-Kelly 1983; Multinational Monitor 1982; UNIDO 1980; Pacific Resource Center 1979; Salaff 1981; Wong 1980; Cho 1984; Arrigo 1980). Further, there is a high incidence of manufacturing jobs among women in countries or regions within countries where export manufacturing is a key sector of the economy. In these cases we can see a growing incidence of manufacturing jobs and, frequently, a declining share of service jobs among women, a trend that diverges from what has been typical in highly industrialized countries and from what has been the case in Third World countries over the last two decades. For example, in Taiwan, only 13.2 percent of women held manufacturing jobs (including transport) in 1965; by 1977, this share had risen to thirty-four percent (Arrigo 1980, 26).

It is worth noting, for example, that in a rather developed state such as Singapore, the largest single concentration of women workers in the late 1950s was in services. By 1978, it was in production and related jobs. Though in absolute numbers the service sector has increased, its percentage of all jobs declined from 34.7 percent in 1957 to 14.9 percent in 1978, a function of the quintupling of production jobs, which accounted for almost thirty-six percent of all jobs in 1978 (Wong 1980, 9). This is clearly a result of the expansion of export production. The conjunction of the weight of this type of production and the distinct employment patterns it promotes have generated an additional pattern that contrasts with what is typical in highly developed countries: there is no bimodality in the age composition of women workers. The labor force participation rates of women twenty to twenty-four years old are very high yet there is (as of yet) no resurgence in participation among women aged forty and over (Wong 1980, 8).

This new pattern diverges significantly from what most of the literature on female migration in the Third World found to be the case in the 1950s, 1960s, and well into the 1970s. The general pattern found was that most women migrants to cities became employed in domestic service and in informal sector activities (Boserup 1970; Schmink 1982; Delaunoy 1975; Shah and Smith 1981; Orlansky and Dubrovsky 1978; Recchini de Lattes and Wainerman 1982; Youssef 1974; Jelin 1979). Further, the evidence points to a displacement of women from manufacturing as the branches typically employing women become modernized, more capital intensive and operate on larger scales of production. (Petritsch 1981; Dauber and Cain 1981; Tinker and Bramsen 1976; Boulding 1980; Parra Sandoval 1975; Institute of Social Studies 1980; Ahmad and Jenkins 1980; Caughman and Thiam 1980). The same pattern is evident in the development of heavy industry: as the latter becomes an increasingly significant component of a given region's or country's manufacturing sector, the share of jobs held by women in this sector declines; for example, the share of women in manufacturing in Brazil declined from 18.6 percent to 11 percent from 1950 to 1970 (Schmink 1982, 6).

The prevalence of women in export manufacturing and the high incidence of manufacturing jobs among women in countries where this type of production is prominent raises a number of questions as to the nature of this development. One element in the explanation is the marked concentration of electronics, garments, textiles, toys, and footwear in export manufacturing—that is, industries that have traditionally employed women. Indeed, the expansion of these industries is beginning to result in changes in the sex composition of rural-to-urban migration streams in areas of Asia and the Caribbean where males used to be prevalent (World Bank Staff 1975; Standing 1975; Arrigo 1980; Kelly 1984). For example, Standing (1975) notes a tendency to substitution of male labor within the nonagricultural sector in Jamaica over the last two decades, with the share of women in manufacturing going from twenty-three to twenty-four percent in the early 1950s to thirty-five percent in 1973 (Standing 1975, 1).

These trends point to the need for certain distinctions. First, the distinction between so-called traditional and modern forms of manufacturing shows women to have experienced declines in their share of jobs as an industry modernizes. However, if we consider the developments in the new industrial zones, perhaps a better formulation would be one that distinguishes between labor-intensive and capital-intensive forms of production. This would allow for the incorporation of both the earlier instances of female employment in certain industries and contemporary cases as diverse as electronics and garments. Further, it overcomes the inadequacy of conceiving of certain industries, notably garments, and certain forms of organization of work, notably sweatshops and industrial homework, as pertaining to the traditional, nonmodern sector, a notion that can easily be read to mean that these forms will become increasingly insignificant as modernization takes place. The growth of labor-intensive manufacturing plants in several Third World countries, as well as the growing use of sweatshops and industrial homework via subcontracting both in the Third World and in highly industrialized countries, all point to the viability of these forms in "modern" contexts. In some instances they would seem to be integral to the functioning of advanced capitalism in the current historical phase (Sassen 1988; see also chap. 7 here). This reading of current developments carries considerable implications for an analysis of women's participation in waged employment. While earlier trends suggested both a tendency toward "modernization" in industry and a corresponding displacement of women from manufacturing, these new trends point to growing participation.

However, this growing participation is posited on certain forms of organization of the work process, forms which generate low-wage jobs where workers' empowerment is often difficult. This raises a question about female migrants as a social category and at this point a second set of distinctions needs to be considered. As Orlansky and Dubrovsky (1978, 6) posit, female migrants are characterized by a double disadvantage, one of sex and one of class. Certainly the little evidence available on remuneration shows women migrants to have the lowest wage expectations (Standing 1975) and actual pay. To this we should add the evidence described earlier on the absence of opportunities for women migrants to be employed in the "modern" sector and their prevalence in domestic service and in informal activities. What emerges clearly is that a large share of women migrants constitute a certain kind of labor. Singer (1974) argues that the employment of women migrants in domestic service in the Third World represents a vehicle for the reproduction of a labor reserve that can be seen as the equivalent of the welfare state in highly industrialized societies. The evidence points to women's exits and re-entries into this type of employment and supports this argument. Domestic service can be seen as providing a livelihood and means for integration into an urban situation. The movement out of domestic service employment and the magnitude of this movement will depend on the characteristics of the job supply (Marshall 1976). It would seem that in the case of export manufacturing the reserve-status stage becomes unnecessary because of the accelerated growth in labor demand. At the same time, we need more empirical studies examining what the employment options are for the women who are fired or resign from manufacturing jobs. Does domestic service—at least in certain locations—become one of the few alternatives and does it, then, function, as a privatized mechanism for social reproduction and maintenance of a labor reserve?

The category of female migrants consists, thus, of several concrete components ranging from reserve status conditions to full participation in waged employment. The key is the systemic link between the formation of various components of this category in particular historico-geographic configurations and broader processes of social change, such as the development of commercial agriculture or the new export-led industrialization. Migrations do not just happen: they are one outcome or one systemic tendency in a more general dynamic of change. The internal transformation of the category is similarly linked, with broader processes of social change. (Some aspects of this change are developed in the preceding chapter here.)

The migrations of young women into the new industrial zones are linked with basic economic transformations in the world economy that assume concrete forms in particular locations. Some aspects of this articulation are quite evident, such as the massive redeployment of labor-intensive segments of production to Third World locations, which has generated a large demand for workers. Others are much less so and require further empirical and conceptual elaboration. One of these aspects is the question as to a possible systemic link between this accelerated growth of export manufacturing and the new immigration to the United States, much of it consisting of women originating in countries that have been the central sites for export manufacturing. This kind of analytic effort would further develop the category of female migrant and incorporate it into a theoretical space that seeks to capture central features of the current phase of world capitalist development.

The coexistence of high employment growth and high emigration in the main countries of origin of the new immigration to the United States is theoretically unsettling. The push factors traditionally used to explain domestic or international migration, most importantly lack of economic growth, are insufficient. In fact, according to most of these there should have been a decline, if anything, in the levels of emigration. Export industries tend to be highly labor intensive, this being precisely one of the rationales for locating factories in low-wage countries. The job creation impact is further accentuated by high concentrations of export manufacturing in certain areas, because of the need for access to transportation abroad and the more cost-effective development of necessary infrastructure and servicing.[2]

Thus the question is, how did a situation of general employment growth contain conditions for promoting emigration? Answering such a question requires a detailed examination of the characteristics of this type of industrial growth, its employment effects, and the cultural-ideological impact on the people it touches. We need to specify the links between the objective conditions represented by rapid, mostly export-led industrialization and emigration, particularly migration to the United States. The evidence clearly documents the existence of industrialization and of immigration into the United States. What is necessary is for conceptual and empirical elaboration of the linkage between these two processes. Because the analysis from which this article is derived is complex, is based on several distinct bodies of data, and at times must rely on inference, there follows a brief description of the main steps involved in the conceptual and empirical elaboration of the links between industrialization and emigration. For each of these steps there is brief discussion of the main findings relevant to an analysis of migration in the major Asian and Caribbean sending countries. These findings represent, in principle, one of several possible outcomes in an examination of the relation between industrialization and migration. (For a full exposition of the analytical framework and a re-elaboration of the available evidence see Sassen 1988.)

First, it is necessary to examine the characteristics of the new industrial growth in less developed countries and to place it in the context of the overall economic organization of a country. A good part of the growth in these countries can only be accounted for by the growth in exports. Access to the world market is a must given fairly limited internal markets. The development of a world market for these countries is intimately linked to a significant growth in direct foreign investment (Tinker and Bramsen 1976; UNIDO 1980; ILO 1960; OECD 1980; 1981; NACLA 1977; see also Pineda-Ofreneo 1982). One distinctive trait about industrial growth in the major new immigrant-sending countries is the weight of export production. While this is a particularly strong trend in the Asian and Caribbean countries, it is also present in Mexico and Colombia, two countries with rather developed industrial economies and large internal markets.

Second, it is necessary to examine the employment effects of these patterns of growth. Export agriculture requires a large supply of low-wage workers at crucial periods of the production cycle. Export-oriented plants are often concentrated for reasons having to do with servicing and transportation, a fact which may tend to accentuate the labor-demand impact. Finally, large agglomerations of firms producing for export generate a range of additional jobs, from the packaging for shipment abroad to the construction and operation of airports and harbors.

Third, it is necessary to examine how these labor needs are met. Both export agriculture and export manufacturing have mobilized large numbers of people into wage labor. The large-scale development of commercial agriculture in Latin America and the Caribbean contributed to the creation of a rural wage labor supply through the displacement of subsistence farmers and small producers. This displacement was also central in promoting rural unemployment and migrations to the cities. On the other hand, because it is highly labor intensive, export manufacturing could have conceivably solved the unemployment problem, particularly among prime aged males. Instead, the evidence overwhelmingly shows that it has drawn new segments of the population into the labor force: mostly young women who under conditions of more gradual industrialization would not have entered the labor force in so massive and sudden a way (Lim 1980; Safa 1981; Gross 1979; Fernandez-Kelly 1983; UNIDO 1980).

Fourth, it is necessary to examine the migration impact, if any, associated with this job creation and labor recruitment. (See UNIDO 1979.) Precisely because of the significant job-creation effect of export-manufacturing and its concentration in a few areas, the extent and impact of the mobilization of young women into the labor force have been considerable. This effect has been further accentuated by the high turnover rates resulting from the employment practices in the plants and the mental and physical fatigue associated with these jobs. A hypothesis that emerges from these patterns is that in areas where there has been a large development of new industrial zones, the large mobilization of women into the labor force has contributed to the disruption of unwaged work structures in communities of origin: the young men are left without mates and partners, the households are left without a key labor factor (but see also, Salaff on the case of Hong Kong 1981).

One could further posit that the disruption of unwaged work structures resulting from an extremely high incidence of young female emigration has increased the pool of unemployed. It may have stimulated the departure of men and women who may not have planned on doing so. At the same time, the high turnover rates in the new industrial zones and the pronounced preference by employers for young women has contributed to high turnover and growing unemployment among women. Incipient Westernization among zone workers and the disruption of traditional work structures combine to minimize the possibilities of returning to communities of origin. In sum, these developments can be seen as having induced the formation of a pool of migrant workers. We need research on each one of these aspects.

Fifth, it is necessary to examine whether these conditions could promote the emergence of emigration as an option actually felt by individuals, particularly migration to the United States. At this point the fact of a strong foreign presence becomes significant. It is not only the concentration of foreign investment in a few areas. It is also the fact that it dominates the new industrial zones objectively and culturally, thereby creating linkages to the countries where the capital originates. Of interest here is the evidence showing that recent migrants have a higher propensity to move again (Morrison 1967; Land 1969; see also Grasmuck 1982), which would suggest that migrants to the new industrial zones will tend to be available subjectively for yet another move. Also of interest is the evidence pointing to the weight of economic incentives in migration (Brigg 1973 reviews the literature on this subject; Standing 1975; Harris and Todaro 1970; Cohen and Sassen-Koob 1982). The familiar image of America as a land of opportunity can operate as a strong pull factor, possibly strengthened by the aura of dynamic growth in the new industrial zones populated with U.S. firms and producing for export to the U.S. market.

Finally, the strong presence of foreign firms facilitates access to information and a sense of familiarity with the potential destination, both aspects found to be important in migration studies (World Bank Staff 1975, 22–23). Indeed, distance is found to be a major deterrent in many studies on migration. Contracts and information about the destination location can overcome it partly. Thus, the migration from South Asian and Caribbean Basin countries to the United States over the last two decades can be seen as a case where the powerful deterrent effect of distance is overcome by the various factors discussed here, from the imagery about the land of promise to the objective linkages represented by employment in U.S. firms located in the Third World. In this context, the liberalization of U.S. immigration policy after 1965 can be seen as the other side of the processes that have built the structural and subjective linkages with several Third World countries. In brief, I am positing that the distinctive traits of export manufacturing—notably its locational concentration, labor intensity, and use of young, mostly first-time entrants into waged employment—make it into one of these processes for structural and subjective linking (Sassen 1988; 1984a,b).

THE NEW LABOR DEMAND: CONDITIONS FOR THE ABSORPTION OF IMMIGRANT WOMEN

The technical transformation of the work process underlying the redeployment of manufacturing and office jobs to less developed areas has also reshaped the job supply in the developed areas. Further, the spatial dispersion of plants and offices has created a need for an expanded, centralized management and servicing apparatus located mostly in highly developed areas. Both of these processes together with the overall shift to a service economy have directly and indirectly, created a significant increase in the supply of low-wage jobs, particularly female-typed jobs, in highly developed countries.

Today, as in the past, the immigration of women is not simply a function of kinship. There are objective conditions that create a demand for female workers given the sex-typing of jobs and the lower wages paid to women. The shift to services and the technically induced downgrading of many jobs have generated an expansion in types of jobs associated with women workers. Taking some liberty with the term, one could argue that there has been not only a growing female labor force participation, but also a feminization of the job supply. The feminization of the job supply in conjunction with the growing politicization of native women may well create a growing demand for immigrant women.

Here I will focus on the general increase in the supply of low-wage jobs and on the particular configuration these trends assume in major cities, these being the main recipient areas of the new immigration.

At the national level the general trends shaping the job supply have brought about a greater inequality in the income distribution of workers over the last decade. The shift to a service economy is generally recognized to result in a greater share of low-wage jobs than is the case with an economy dominated by a strong manufacturing sector (Singelmann 1978; Bluestone, Harrison, Gorham 1984). Second, some of the fastest-growing service industries are characterized by a larger than average concentration of low-wage and high-income jobs, which means we can expect an even stronger polarization (Stanback and Noyelle 1982). Third, there has been what I call a downgrading of the manufacturing sector; major new industries, notably in high technology, have large shares of low-wage jobs in production and assembly while several of the older industries have undergone a social reorganization of the work process characterized by a growth in nonunion plants and rapid growth of sweatshops and industrial homework (NY State Department of Labor 1979; 1980; 1982a; 1982b; Sassen 1981a; 1981b; Balmori 1983; Morales 1983; Marshall 1983; Benamou 1985). Fourth, the technological transformation of the work process, in part underlying the above trends, has further added to polarization by either upgrading or downgrading a vast array of middle-income jobs: mechanization and computerization have transferred skills to machines and have shifted certain operations from the workplace to the computer room or designer's studio.

This polarization is evident when we compare 1970 and 1980 census data on earnings. The two highest earnings classes increased their total share from thirty-two percent to thirty-seven percent while the two lowest classes increased their share from thirty-two to 38.5 percent. Correspondingly the two middle-earnings classes reduced their share by eleven percent. When we control for sex these trends are even more pronounced in the case of women. Thus, while forty-two percent of all women as compared to 34.4 percent of all men held jobs in the two lowest earnings classes in 1970, this share had increased to fifty-two percent for women and only to 35.7 percent for the men by

1980. Men and women lost about equal shares in the two middle-income strata. And all the gains in the two highest income strata were obtained by men, while women actually lost some representation (see Table 5.1).

All these trends are operating in the major cities that have received most of the immigrants. Indeed, for several reasons I should expect these trends to be even more intense in such cities (Sassen 1984a). First, the locational concentration of major new growth sectors in such cities entails a disproportionate concentration of industries with highly polarized income distributions. The data on earnings classes show that almost half of all workers in the producer services are in the next to lowest earnings class compared with seventeen percent in manufacturing (Stanback et al., 1981). The producer services are the economic core of such cities as New York and Los Angeles, and one of the most dynamic sectors in the economy as a whole.

There also is an indirect creation of low-wage jobs associated with a polarized income distribution. It takes place in the sphere of social reproduction as indicated by consumption. The expansion of the high-income workforce in conjunction with the emergence of new cultural forms has led to a process of high-income gentrification that rests, in the last analysis, on the availability of a vast supply of low-wage workers. As I have argued at greater length elsewhere (Sassen 1981b) high-income gentrification is labor intensive. This contrasts with the typical middle-class suburb, which represents a capital in-tensive process – tract housing, road and highway construction, de-pendence on private automobile or commuter trains, heavy reliance on appliances and household equipment of all sorts, large shopping malls with self-service operations. High-income gentrification re-places much of this capital intensity with workers directly and indi-rectly. Behind the gourmet food stores and speciality boutiques that have replaced the self-service supermarket and department store lies a very different organization of work. Similarly, high-income resi-dences in the city depend to a much larger extent on hired mainte-nance staff than the middle-class suburban home with its heavy input of family labor and of machinery, epitomized by the ever-running lawn mower.

A different type of organization of work is present both in the retail and in the production phase. High-income gentrification generates a demand for goods and services that are typically not mass-produced

Table 1

Distribution of Total U.S. Labor Force* Among Earnings Classes, 1970 and 1980

Earning Classes*	Distribution of Total U.S. Labor Force %							
	1970				1980			
	Total		Female	Male	Total		Female	Male
1.60 and above	11.3		7.5	9.4	12.9		4.8	11.0
1.59 to 1.50	20.9	32.2	18.6	18.9	24.2	37.0	14.5	20.7
1.29 to 1.00	18.9		21.5	23.1	12.8		12.8	15.6
.99 to .70	16.9	55.8	10.5	14.3	11.7	24.5	15.8	17.0
.69 to .40	22.8		13.5	15.4	25.2		16.7	11.8
.39 and below	9.2	32.0	28.4	19.0	13.3	38.5	55.4	23.9

Source: Based on U.S. Bureau of the Census, 1982. *Money Income of Households, Families and Persons in the United States: 1980.* (Current Population Reports: Series P-60, No. 132); and U.S. Bureau of the Census, 1972, *Money Income of Households, Families and Persons in the United States: 1970.*

Notes: *Civilian workers 14 years and over by total money earnings.

*Earnings classes are derived from the application of 1975 average earnings for each major occupation within each industry group. A basic assumption is that the relative income at 1975 levels for each occupational-industrial subgroup is constant—in this case from 1970 to 1980. I followed the method used by Stanback and Noyelle (1982) in their comparison of 1960 and 1975 earnings for industry-occupational cells. The total earnings distribution obtained is then divided into quintiles. The major industry groups are Manufacturing, Construction, Distributive Services, Retail, Producer Services, Consumer Services, Nonprofit Services (Health and Education), Public Administration. Not included are Agriculture, Fisheries and Mining. The major occupational groups are Professional, Technical, Manager, Office Clerical, Nonoffice Clerical, Sales, Craft Workers, Operatives, Service Workers, Laborers.

or sold through mass outlets. Customized production, small runs, speciality items, fine food dishes are generally produced through labor-intensive methods and sold through small, full-service outlets. Subcontracting part of this production to low-cost operations, be they sweatshops or households, is common.

Second, there is a proliferation of small, low-cost service operations made possible by the massive concentration of people in such cities in addition to a large daily inflow of nonresident workers and of tourists. The ratio between the number of these service operations and the resident population is most probably significantly higher than in an average city or town. Further, the large concentration of people in major cities will tend to create intense inducements to open up such operations as well as intense competition and marginal returns. Under such conditions the cost of labor is crucial and hence the likelihood of a high concentration of low-wage jobs. The overall outcome for the job supply and the range of firms involved in this production and delivery is rather different from that characterizing the large department stores and super markets which tend to buy from mass producers often located at great distances from the retail outlets. Mass production and mass distribution outlets facilitate unionization both in production and in sales. The changing organization of work creates conditions that make immigrants a desirable labor supply.

Third, for these same reasons together with other components of demand, the relative size of the downgraded manufacturing sector will tend to be larger in larger cities (although such a downgraded manufacturing sector may not necessarily be present in *every* urban environment). The expansion of a downgraded manufacturing sector in major cities is the result of several concrete developments besides the more general processes of social and technical transformation cited earlier. First, labor-intensive industries were differentially affected by capital flight from the cities. In the case of New York's garment industry, the largest employer in the city's manufacturing sector, the bigger shops with mechanized branches, specialized shops, and the industry's marketing and design operations have remained in the city. (See Table 5.2) It is worth noting that the garment industry in Los Angeles added 80,000 jobs from 1970 to 1980, a fact often overlooked in analyses of that region as a high-tech center. Further, the changing structure of consumption has also affected the garment industry (Sassen 1984); the greater demand for specialty items and limited-edition

Table 2

Low Wage, Unskilled Jobs, Likely to Employ Immigrants:
Select Service Industries, New York City, 1978[a]

	Employment in Select Service Industries			
	Finance, Insurance Real Estate[b]	Business Services[c]	Other Service Industries[d]	Total
Managers, Professionals and Technical	104,460	65,800	140,600	310,860
Services				
Low-Wage Jobs	30,520	52,430	40,900	123,850
Total	36,980	54,950	83,520	175,450
Maintenance				
Low-Wage Jobs	9,150	1,980	19,590	30,720
Total	12,700	15,880	45,510	74,090
Clerical				
Low-Wage Jobs	1,420	5,020	3,450	3,890
Total	201,630	102,140	80,710	384,480
Sales	23,980	10,180	4,490	38,560
Total all Occupations	379,660	248,950	354,830	983,440
Total Low-Wage Jobs[e](N)	41,090	59,430	63,940	164,460
% of Total	10.8%	23.9%	18.9%	16.7%

Source: Based on New York State Department of Labor, Division of Research and Statistics, *Occupational Employment Statistics: Services, New York State, April–
June, 1978*, 1980, and New York State Department of Labor, Division of
Research and Statistics, *Occupational Employment Statistics: Finance, Insurance, and Real Estate, New York State, May–June 1978*, 1979.

Notes: [a]This is derived from a survey by the New York State Department of Labor
(1980, 1979). The sample was drawn from establishments (only those covered
by New York State Unemployment Insurance Law) in select service industries.
Excluded from the sample were the following service industries: educational
services (SIC 82), private households (SIC 88), and the hospitals industry sub-
groups (SIC 806). Private households and hospitals contain significant numbers of low-wage jobs known to be held by immigrants. Also excluded from the
sample were establishments and activities which include significant numbers
of low-wage jobs known to employ immigrants, notably, restaurants.
[b]SIC codes 61–65.
[c]SIC codes 73, 81.
[d]SIC codes 70, 72, 75–80, 83, 84, 86, 89.
[e]The jobs identified as low-wage are only a segment of all low-wage jobs. They
are those that lack langugage proficiency requirements, are not part of a well-
defined advancement ladder and are not usually part of a highly unionized
occupation.

garments has promoted the expansion of small shops and industrial homework in cities because small runs and vicinity to design centers are important locational constraints. A parallel argument can be made for other industries, notably furniture, furs, and footwear. Also immigrant-owned plants have rapidly grown in number in view of easy access to cheap labor and, most importantly, a growing demand for their products in the immigrant communities and in cities at large.

The expansion of the low-wage job supply contains conditions for the absorption of immigrants. It coincides with a pronounced increase in the overall numbers of immigrants, both women and men. Slightly over half of all immigrants legally admitted during the 1960s and 1970s were women. While the share of women in total immigration remained constant, their numbers increased markedly, going from one million in the decade of the 1950s, to over two million in the 1970s (see Tables   3 and   4). This may or may not contradict the common view that most undocumented workers are men insofar as the census would inevitably fail to count those who may have been in the country in the intercensal periods and left before 1980.

Although immigrant women's participation rate in the labor force is generally lower than that of immigrant men and native women, their occupational concentration is far more pronounced. If we consider the five states in which most immigrants are living (New York, California, Texas, Florida, and Illinois) the sharpest difference in occupational distribution is between native and immigrant women in operative jobs; only about eight percent of native compared with twenty to twenty-five percent of immigrant women held operative jobs according to the 1980 census (Bach and Tienda 1984). Nowhere does the occupational distribution of men contain this large a divergence between natives and immigrants. Probably the second largest difference is in clerical jobs: thirty-seven to forty percent of native women held such jobs in 1980, compared with twenty-five to thirty percent of immigrant women.

About half of all immigrant women are concentrated in two occupations, operative and services. There are variations by nationality. Nearly seventy percent of all Hispanics in the five states that accounted for most immigrants held operative, service, or laborer jobs. The figure for Asians who arrived during the 1970s was forty percent (Bach and Tienda 1984, 13–14). The figure for all women workers in the United States holding these types of jobs was twenty-nine percent

Table 3

Immigrants Admitted by Sex, 1951–1979 (in thousands)

	1951–1960	1961–1970	1971	1972	1973	1974	1975	1976	1977	1978	1979	1971–1779
Number Admitted	2,515	3,322	370.5	384.7	400.1	394.9	386.2	398.6	462.3	601.4	460.3	3,962
Men	859	1,488	172.5	179.7	186.3	184.5	180.7	184.9	216.4	286.4	219.5	1,859
Women	1,014	1,834	197.9	204.9	213.7	210.3	205.5	213.8	245.9	315.1	240.8	2,103

Source: Immigration and Naturalization Service, Annual Report (various years).

Table 4

Estimates of Illegal Aliens Counted in the 1980 Census by Sex and Period of Entry for
All Foreign-Born Persons and Persons Born in Mexico
(population in thousands)

	All countries			Mexico			All other countries		
Period of Entry	Both sexes	Male	Female	Both Sexes	Male	Female	Both sexes	Male	Female
Entered since 1960*	2,047	1,097	950	931	531	400	1,116	566	549
Entered 1975–1980	890	494	396	476	278	198	413	216	197
Entered 1970–1974	551	297	254	280	159	121	270	138	132
Entered 1960–1969	570	290	281	158	77	61	432	212	220

Source: Warren and Passel (1983).

(U.S. Department of Commerce 1983). The incidence of low-wage jobs among Asians may be growing, pointing to the possibility of a new phase in Asian migration after the earlier phase dominated by middle-class origins and high levels of education. At the other extreme, fewer immigrant women than native women hold professional jobs: the share among the first was nine to ten percent, among the second, fourteen to sixteen percent.

The evidence by industry shows a similarly high concentration in certain sectors. The share of immigrant women in transformative industries (garment, textiles, and food, principally) ranged from twenty-four to thirty-four percent, which was about ten to fifteen percent higher than that of native women. The second largest single concentration was in the five main social services, where from twenty-two to twenty-seven percent of all immigrant women in the five main states can be found. A significantly higher share of native women are in this grouping, ranging from thirty-two to thirty-seven percent. The differences between native and immigrant women are less pronounced in the other industry groups. From twenty-three to thirty percent of immigrant women are in the producer and distributive services, a share slightly lower than that of native women. These services are a key component in the economies of large cities (Stanback and Noyelle 1982; Sassen 1984), suggesting the possibility of an interaction effect between demand and supply factors – that is, a growing demand for low-wage female workers in these expanding sectors alongside a growing supply of immigrant women workers.

These trends tend to be confirmed by localized studies. For example, using the data from the Fordham University Survey of Colombians and Dominicans in New York City, Castro (1982) found that the incidence of blue-collar jobs among Colombian women in New York City was significantly higher than that among native women in the U.S. and than that among women in Colombia. Cohen and Sassen-Koob (1982) similarly found a very high incidence of women in blue-collar jobs; of all Hispanics in the survey holding blue-collar jobs, almost forty-one percent were women. This is a high figure compared with that for the United States as a whole, where women are one-sixth of all blue-collar workers (U.S. Department of Commerce 1983) (see Table 5.5).

The expansion of a downgraded manufacturing sector, be it the garment sweatshops in New York city or the high-tech production

Table 5

Occupational Distribution by National Origin and Sex,
Queens (NYC), 1980
(percentages)

	Colombian	Puerto Rican	Other Hispanics	All Hispanics
White Collar, Total	100.0	100.0	100.0	100.0
Male	44.4	28.6	41.7	37.0
Female	55.6	71.4	58.3	63.0
Blue Collar, Total	100.0	100.0	100.0	100.0
Male	62.5	66.7	55.2	59.2
Female	37.5	33.4	44.8	40.8
Services, Total	100.0	100.0	100.0	100.0
Male	44.4	25.0	43.5	36.5
Female	55.6	75.0	56.5	63.5

Source: Cohen and Sassen-Koob (1982).

plants in the Los Angeles region, can be seen to generate a demand for low-wage women workers. Immigrant women have clearly emerged as a labor supply for these kinds of jobs. It is well known that the garment, furs, and footwear sweatshops rely heavily on immigrant women. The employment of immigrant women in California's high-tech production and assembly operations has been well documented (Solorzano 1983).

Similarly, the expansion of low-wage service jobs, particularly pronounced in major cities for reasons discussed above, generates a demand for low-wage workers. Also in this case immigrant women can be seen as a desirable labor supply. Even more so than in the case of the downgraded manufacturing sector, many of these jobs have been historically and/or culturally typed as women's jobs.

There is, then, a correspondence between the kinds of jobs that are growing in the economy generally, and in major cities particularly, and the composition of immigration—largely from low-wage countries and with a majority of women. This correspondence does not necessarily entail the actual employment of immigrant women in such jobs. However, the available evidence on immigrant women shows them to be disproportionately concentrated in operative and service jobs and disproportionately located in certain states, notably New York and California, and then especially in major cities.

CONCLUSION

The expanded incorporation of Third World women into wage labor is a global process that assumes specific forms in different locations. These forms and locations may seem unrelated and disparate. I examined two instances of this incorporation and the possibility of a systemic relation between them. The two instances are: 1) the recruitment of women into the new manufacturing and service jobs generated by export-led manufacturing in several Caribbean and Asian countries; for a number of reasons this type of industrialization has drawn mostly young women without much prior wage-laboring experience; 2) the employment of immigrant women in highly industrialized countries, particularly in major cities which have undergone basic economic restructuring; waged employment represents for many immigrant women a first labor market experience, but it is increasingly becoming the continuation of patterns already initiated in countries of origin, among which, possibly, the recruitment of women into export manufacturing in the main immigrant-sending countries.

The study of women migrants has typically focused on their family situation and responsibilities and on how gender is affected by the migration to a highly industrialized country. I sought to add another variable by linking female immigration to basic processes in the current phase of the capitalist world economy. Global processes of economic restructuring are one element in the current phase of Third World women's domestic and international migration. Although many of these women may have become domestic or international migrants as a function of their husbands or families' migration, the more fundamental processes are the ones promoting the formation of a supply of women migrants and a demand for this type of labor. Some of the conditions that have promoted the formation of a supply of migrant women in Third World countries are one expression of the broader process of economic restructuring occurring at the global level. The particular expression in this case is the shift of plants and offices to Third World countries. Similarly with conditions that have promoted a demand for immigrant women in large cities within the United States. The particular expression in this case is the general shift to a service economy, the downgrading of manufacturing – partly to keep it competitive with overseas plants – and the direct and indirect demand for low-wage labor generated by the expansion of management and control functions centered in these large cities and necessary for the regulation of the global economy. All of these trends are contributing toward informalization in various sectors of the economy of large cities in highly developed countries. Further, the feminization of the job supply and the need to secure a politically adequate labor supply combine to create a demand for the type of worker represented by immigrant women. This suggests that gender cannot be considered in isolation of these structural arrangements and that gender alone is insufficient to specify the conditions of migrant women whether within their countries of origin or outside.

NOTES

1 This chapter is derived from the author's *The Mobility of Labor and Capital: A Study in International Investment and Labor Flow* (Cambridge University Press, 1988). Neither the larger project nor this chapter could have been carried out without the outstanding research assistance of Soon Kyoung Cho.

SECTION III

BAD SERVICE

7

SERVICE EMPLOYMENT REGIMES AND THE NEW INEQUALITY[1]

Beyond the multiple causes that produce inequality and poverty through lack of employment, I argue that major changes in the organization of economic activity over the last fifteen years have also emerged as a source of general economic insecurity and, particularly, of new forms of employment-centered poverty.

This is a broad subject; here I will confine myself to three processes: 1) the growing inequality in the profit-making capacities of different economic sectors and in the earnings capacities of different types of workers; 2) the polarization tendencies embedded in the organization of service industries and the casualization of the employment relation; and 3) the production of urban marginality, particularly as a result of new structural processes of economic growth rather than those producing marginality through abandonment. These three dynamics are not necessarily mutually exclusive. I will examine how they operate in major cities. One of the working hypothesis in this chapter is that in global cities the impacts of economic globalization operate in part through these three dynamics. Such an analysis thus becomes a heuristic for capturing the ways in which economic globalization may or may not contribute to urban poverty in such cities.

Cities, particularly cities that are leading business centers, are a nexus where many of the new organizational tendencies come together. Many service activities have been decentralized through the new information technologies, and many other services dependent on vicinity to buyers follow distribution patterns of populations, firms, and governments. But cities are key sites for the production of the most advanced services and predominantly export-oriented services, and for service firms that operate in dense networks of firms. Cities are also key sites for the various labor markets these service firms need. They are the sites where the polarization tendencies embedded in the organization of service industries come to the fore and have distinctive impacts on urban economic and social configurations; these outcomes are sharpened in very large cities by the disproportionate concentrations of low-wage service jobs catering to commuters, tourists, as well as a mass of low-income residents. Many of these tendencies assume concrete forms in the urban landscape.

The first section focuses particularly on the major systemic tendencies in the organization of the economy and how they materialize in cities. The second section focuses on polarization tendencies in the service sector. And the third section briefly examines some of the impacts of these trends on urban space.

Throughout much of this chapter the empirical focus is on the United States. To a considerable extent these trends toward greater inequality and insecurity are most advanced in the United States because the government has never been as concerned with regulating economic and social conditions as is typical in Western European countries. An important research question is how far the European countries will go toward deregulation of the economy and thereby stimulate some of these new trends.

INEQUALITY IN PROFIT-MAKING AND EARNINGS CAPACITIES

Inequality in the profit-making capacities of different sectors of the economy and in the earnings capacities of different types of workers is a basic feature of advanced economies. However, the orders of magnitude evident today distinguish current developments from those of the post-war decades. The extent of inequality and the systems in which it is embedded and through which these outcomes are produced are engendering massive distortions in the operations of various markets, from investment to housing and labor.

From the perspective of employment regimes, we need to understand what are the major processes lying behind the possibility for the increased inequality in profit making and earnings capacities. In the case of major cities they are: 1) the ascendance and transformation of finance, particularly through securitization, globalization, and the development of new telecommunications and computer networks technologies; and 2) the growing service intensity in the organization of the economy generally which has vastly raised the demand for services by firms and households. Insofar as there is a strong tendency toward polarization in the technical levels and prices of services as well as in the wages and salaries of workers in the service sector, the growth in the demand for services contributes to polarization and, via cumulative causation, to reproduce these inequalities. (For a fuller development of this argument, see Sassen 1994a, chap. 4.) Here I will particularly focus on these two major systemic tendencies in the economy and on how they materialize in cities.

The superprofit-making capacity of many of the leading service industries is embedded in a complex combination of new trends: technologies that make possible the hypermobility of capital at a global scale; market deregulation which maximizes the implementation of that hypermobility; financial inventions such as securization which liquify hitherto unliquid or relatively unliquid capital and allow it to circulate faster and hence make additional profits; the growing demand for services in all industries along with the increasing complexity and specialization of many of these inputs have contributed to their valorization and often overvalorization.

The ascendance of finance and specialized services, particularly concentrated in large cities, creates a critical mass of firms with extremely high profit-making capabilities. These firms contribute to bid up the prices of commercial space, industrial services and other business needs, and thereby make survival for firms with moderate profit-making capabilities increasingly precarious. Among the latter, informalization of all or some of a firm's operations can emerge as one of the more extreme responses, further contributing to polarization in the urban economy. More generally, we see a segmentation between high-profit-making firms and relatively modest-profit-making firms.

The growth in the demand for service inputs, and especially bought service inputs, in all industries is, in my reading, perhaps the most fundamental condition making for change in advanced economies (see Sassen 1994: chap. 4). It has had pronounced impacts on the earnings distribution, on industrial organization and on the patterns along which economic growth has spatialized. It has contributed to a massive growth in the demand for services by firms in all industries, from mining and manufacturing to finance and consumer services, and by households, both rich and poor.

The growing importance of services in economic organization can be seen in various types of data. All advanced economies have shown the most pronounced job growth in the so-called producer services (Castells and Aoyoma 1994; Sassen 1994a, Table 4.1). In the United States, the sectors with the largest share of new growth from 1973 to 1987 were finance, insurance, and real estate, which accounted for over eleven percent of all new jobs; in the 1980s these sectors accounted for twelve percent and business services for almost fourteen percent of new jobs (though they are only two percent of total jobs). At the other end of the spectrum, eating and drinking places, and retail each accounted for over ten percent of new jobs in the 1990s.[2] Another measure can be found in the value of bought service inputs in all industries. For this purpose I analyzed the national accounts data over different periods beginning with 1960 for several industries in manufacturing and services. The results showed clearly that this value increased markedly over time (see Sassen and Orloff, forthcoming; and see note 6 in chap. 8 here.)

There are broader and more generalized tendencies toward a deeply embedded dualization in economic organization that are particularly evident in global cities. These general trends have to do with the enormous differentiation within each of the traditional categories, particularly manufacturing and services, depending on the intensity of the use of computers, information, and control technologies in industry organization, and on whether an industry produces important inputs for other industries. Appelbaum and Albin (1990) have, in as far as this is possible given current data limitations, reclassified industries in terms of this variable across all major sectors of the economy.[3] Within the service sector, one grouping of industries can be characterized as "knowledge and information intensive" and another subsector as labor intensive, and typically as having low productivity (Appelbaum and Albin 1990). The same can be found for manufacturing and other major sectors. Overall the employment, occupational, educational, and earnings characteristics in each subsector tend to vary significantly. I return to a discussion of Appelbaum and Albin's findings – the sole study of its kind – in the next section.

Both the growing service intensity in the organization of the economy and the increased use of advanced technologies across all major sectors in the economy have a significant impact on the urban economy. Both entail a growing weight of specialized services in the economy. Insofar as cities are preferred locations for the production of specialized services, cities reemerge as significant production sites in advanced economies. This is a role they had lost to some extent when large-scale standardized mass manufacturing was dominant and necessarily left cities because of space requirements.

We see in cities the formation of a new urban economic core of financial and service activities that comes to replace the older typically more manufacturing-oriented core of services and production activities. In the case of cities that are major international business centers, the scale, power, and profit levels of this new core suggest that we are seeing the formation of a new urban economy. Even though these cities have long been centers for business and banking, since the early 1980s there have been dramatic changes in the structure of the business and financial sectors, as well as sharp increases in the overall magnitude of these sectors and their weight in the urban economy. This has had significant economic and social effects on cities in the United States in the 1980s, a development also evident as of the mid-1980s in major European cities (see, for example, Kunzmann and Wegener 1991; Frost and Spence 1993; *Le Debat* 1994; Sassen 1994a, chapters 2, 3 and 5).[4]

This growth in services for firms is evident in cities at different levels of national urban systems. Some of these cities serve regional or subnational markets; others serve national markets and/or global markets. The specific difference that globalization makes in the context of the growing service intensity in the organization of the economy is to raise the scale and the complexity of transactions. This feeds the growth of top-level multinational headquarter functions and the growth of advanced corporate services. But even though globalization raises the scale and complexity of these operations, they are also evident at smaller geographic scales and lower orders of complexity, as in the case with firms that operate regionally. Thus while regionally oriented firms need not negotiate the complexities of international borders and the regulations of different countries, they are still faced with a regionally dispersed network of operations that requires centralized control and servicing, and with a growing need to buy insurance, legal, accounting, advertising and other such services. In this context, globalization becomes a question of larger scale and added complexity: firms that operate across borders have more complicated servicing needs.

The ascendance of this specialized services-led economy, particularly the new finance and services complex, engenders what may be regarded as a new economic regime because although this sector may account for only a fraction of the economy of a city, it imposes itself on that large economy. One of these pressures is toward polarization, as in the case with the possibility for superprofits in finance which in turn contributes to devalorize manufacturing insofar as the latter cannot generate the superprofits typical in much financial activity.

One of the key outcomes of this transformation has been the significant growth of a high-income population particularly concentrated in cities and intimately linked to the ascendance of expertise and specialization in the organization of the economy. This ascendance of expertise in economic organization in turn has contributed to the valorization of specialized services and professional workers. And it has contributed to mark many of the "other" types of economic activities and workers as unnecessary or irrelevant to an advanced economy. As I have sought to show at length elsewhere, many of the "other" jobs are in fact an integral part of internationalized economic sectors, but not represented as such. This creates a vast number of both low-income households and households earning very high incomes. The next two sections examine these issues in greater detail.

POLARIZATION TRENDS IN SERVICE EMPLOYMENT

The growth of services in terms of both jobs and firm inputs needs to be unbundled in order to capture the impact on questions of inequality and new forms of employment-centered poverty. Key issues are the types of jobs being created and the systemic tendencies organizing the service sector which are setting the terms of employment for today and tomorrow. Jobs and organization are, clearly, overlapping and mutually shaping factors. However, they do not overlap completely: the labor markets associated with a given set of technologies can, in principle, vary considerably and contain distinct mobility paths for workers. Nonetheless, today, sector organization, types of jobs, and labor-market organization, are all strengthening the tendencies toward polarization.

Dualization in the Organization of Service Industries

Among the major systemic tendencies in the organization of the service sector contributing to polarization is the disproportionate grouping of service industries at either end of the technology spectrum. In the United States, service industries that can be described as information and knowledge intensive have generated a significant share of all new jobs created over the last fifteen years and have absorbed a disproportionate share of college graduates. Most of the other jobs created in the service sector fall at the other extreme. Appelbaum and Albin (1990) find that the first subsector generated over nine million jobs from 1973 to 1987, while the second subsector added 11.2 million jobs. Each of these subsectors accounts for a considerable share of U.S. jobs, with the first accounting for almost thirty percent of all U.S. jobs, and the second subsector for thirty-nine percent.[5]

These conditions of sharp growth at either end of the technology spectrum are continuing into the 1990s. Based on the data for 1992, the U.S. Bureau of Labor Statistics (BLS) projects a massive growth of low-wage service jobs, including service jobs catering to firms. Three service industries alone will account for about half of total U.S. employment growth between 1992 and 2005: retail trade, health services, and business services. Using the most detailed occupational classification (223 categories), the largest increases in terms of numbers of jobs are, in descending order: retail sales workers, registered nurses, cashiers, truck drivers, waiters and waitresses, nursing aides, janitors, food preparation workers, and systems analysts.[6] Most of these jobs do not require a high school education and they are mostly not very highly paid. Nor does the BLS expect an increase in the median weekly wage of workers.

At the other extreme are jobs requiring a college degree. Their share was twenty-three percent in 1992 and is projected to rise only by one percent to twenty-four percent by 2005. Appelbaum and Albin (1990) found that the knowledge- and information-intensive service subsector absorbed more than 5.7 million college-educated workers from 1973 to 1987. By 1987, over forty percent of workers with a college degree were employed in the service industries, compared to seventeen percent in the other service subsector. Indeed in the latter, sixty percent of workers have never attended college. Further, twenty percent of workers with post-college education were in information- and knowledge-intensive service industries, compared to six percent in the other service subsector.

Parallel segmentation is evident in terms of occupation. Managerial, executive, and administrative occupations account for seventeen percent of all jobs in information- and knowledge-intensive service industries, which is double the percentage for other services. On the other hand, the latter subsector had, at 9.4 percent, three times the share of supervisors as were found in the former. Information-, clerical-, and computer-related-equipment operators were also most present in information- and knowledge-intensive services, 8.5 per cent compared to 4.7 percent in other services. Service and sales occupations are forty percent in other services, but only sixteen percent in information- and knowledge-intensive services. If we add up professionals, executives and kindred occupations, we can see that they account for thirty-four percent of workers in this subsector, compared to 14.6 percent in other services.

The two broad occupational categories projected by the BLS to increase are professional specialty occupations and service occupations. The BLS data and projections show that the incomes in these two occupations in 1992 were on opposite ends of the earnings spectrum; earnings for service workers were about forty percent below the average for all occupational groups in 1992. In combination with growth trends in industries and occupations, this points to a maintenance and even increase in inequality in earnings, since most new jobs will be in low-paying service jobs and some of the professional specialty jobs may raise their levels of specialization and pay.

Appelbaum and Albin (1990) found that the differences they identified within the service sector are also evident in earnings. About thirty-seven percent (or 5.3 million jobs) of total new job growth in the United States from 1979 to 1987 was in a group of service industries within the labor-intensive subsector where the median earnings of full-time year-round workers in 1986 was $15,500. This is $7,000 less than the median of $22,555 of all full-time workers in this subsector (and almost $9,000 less than the median in durable goods manufacturing). Thus, most new jobs in the labor-intensive subsector were in industries paying median wages and salaries under $15,500. Further, these jobs were thirty-seven percent of new job growth in the 1980s, which is an increase over the twenty-nine percent share they had in the 1970s, signaling deterioration in the earnings of a growing share of workers in services. In contrast, public-sector low-wage jobs, which are better paid and have more fringe benefits, saw a fall in their share of all new jobs, accounting for twenty-six percent of jobs created in the 1970s and twenty-two percent in the 1980s (or 3.2 million new jobs). The lowest paid hourly workers are part-time workers in the labor-intensive service industries, followed by full-time hourly workers in knowledge- and information-intensive service industries.[7] At the other end, the highest paid full-time hourly workers are in knowledge- and information-intensive manufacturing, followed by all other manufacturing.

A crucial and familiar form of segmentation is by sex. Seven out of every ten new jobs from 1973 to 1987 have been filled by women. Over eighty percent of women hold jobs in service industries compared with about fifty-five percent of men. The gendering of the employment transformation can be captured in the fact that women have more jobs in knowledge- and information-intensive industries than men: about thirty-four percent of jobs held by women are in these industries compared with about twenty-five percent of jobs held by men. Differences by sex are also evident in terms of education. Thus, thirty-eight percent of women workers and forty-eight percent of men in information- and knowledge-intensive services have a college degree, compared with respectively fifteen percent and twenty percent in other services. Median earnings of women are higher in knowledge- and information-intensive services and manufacturing than in all other sectors, but they are always lower than the median for men in each sector.

The Casualization of the Employment Relation

In principle, the trends described earlier toward polarization in the job characteristics of the service sector could have left labor-market organization unaffected. But they have not. We see a tendency toward a greater casualization of the employment relation. This is to say, it is not just a matter of an expansion of what are typically considered casual or unsheltered jobs, but a more fundamental transformation, one which also includes a growing array of high-paying professional jobs.

Two tendencies stand out. One is the weakening role of the firm in structuring the employment relation. More is left to the market. A second tendency in this restructuring of the labor market is what could be described as the shift of labor-market functions to the household or community (see Sassen 1995). Let me elaborate on each of these briefly.

Among the empirical referents for the weakening role of the firm in structuring the employment relation is the declining weight of internal labor markets. It corresponds to both the shrinking weight of vertically integrated firms and the restructuring of labor demand in many firms toward bipolarity – a demand for highly specialized and educated workers alongside a demand for basically unskilled workers whether for clerical, service, industrial service, or production jobs.

The shrinking demand for intermediate levels of skill and training has in turn reduced the need and advantages for firms of having internal labor markets with long promotion lines that function as training-on-the-job mechanisms. It has also reduced the need for firms to have full-time, year-round workers. And it has contributed to the rapid rise of employment agencies as intermediaries in the labor market; such agencies take over the demand and supply of a growing range of skills and occupations under highly flexible conditions. We can see here a coincidence – and the possibility of systemic linkages – between a de-valuing of a growing range of jobs and a feminization of employment.

These tendencies appear to be particularly evident in labor-intensive service industries, where the levels of skill required are often lower than in manufacturing. The higher growth of service as compared to manufacturing jobs thus carries additional consequences for the casualization of the employment relation.

Perhaps one of the most familiar and dramatic trends is the growth in part-time jobs. Over sixty percent of all part-time workers in the U.S. labor force are in labor-intensive services, which is also the sector that is expected to add the largest share of new jobs over the next decade.[8] Service workers are twice as likely to be in part-time jobs as average workers; involuntary part-time employment has grown significantly over the past decade (Carre 1992).

The terms of employment have been changing rapidly over the last fifteen years for a growing share of workers. In my reading, the overall tendency is toward a casualization of the employment relation that incorporates not only the types of jobs traditionally marked as "casual" jobs, but also jobs at a high professional level which in many regards are not casual. It might be useful to differentiate a casualized employment relation from casual jobs in that the latter connotes such added dimensions as the powerlessness of the workers, a condition which might not hold for some of the highly specialized professional part-time or temporary workers. This is a subject that requires more research. (see Sassen 1994a, chap. 6).

The second tendency in the restructuring of labor markets I want to point out is the shift of labor-market functions to the household or community. This is perhaps most evident in the case of immigrant communities. But it is also present in types of labor markets that are not necessarily embedded in communities or households. It also represents a feminization of the costs of some aspects of labor-market operation.

There is a large body of evidence showing that once one or a few immigrant workers are hired in a given workplace, they will tend to bring in other members from their communities as job openings arise (Portes 1995; Mahler 1996). There is also evidence showing great willingness on the part of immigrant workers to help those they bring in with some training on the job, teaching the language, and just generally socializing them into the job and workplace. This amounts to a displacement of traditional labor-market functions such as recruitment, screening, and training from the labor market and the firm to the community or household. The labor market can then be reconceived as an activity space that contains a space dependency between employers and the community/household.[9]

Elsewhere (1995) I have examined how this space dependency between employers and low-wage workers contributes to the formation of distinctive localized labor markets and the extent to which the networks thus constituted also have the effect of restricting job opportunities for these workers. The formation of such localized labor markets and the enclosure of workers in these networks becomes particularly significant with the breakdown of internal labor markets in firms and trend toward bipolarity in skill requirements generally in service industries. The overall effect is to reduce further the chances for upward mobility. While in the case of immigrant workers this general dynamic is particularly clear and transparent, it actually affects a growing share of all low-wage workers.

In this restructuring of the labor market lie conditions for the growth of employment-centered insecurity and poverty and for urban marginality. The casualization of the employment relation weakens and even eliminates the claims by workers on the firms that employ them and hence can be seen as a weakening of the position of labor in the economy and, at the limit, its institutional marginalization. Second, the displacement of labor-market functions to the community or household raises the costs of participating in the labor force for workers, even if these costs are often not monetized.[10] These are all subjects that require new research given the transitions that we are living through.

CONCLUSION

Developments in cities cannot be understood in isolation from fundamental changes in the larger organization of advanced economies. One way of conceiving of these transformations is as systemic transitions between different modes of social and economic organization. Thus we are seeing a transition from the relative obsoleteness of urban economies during the dominance of Fordism, to the revalorization of strategic components of urban space because of the increased service intensity in the organization of the economy.

The new urban economy not only strengthens existing inequalities but sets in motion a whole series of new dynamics of inequality. The new growth sectors – specialized services and finance – contain capabilities for profit making vastly superior to those of more traditional economic sectors. Many of the latter are essential to the operation of the urban economy and the daily needs of residents, but their profitable survival is threatened in a situation where finance and specialized services can earn superprofits.

We see sharp increases in socioeconomic and spatial inequalities within major cities. This can be interpreted as merely a quantitative increase in the degree of inequality. But it can also be interpreted as social and economic restructuring and the emergence of new social forms and class alignments in large cities of highly developed countries: the growth of an informal economy; high-income commercial and residential gentrification; and the sharp rise of homelessness.

The observed changes in the occupational and earnings distribution are outcomes not only of industrial shifts but also of changes in the organization of firms and of labor markets. There has been a strengthening of differences within major sectors, notably within services. One set of service industries tends toward growing capital–labor ratios, growing productivity, intensive use of the most advanced technologies; the other, toward continued labor intensity and low wages. Median earnings and median educational levels are also increasingly diverging for each of these subsectors. These characteristics in each group of industries contribute to a type of cumulative causation within each group. The first group of industries experiences pressures toward even higher capital-labor ratios and productivity levels given high wages, while in the second group of industries, low wages are a deterrent toward greater use of capital-intensive technologies, and low productivity leads to even more demand for very low-wage workers. These conditions in turn reproduce the difference in profit-making capacities embedded in each of these subsectors.

When we speak of polarization in the use of land, in the organization of labor markets, in the housing market and in the consumption structure, we do not necessarily mean that the middle class is disappearing. We are rather referring to a dynamic whereby growth contributes to inequality rather than expansion of the middle class, as was the case in the two decades after World War II in the United States and in many of the developed economies. Where the middle class represents a significant share of the population it is an important channel through which income and lifestyle coalesce into a dominant social form. In many of today's leading urban economies we see a segmenting of the middle class that has a sharper upward and downward slant than had been the case in other periods. The conditions that contributed to middle class expansion and politico-economic power–the centrality of mass production and mass consumption in economic growth and profit realization–have been displaced by new sources of growth. This is not simply a quantitative transformation; we see here the elements for a new economic regime.

NOTES

1   A version of this chapter first appeared in *Urban Poverty and the Underclass*, ed. Enzo Mingione (London: Blackwell, 1996).

2   By 1987, business services provided 5.2 million jobs, or five percent of total jobs, and had
    become a larger employer than construction and almost as large as transport and public utili-
    ties, and wholesale trade. Almost half of the new jobs in business services came from personnel
    supply services, and computer and data processing (see Bednarzik 1990).

3   Appelbaum and Albin have proposed a taxonomy of firms and industries into broad sectors on
    the basis of "information and knowledge intensity" – "a multidimensional property of firms and
    industries, reflecting the nature of the output produced, the extent of computer rationalization
    of the production process, and the organizational adaptation to information and computation
    technologies" (1990, 32).

4   Manufacturing remains a crucial sector in all these economies, even when it may have ceased
    to be a dominant sector in major cities. Some have argued that the producer services sector
    could not exist without manufacturing (Cohen and Zysman 1987; Markusen and Gwiasda 1994).
    There is no consensus around this issue (see, for example, Noyelle and Dutka 1988; Drennan
    1992). Drennan (1992) argues that a strong finance and producer service sector is possible in a
    city like New York notwithstanding decline in its industrial base and that these sectors are so
    strongly integrated into the world markets that articulation with the larger region becomes
    secondary. In a variant on both positions, I have long argued that manufacturing indeed feeds
    the growth of the producer services sector, but that it does so whether located in the area in
    question, somewhere else in the country, or overseas. Even though manufacturing – and min-
    ing and agriculture, for that matter – feeds growth in the demand for producer services, their
    actual location is of secondary importance in the case of global-level service firms. Second, the
    territorial dispersal of plants, especially if international, actually raises the demand for pro-
    ducer services insofar as it raises the complexity of management and financing for multisite
    firms. The growth of producer services firms headquartered in New York or London or Paris
    can be fed by manufacturing located anywhere in the world as long as it is part of a multina-
    tional corporate network. Third, a good part of the producer services sector is fed by financial
    and business transactions that either have nothing to do with manufacturing, as is the case in
    many of the global financial markets, or for which manufacturing is incidental, as in much
    merger and acquisition activity, which is centered on buying and selling firms rather than the
    buying of manufacturing firms as such.

5   Information- and knowledge-intensive manufacturing in the United States accounts for only 3.2
    percent of U.S. employment; the rest of manufacturing, for about twenty-seven percent. Note
    that women are far less represented in the "rest of manufacturing" subsector than in the
    former; this is partly due to the feminization of the electronics assembly line.

6   Retail trade is expected to add the largest number of jobs, 4.5 million. Nearly half of these jobs
    will be for food service workers (cashiers and salespersons in eating and drinking places: these
    are not well-paid jobs, nor do they demand high levels of education). Next comes health ser-
    vices with an added 4.2 million jobs; within these the fastest-growing type of job is home care
    service, again mostly a low-paying job. Next are business services, with 3.1 million new jobs,
    which includes both low-wage and high-wage industries. One of the growth industries in busi-
    ness services is personnel supply services, such as temporary employment agencies; another
    growth sector is transportation, particularly trucking and warehousing.

7   Average hourly wages have been stagnant in the United States since 1973, notwithstanding a
    rapid increase in the salaries of new professionals. And as has been documented in the 1990
    census, income inequality increased over the previous twenty years.

8   Almost thirty percent of all jobs in labor-intensive services are part time, compared to seven-
    teen percent in information- and knowledge-intensive services. Part-time jobs are highly con-
    centrated: restaurants and hotels, retail, and education account for forty-five percent of all
    part-time jobs, but only twenty-five percent of all jobs in the economy. Nearly half of all work-

ers in retail are part time, compared with ten percent in administrative, managerial and supervisory occupations.

9   This space dependency is centered on the relation between workplace and household, and between workplace and community. The exchange dynamic – a component of all markets – is therewith displaced from the center of labor-market operation where it is situated in the neo-classical model (see Sassen 1995). When it comes to international labor migration, this reconceptualization views the act of migrating as a move from one particular local labor market (in the country of origin) to another particular local labor market (in the country of destination). This specific job search pattern has the effect of altering the geographic dimension often implied by job search models, especially among low-wage workers who have been found to have little geographic mobility. However, notwithstanding this wide-ranging area within which many immigrants search for jobs, they are actually largely moving within a very confined institutional setting, that is, a *local* labor market, even when they travel long distances and improvise informal transportation systems. This is another way of conceptualizing the role of networks. These networks of immigrants have spatial patterns, but they are not characterized by geographic proximity. Further, while they may cover immense distances they do not necessarily offer great opportunities for mobility nor place immigrants in particularly competitive positions vis-à-vis natives in terms of upward job mobility. This effect is strenghtened by the polarization tendencies evident in the distribution of jobs in services – rather than, for instance, long upward mobility chains that connect low-level jobs to high-level jobs.

10 There is an interesting parallel here with one of the components of the service economy, that is, the shift of tasks traditionally performed by the firm onto the household: for example, furniture and even appliances sold unassembled to be put together by the buyer (Gershuny and Miles 1983).

8

THE INFORMAL ECONOMY: BETWEEN
NEW DEVELOPMENTS AND OLD REGULATIONS

———

Т he growth of an informal economy in the large cities of highly developed countries prompts new questions about the relationship between economy and regulation today. As I shall employ the term, the "informal economy" refers to those income-generating activities occurring outside the state's regulatory framework that have analogs within that framework. The scope and character of the informal economy are defined by the very regulatory framework it evades. For this reason, the informal economy can only be understood in terms of its relationship to the formal economy – that is, regulated income-generating activity.

The main theories of economic development – whether proffered by the modernization or the Marxist schools of thought – do not foresee the inevitable emergence of an informal economy in highly developed countries. Such theories do allow for criminal activities and underreporting of income in advanced economies; these activities do not signal the presence of any novel or unexplained economic dynamic. Income underreporting, for instance, is acknowledged as an inevitable response to the state's implementation of a tax system. Nevertheless, the main theories of economic development have yet to explain adequately the phenomenon of the informal economy in advanced capitalist (usually urban) societies.

Until recently, theorization about the informal economy has focused on the shortcomings of less developed economies: their inability to attain full modernization, to stop excess migration to the cities, and to implement universal education and literacy programs.[1] The growth of an informal economy in highly developed countries has been explained as the result of immigration from the Third World and the replication here of survival strategies typical of the home countries of migrant workers. Related to this conception is the notion that "backward" sectors of the economy such as the garment industry remain backward (or even continue to exist) because a large supply of cheap immigrant labor is available. Both of these views imply that if there is an informal economy in highly developed countries, it is solely attributable to Third World immigration and the existence of backward sectors of the economy, not to the nature of the current phase of advanced economies.

Rather than simply assume the truth of such an argument, we must critically examine the role that Third World immigration might or might not play in the informalization process. Although immigrants, insofar as they tend to form communities, may be in a favorable position to seize the opportunities presented by informalization, immigrants do not necessarily *create* such opportunities. Instead, the opportunities may well be a structured outcome of the composition of advanced economies. The argument presented here is that informalization must be seen in the context of the economic restructuring that has contributed to the decline of the manufacturing-dominated industrial complex of the post-war era and the rise of a new, service-dominated economic complex.[2] The specific mediating processes that promote informalization of work are: 1) increased earnings inequality, and the concomitant restructuring of consumption in high-income and very low-income strata; and 2) the inability of providers of many of the goods and services that are part of the new consumption to compete for necessary resources in urban contexts, where leading sectors have sharply bid up the prices of commercial space, labor, auxiliary services, and other factors of production going partly or wholly informal is an option. Not immigrants, but the growing inequality in earnings among consumers, and the growing inequality in profit-making capabilities among firms in different sectors in the urban economy, have promoted the informalization of a growing array of economic activities. These shifts in earnings and profit-making capabilities are integral conditions for the current phase of advanced capitalism developing in major cities. The new, advanced services complex, typically oriented toward world markets and capable of generating extremely high profits, dominates these cities. The conditions giving rise to informal economies in these cities cannot be said to be imported from the Third World.

To explain the source of informal economies in advanced urban societies, I consider the differential impact that 1) immigration and 2) conditions in the economy at large may have on the formation and expansion of informal income-generating processes. Each of these factors has specific implications for research and policy development. If conditions in the economy at large have a greater impact on the development of informal economies, then we need to deepen our understanding of the nature of advanced capitalism. But if immigration has the greater impact, then we may indeed find adequate the current development theories of advanced economies or the postindustrial society, which allow no room for phenomena such as informalization. Similarly, the primacy of immigration would suggest, at its crudest, that policy makers should control immigrant activity in order to eradicate the informal economy. If, however, conditions in the economy at large are primary, as I argue, then policy makers should stop approaching the informal economy as an anomaly. They should instead view the informal economy as a necessary outgrowth of advanced capitalism. Rather than treat its components as isolated deviations from the norm, policy makers should recognize that a new norm has developed; rather than attempt to make this new norm fit the regulations developed decades ago, they should develop new regulations to fit this norm.

Elsewhere, I have argued that it might be useful to think in terms of regulatory "fractures," rather than regulatory "violations." Increasingly, economic processes diverge from the model for which extant regulations were designed. As these divergences take on a recognizable shape of their own, it becomes meaningless to speak of regulatory violations; informal economic activity as here described is not a scattering of isolated deviations, but a recurrent pattern. The difficulty, if not impossibility, of acknowledging the existence of an informal economy in today's regulatory framework without criminalizing that economy is an instance of what I have referred to as a regulatory "fracture."[3]

In order to identify systemic links between informalization and structural conditions in advanced capitalism, I shall discuss the effects of major growth trends in shaping different types of jobs, firms, and subcontracting patterns that induce or are themselves susceptible to informalization.[4] There is no precise measurement of informalization, and the evidence of this process cannot be culled from one neat set of data. However, pairing systemic trends with the available evidence provides us with a basic understanding of the patterns and scope of informalization and the conditions that foster its growth.

SPECIFYING THE INFORMAL ECONOMY

We can only obtain an operational definition of the informal economy[5] against the backdrop of an institutional framework for economic activity in which the state intervenes explicitly to regulate the processes and products of income-generating activities according to a set of enforceable legal rules. Nevertheless, the informal economy (as I use the term) does not include every transaction that happens to evade regulation. The concept excludes certain types of income-generating activities, such as teenage babysitting, that we almost expect to escape regulation. What makes informalization a distinct process today is not these small cracks in the institutional framework, but rather the informalization of activities generally taking place in the formal economy. For example, a student of the informal economy would find a sweatshop most interesting because it operates against a background in which people expect such enterprises to comply with regulation. Today's sweatshops may look similar to the sweatshops of the last century. Yet, the implementation of various health and labor regulations since then is what makes today's sweatshops a different form of labor/employer relation than their counterparts of one hundred years past, when no such regulations existed and the vast majority of manufacturing took place in sweatshops. The type of social relation represented by sweatshop work is defined by its historical context, in this case one where the activity of manufacturing has been regulated for decades.

While there are certain activities that lend themselves more to informalization than others, it is not the intrinsic characteristics of those activities, but rather the boundaries of state regulation, that determine their informalization. As these boundaries vary, so does the definition of what is formal and what is informal. The informal economy is not a clearly defined sector or set of sectors. Neither is the informal economy a fixed set of activities undertaken solely for survival. Indeed, the shape of the informal economy changes according to the opportunities created and constraints imposed by the formal economy. The key to an analysis of the informal economy, then, is not so much a precise description of the particular activities it encompasses at any given moment, as a description of the basic dynamics that make possible or even induce informalization, despite regulatory policies and pressure from institutions such as labor unions and enforcement agencies.

It is important here to keep in mind the distinction between what can be considered elements central to a theorization of informalization in advanced economies and the fact of possibly fairly generalized informal practices. The first seeks to identify what is distinct and can be used to specify the nature of the process in highly developed countries with extensive regulatory frameworks. Thus the finding that over half of all US households consume food produced informally (Institute for Social Research, 1987) does not by itself specify the informal economy. Generally, the findings about US household use of informally produced and/or distributed services and goods describe a far more widespread condition than can be read as carrying theoretical meaning. For instance, over twenty-seven percent of US households bought informally produced home repairs, almost twenty-one percent bought goods from informal sidewalk vendors, 15.5 percent bought informal lawn and garden services, and so on.

Professors Manuel Castells and Alejandro Portes have identified certain elements of the work process, such as status of labor, work conditions, and form of management, as factors that often evade regulation in the informal economy. Although each of these elements may escape the state's institutional framework, the unregulated status of any one is neither necessary nor sufficient to characterize the overall work process as part of the informal economy.[6] The status of labor, for example–the identities of the employees in an enterprise, whether aliens or citizens–does not determine the formality or informality of the enterprise. In principle, an undocumented immigrant may be employed in a fully regulated job in the formal economy in full compliance with the laws, while a legal citizen may be employed in an informal shop.[7] Although it is true that in the United States we have found a large number of undocumented immigrants in the informal economy,[8] it is also true that many of the illegal homeworkers in the Netherlands, for example, are Dutch citizens,[9] and many of the workers in the unregulated factories of Emilia-Romagna in Italy are Italian citizens.[10] Thus, the expansion of informalization does not, in principle, depend on the existence of an immigrant labor force. Further, in terms of the conditions of work, informal work is, in itself, licit work. But if it is done in the home when there is a ban on doing such work in the home, or if it is done in factories which violate various codes, the work becomes illegal. A factory or a shop that fails to comply with health, fire, labor, tax, zoning, or other such regulations is part of the informal economy, even if all the workers are properly documented.

Measuring the size and geographical scope of the informal economy is particularly difficult because of its shifting boundaries and interaction with the formal economy. However, the measurement problem does not preclude analysis. Informalization is a process whose particular empirical content varies, but whose analytic meaning remains fairly constant when specified along the lines set out above. The process of informalization across different sectors reflects common trends that help to explain the mechanics of that process.

CONDITIONS FOR INFORMALIZATION IN ADVANCED ECONOMIES

The forms economic growth assumed in the post–World War II era – notably capital intensity, standardization of production, and suburbanization-led growth – contributed to the vast expansion of a middle class and deterred and reduced informalization. The cultural forms accompanying these processes shaped the structures of everyday life insofar as a large middle class engages in mass consumption and thus contributes to standardization in production. Large-scale production and mass consumption were conducive to higher levels of labor unionization and worker empowerment than had existed before World War II. It was in that post-war period, extending into the late 1960s and early 1970s, that the incorporation of workers into formal labor market relations reached its highest level.[11]

The decline of mass production as the main engine of national growth and the shift to services as the leading economic sector contributed to the demise of a broader set of social arrangements, particularly a weakening of the larger institutional framework that shaped the employment relationship. This context is important in understanding the conditions for informalization in advanced economies. The groups of service industries that were the driving economic force in the 1980s were characterized by greater earnings and occupational dispersion, weak labor unions, and mostly unsheltered jobs in the lower-paying echelons.[12] Along with the decline in manufacturing, these trends altered the institutional framework that shaped the employment relationship in the 1980s. Changes in the employment relationship reshaped social reproduction and consumption trends which, as discussed below, have had a feedback effect on economic organization and earnings. Although in the earlier period a similar feedback effect helped reproduce the middle class and formalization of the employment relationship, currently it reproduces growing earnings dispersion and the casualization of the employment relationship.

The overall result of the transformation of the economic structure is a tendency toward increased economic polarization. The ascendance of finance and specialized services, particularly concentrated in large cities, creates a critical mass of firms with extremely high profit-making capabilities. These firms bid up the prices of commercial space, industrial services, and other factors of production, such as energy and business services. The high profit-making firms thereby make survival for firms with moderate profit-making capabilities increasingly precarious. My research indicates that even when moderate profit-making firms have a stable, or even increasing, demand for their goods and services from households and other firms, operating informally is often one of the few ways in which they can survive. In short, the sectors in which these firms operate may be thriving, demand may be sufficiently high to attract new entrants into the sector, but despite the high demand, the only way to succeed may be to operate informally.[13] Alternatively, firms with limited profit-making capabilities may subcontract part of their work to informal operations. This alternative allows the contracting firm to operate formally *and* reduce its costs of operation.[14]

The polarization I have described does not simply constitute a quantitative transformation; it posseses the elements of a new economic regime.[15] As indicated above, the tendency toward polarization assumes distinct forms in 1) structures of social reproduction; 2) organization of the labor process; and 3) spatial organization of the economy.

Increased economic polarization affects not only businesses, but also patterns of social reproduction and consumption. Although the middle class still constitutes the majority, the conditions that contributed to its expansion and political-economic power – the centrality of mass production and mass consumption in economic growth and profit realization – have been displaced by new sources of growth that feed the top and the bottom of the income structure. The expansion of a low-income population fuels the demand for very cheap goods and services; the informal economy can help satisfy that demand and, indeed, it can compete against low-priced imports in these markets. The expansion of a high-income stratum in cities promotes demand for customized goods and services; this market includes the rise of a designer culture in all forms of consumption, from food and clothing to furniture and home renovation. The production and/or distribution of customized goods and services frequently draws on the informal economy at some point in the work process.

The rapid growth of industries with strong concentrations of high- and low-income jobs has assumed distinct forms in the consumption structure, which in turn has had a feedback effect on the organization of work and the types of jobs being created. The expansion of the high-income workforce, in conjunction with the emergence of new cultural forms, has led to a process of high-income gentrification that ultimately depends on the availability of a vast supply of low-wage workers.[16] High-income gentrification is labor intensive, whereas middle-income suburbanization is capital intensive. The latter phenomenon is characterized by tract housing, road and highway construction, dependence on private automobile or commuter trains, marked reliance on appliances and household equipment of all sorts, and large shopping malls with self-service operations.[17] High-income gentrification replaces many of these capital-intensive projects with operations that rely heavily on workers, directly and indirectly. Similarly, high-income residents in cities depend to a much greater extent on hired maintenance personnel than do middle-class suburban households, with their concentrated input of family labor and machinery.

Behind the gourmet food shops and specialty boutiques that have replaced many self-service supermarkets and department stores in cities, lies an organization of work that is very different from that prevailing in large, standardized establishments. This difference in the organization of work is evident both in retail and production phases. High-income gentrification generates a demand for goods and services often unsuitable for mass production or mass retailing. Customized production, small runs, specialty items, and fine food dishes are generally produced through labor-intensive methods and sold through small, full-service outlets. Subcontracting part of this production to low-cost operations, including sweatshops and households, is common. The types of firms and labor that serve this market are distinct from the large department stores and supermarkets that serve the middle-income market. Department stores and supermarkets typically sell standardized products, which they acquire from large, standardized factories located outside the city or the region. Proximity to retailers is of far greater importance to customized producers. These producers rely heavily on specific customer input in designing their product line, and their small scales of production raise the relative costs of transportation and national distribution. Further, unlike mass production and distribution, customized production and distribution do not facilitate labor unionizing.

The expansion of the low-income consumer population in large cities has also contributed to the proliferation of small operations and the move away from large-scale standardized factories and large chain stores for the low-priced goods. The consumption needs of the low-income population are met in large part by small manufacturing and retail establishments that rely on family labor and often fall below minimum safety and health standards. Cheap, locally produced sweatshop garments, for example, compete with low-cost Asian imports. A growing range of products and services, from low-cost furniture made in basements to "gypsy cabs" and family day care, is available to meet the demand of the growing low-income population.[18]

In any large city, there also tends to be a proliferation of small, low-cost service operations made possible by the massive concentration of people in such cities and the daily inflow of commuters and tourists. Sheer numbers of people, as well as fierce competition and low returns, create strong inducements to open such operations. Under such conditions, the cost of labor is crucial and enhances the likelihood that there will be a high concentration of low-wage jobs.[19]

There are numerous examples of how the increased inequality in earnings reshapes the consumption structure and how this, in turn, affects the organization of work. The impact of the shift in demand appears in both the formal economy and the informal economy. (Recall that, by my definition, activities in the informal economy have counterparts in the formal economy.[20]) However, the size of businesses serving either high-income or low-income customers is typically smaller than that of businesses serving the large middle class. The reduction in size, and the accompanying loss of economies of scale and scope, sometimes make it advantageous for businesses to operate in the informal economy, and often requires them to do so. Responses to this shift in demand include the increase in highly customized woodwork in homes and shops in gentrified neighborhoods, the increase in low-cost rehabilitation of homes and shops in poor neighborhoods, and the increase in homeworkers and sweatshops making either very expensive designer products for boutiques or very cheap products.

Income polarization is also expressed spatially. Services in the formal economy for high-income customers have proliferated, as have services in the informal economy for low-income customers. Taxi services and banking services illustrate this pattern. The creation of a special, fully registered limousine line that exclusively services New York City's financial district stands in stark contrast to the increase in gypsy cabs servicing low-income neighborhoods, where registered cab drivers typically refuse to go.[21] The spatial impact of income polarization is also evident in the distribution of bank branches. A recent study presented to the New York State Legislature that addressed commercial bank branch closings and openings in the New York metropolitan area[22] revealed a wave of bank branch closings even larger than the one that took place in the early 1980s.[23] While the earlier rash of branch closings was concentrated in low-income areas, the latest wave affected the more modest segments of middle-income areas.[24] Five major New York City banks accounted for all but one of the closings of commercial branches in New York City neighborhoods with minority populations greater than fifty percent.[25] During the same period, branch services increased in the suburbs and in high-income areas in New York City.[26] Banks also opened numerous "personal financial centers" or "private banking centers" in affluent areas of New York City. In some of these branches a minimum account balance of $25,000 was required to use the teller service. Bank closings and openings illustrate a strong trend toward offering fewer services to poor and middle-class neighborhoods, while offering an increased array of specialized services to affluent neighborhoods. One response to this trend in low-income areas can be seen in the rapid proliferation of formal and informal check-cashing operations and various forms of informal credit operations.

In sum, the kinds of growth trends described earlier favor the informalization of a broad range of activities. Inducements to informalization particularly evident in major cities include: 1) the increased demand for highly priced customized services and products by the expanding high-income population; 2) the increased demand for extremely low-cost services and products by the expanding low-income population; 3) the demand for customized services and goods or limited runs from firms that are either final or intermediate buyers, with a corresponding growth of subcontracting; and 4) the increasing inequality in the bidding power of firms in a context of acute pressures on land due to the rapid growth and strong agglomerative pattern of the leading industries. The continuing demand for a range of goods and services typically produced in firms with low profit rates, and that find it increasingly difficult to survive given rising rents and costs of production, promotes informalization in a broad range of activities and spheres of the economy. The existence of an informal economy, in turn, becomes attractive for firms seeking to reduce costs. Firms that do not necessarily need to operate informally in order to survive may nevertheless turn to the informal economy for subcontracts in order to increase profit margins and enhance flexibility.

PATTERNS OF INFORMALIZATION
AND THEIR IMPLICATIONS: A SUMMARY

My field research in New York City[27] has revealed several recurring patterns in the process of informalization. The first pattern concerns the source of demand for informally produced or distributed goods and services.[28] Most of the demand for informally produced goods in the garment, furniture, construction, packaging, and electronics industries comes from firms that operate in the formal economy. Other informally produced goods and services cater to the communities in which such activities are performed. Immigrant communities are a leading example, and probably account for much of this second type of demand.

The second set of patterns I have identified concerns factors influencing the supply of, and demand for, informally produced and distributed goods and services. One of these factors is pressure in certain industries, notably apparel, to reduce labor costs, given massive competition from low-wage Third World countries. Informal work in this instance combines very low wages with substandard conditions.

The construction industry also illustrates this pattern. One factor influencing supply and demand in the construction industry in New York City is the rapid increase in the volume of renovations, alterations, and small-scale new construction as many areas of the city that were once low-income, often dilapidated neighborhoods have been transformed into higher-income commercial and residential areas. In many other cities in the United States, such a transformation would have involved a massive program of new construction; in New York City, it was accomplished mostly by rehabilitating old structures. The volume of work, its small scale, its labor intensity and high skill content, and the short-term nature of each project all were conducive to a heavy incidence of informal construction and rehabilitation work.

Another important factor affecting supply and demand is the failure of enterprises operating in the formal economy to meet the demands of certain low-income consumers. Either their prices are too high for these consumers, their locations are inaccessible, or – where a service inherently requires the seller to come to the buyer, as in the case of taxicabs – the seller provides no service at all to low-income consumers. Informal operations step in to meet the demand that regulated suppliers have failed to meet. For instance, informal neighborhood centers provide child-care services, and low-cost furniture manufacturing shops supply local low-income residences.

The existence of a cluster of informal businesses in a neighborhood may eventually generate agglomeration economies that induce additional entrepreneurs to move in or set up businesses. One observes the formation of auto-repair "districts," vendors "districts," or clusters of both regulated and informal small-scale manufacturers in areas not zoned for manufacturing. These districts can become magnets; they signal to other would-be entrepreneurs that the cost of entry in certain neighborhoods is lower than in the formal economy, and that there is a market in those locations for their goods and services. If the informal businesses choose their locations according to proximity to a relatively cheap labor supply, they signal to other businesses the existence of an informal "hiring hall."

A third set of patterns evident in the informal economy concerns the influence of locational constraints. For some firms, access to cheap labor is the primary reason for choosing a New York City location. While New York City may bring with it collateral benefits, such as access to the city's final or intermediate markets, these firms are driven primarily by labor costs. Drawing on low-wage immigrant workers allows these firms to compete with Third World factories in markets that have rapid production turnover times. New York City is not the only possible location for these firms. Several New Jersey counties have seen a rapid growth in garment sweatshops and homework, as the Hispanic population has expanded.[29]

For other firms, the choice of location is not simply a question of cheap labor supply. Many shops engaging in customized production or operating on subcontracts are bound to New York City for some or all of the following reasons: 1) demand is local and typically client-specific; 2) the nature of the business requires proximity to design and specialized services and a quick turnover between completion of design and production; 3) the firms rely on the purchasing patterns associated with a highly dynamic overall economic environment; and 4) the firms cater to the specific tastes of local immigrant communities. Firms constrained by these factors must stay in New York City in order to have a clientele, whether of households or other firms. However, staying in New York City effectively may mean that these firms must operate informally. The high cost of doing business in the city, particularly the cost of land, can force small-scale customized manufacturers to set up shop in spaces not zoned for manufacturing.

A fourth pattern in the process of informalization concerns variety of jobs. Many of the jobs in the informal economy are unskilled, offering no training opportunities and involving repetitive tasks. Other jobs demand high skills or acquisition of a skill. The growth of informalization in the construction and furniture industries has required a re-skilling of workers in those sectors. There is no wage level typical of the informal economy. Generally, however, employers or contractors seem to save compared with what they would have to pay in the formal market for such skills.

INFORMALIZATION AND POOR COMMUNITIES

My observations about New York City prompt two policy questions concerning the growth of informal economies in that city's low-income communities.

First, how should government deal with the growing informal economy? The easiest course of action is to criminalize all economic activities that evade regulation, imposing fines and closing the renegade operations. New York City has enacted such a policy.[30] City authorities closed newsstands and small restaurants in low-income communities. The result was disappearance of the few available economic activities and loss of the few public space anchors in these communities. From an economic perspective, criminalization makes no sense. Instead of criminalization, cities like New York must find policy formulas that help reduce the tension between these new economic conditions and a regulatory framework rooted in an earlier economic era. Such policy formulas would encompass a range of interactions between government and economy. As one illustration, zoning legislation might be used to address the polarization in profit-making capacities that has become systemic in advanced economies. Zoning laws could allow firms in low-profit sectors to compete for space and other inputs in a place like Manhattan. Thus, the so-called West Side Industrial Zone in Manhattan keeps rents low and makes it possible for a wide range of industrial services to locate in the borough, close to their clients.[31] Rezoning to allocate greater space to corporate offices – a major goal of New York City government in the 1980s – would likely force many of these industrial service firms to close or go partially or fully informal.

Policies such as zoning certain areas specifically for low-profit-sector use could be designed so as to induce an "upgrading" of informal activities by bringing these activities within the regulatory framework while minimizing costs to entrepreneurs. Upgrading is likely to demand greater flexibility in the implementation of existing codes and acknowledgment by city officials that compliance may require several phases. Lower thresholds of regulatory compliance would be applied to new, small-scale businesses in low-income communities than to well-established businesses that have had an opportunity to recover start-up costs. To encourage compliance with modified regulations and enforcement practices, city officials offer informal operations technical and financial assistance as part of the long-term upgrading process. Beyond mildly accommodating policies, one might even envision a more drastic redrawing of regulatory frameworks, on the theory that current developments have rendered the old framework obsolete.[32]

The second question prompted by my study of New York City is: Why should we bother to upgrade the informal economy in low-income communities?

The informal economy is one of the few forms of economic growth evident in these communities. With the decline of manufacturing and the ascendance of finance and specialized services, economic growth has become disproportionately concentrated in central business districts and suburban office complexes. Economic growth, one might conclude, has abandoned low-income communities. We need to find anchors to regenerate these communities, to reconstitute neighborhood sub-economies. This task becomes particularly important absent any sign that mainstream patterns of economic growth will find ways of locating growth in these communities. Informal economies bridge the divide between new high-income middle-class neighborhoods and low-income neighborhoods, a divide widened by the flight of the middle class from the cities. Further, informal economic activity fights the spread of crime and delinquency born out of despair and the absence of options.

We must harness the economic energy represented by small-scale ventures, and we must upgrade them. Upgrading can only happen through the support of government or public–private partnerships. Much has been said about enterprise zones, which give incentives to firms to move *into* a neighborhood. I would propose concentrating instead on low-income "community zones," which would support firms *already operating* in low-income communities. Community empowerment zones, proposed by the current administration, go a considerable way in this direction. Destroying the incipient mini-complex of neighborhood firms represented by the informal economy is, I think, a mistake, because neighborhood firms are one of the few forms of economic growth evident in these communities.

CONCLUSION

The roots of the informalization of various activities are to be found in the currently prevailing characteristics of the economy in general and of large urban economies in particular. The decline of the middle class, the growth of a high-income professional class, and the expansion of the low-income population, have all had a pronounced impact on the structure of consumption. The organization of work, in turn, has evolved to meet the new consumption demand. Part of the demand for goods and services feeding the expansion of the informal economy comes from the mainstream economy and from the fragmentation of what were once mostly homogeneous middle-class markets. Another part of this demand comes from the internal needs of low-income communities that are increasingly incapable of buying goods and services in the mainstream economy.

A second major trend is the growing inequality in the profit-making capacity of different sectors. The ascendance of high-profit industries, such as finance and specialized services, as the dominant sector in major urban economies has raised the price of commercial space and other business costs in the downtown districts of large cities. Small, low-profit firms can hardly afford to compete for space, even when they enjoy an effective demand for their products or services in the city. One way of reconciling these contradictory conditions is to go informal, that is, to use spaces not zoned for commerce or manufacturing, such as basements in residential areas, or to use spaces that are not up to state-mandated health, fire, and safety standards.

A third major trend concerns the organization of space in today's economy, particularly in large cities. The leading sectors of the economy tend to be concentrated in downtown city districts and in suburban office complexes. There is hardly any economic growth taking place in low-income communities. This unbalanced spatial distribution of growth is much stronger today, as it has been over the last fifteen years, than in earlier historical periods. The emergence of semi-formal neighborhood economies has been one response to this imbalance.

These trends in consumption, profit-making capacities, and spatial organization indicate that the expansion of the informal economy in the United States is rooted partly in conditions that are integral to the contemporary phase of an advanced market economy such as that of the United States. The approach to the informal economy that policy makers should adopt depends, at least in part, on whether the informal economy is attributable primarily to structural characteristics of advanced capitalism or is instead an anomaly attributable to Third World immigration. Simply criminalizing informal work may be effective if the informal economy is essentially an anomaly. But if, as I have argued, informalization is embedded in the structure of our current economic system, particularly manifest in large cities, then criminalization may not be the most effective policy. Informalization emerges as a set of flexibility-maximizing strategies employed by individuals, firms, consumers, and producers in a context of growing inequality in earnings and in profit-making capabilities. Its expansion invites us to focus on the broader fact of a growing set of problems in the relationship between new economic trends and old regulatory frameworks.

NOTES

1 See, e.g., W. Arthur Lewis, *The Theory of Economic Growth* (1955).

2 This has been a central hypothesis organizing much of my research on the informal economy. See, e.g., Saskia Sassen, The Global City: New York, London, Tokyo 283–99 (1991).

3 See, e.g., Saskia Sassen, Cities in a World Economy (1994). A number of instances fit this notion of a problematic dynamic between regulation and economy. For example, I use the concept "fracture" to capture the specific dynamic produced by global processes operating in particular localities. One result of this development is that both "regulation" and "violation" become problematic categories and, at the limit, do not apply. We might think of the void analytically as a borderland, rather than a borderline – a terrain for action/activity that remains underspecified, at least from the perspective of regulation. Global cities are particularly strategic terrains for the emergences or shaping of regulatory fractures. Saskia Sassen, *The Global Movement of Capital and Labor*, Paper Presented in the American Society of International Law, International Economic Law Interest Group Workshop on Interdisciplinary Approaches to International Economic Law (Feb. 24, 1994) (on file with author).

4 For a full account of research findings over the last ten years, see Sassen, *The Global City, supra* note 2; The Informal Economy in Low-Income Communities in New York City (1987) (research report on file with Urban Planning Dep't, Columbia Univ.); Saskia Sassen and Robb Smith, "Postindustrial Growth and Economic Reorganization: Their Impact on Immigrant Employment," in *U.S.–Mexico Relations: Labor Market Interdependence* 372–93 (1992). Sassen and Wendy Grover, Unregistered Work in the New York Metropolitan Area (research report on file with Urban Planning Dep't, Columbia Univ., 1986); Sassen and M.P. Fernandez-Kelly, "Hispanic Women in the Apparel and Electronics Industries in the New York Metro Region and in Southern California" (final report presented to the Revson, Ford and Tinker Foundations, 1992). All findings described in this Essay are based upon these earlier research projects.

5 The "informal economy' is one of several kinds of economic activity that fall under the rubric of the "underground economy." We can distinguish at least three very different components of the underground economy. First, the underground economy includes criminal activities, which by their very nature could not be carried out above ground. Second, the underground economy includes tax evasion on licit forms of income. In the United States today, the available information shows a large jump in the amount of unreported income, especially compared to the 1950s, 1960s and early 1970s. The IRS projected in 1990 that the tax gap for 1992 would be $114 billion, two-thirds of which is attributable to individuals. See Internal Revenue Service, Income Tax Compliance Research: Net Tax Gap and Remittance Gap Estimates, Publication 1415 (Supp. to Publication 7285) (Apr. 1990), cited in Cong. Q. Research, Mar. 1994, at 203. Third, the underground economy includes the informal economy, which contributes to the tax gap, but which is distinguishable from income underreporting.

6   See Manuel Castells & Alejandro Portes, "World Underneath: The Origins, Dynamics, and Effects of the Informal Economy," in *The Informal Economy: Studies in Advanced and Less Developed Countries*, edited by Alejandro Portes et al. (1989), 11.

7   Sanctions against employers under the Immigration Reform and Control Act of 1986, Pub. L. No. 99–603, 100 Stat. 3359, alter this proposition in those cases where an employer knowingly hires an undocumented worker. The informality then consists in the form of management.

8   See, e.g., M. Patricia Fernandez-Kelly and Anna M. Garcia, "Informalization at the Core: Hispanic Women, Homework, and the Advanced Capitalist State," in *The Informal Economy, supra* note 6, at 247; Saskia Sassen-Koob, "New York City's Informal Economy," in *The Informal Economy, supra* note 6, at 60; Alex Stepick, "Miami's Two Informal Sectors," in The Informal Economy, *supra* note 6, at 111.

9   See P. H. Renooy, *Twilight Economy: A Survey of the Informal Economy in the Netherlands* (Faculty of Economic Sciences, Univ. of Amsterdam ed., 1984).

10 See Vittorio Capecchi, "The Informal Economy and the Development of Flexible Specialization in Emilia-Romagna," in The Informal Economy, *supra* note 6, at 189.

11 Bennett Harrison and Barry Bluestone, *The Great U-Turn: Corporate Restructuring and the Polarizing of America*, chapter 1 (1988).

12 For a comparison of the distinct manner in which these processes took place in the United States, the United Kingdom, and Japan, see Sassen, *The Global City, supra* note 2, at chapters 8 & 9.

13 These conclusions are based on research described in note 4, *supra*.

14 Subcontracting chains that end in informal operations are very common in several industries, including apparel, construction, and cleaning services. See generally Christian Zlolniski, "The Informal Economy in an Advanced Industrial Society: Mexican Immigrant Labor in Silicon Valley," 103 *Yale L. J.* 2305 (1994).

15 See Sassen, *The Global City, supra* note 2, at chapters 9 & 10.

16 See Saskia Sassen, *The Mobility of Labor and Capital: A Study in International Investment and Labor Flow, chapter* 5 (1988).

17 See Paul Blumberg, *Inequality in an Age of Decline* (1980).

18 See Sassen-Koob, *The Informal Economy in Low-Income Communities in New York City, supra* note 4.

19 This tendency was confirmed, for instance, by Sheets, Nord, and Phelps, who found that each one percent increase in retail jobs resulted in a 0.88 percent average increase in below-poverty-level jobs in the 100 largest metropolitan areas in 1980. See Robert G. Sheets et al., The Impact of Service Industries on Underemployment in Metropolitan Economies 73 (1987).

20 See *supra* p. 156.

21 See Elliott Sclar et al., "The Nonmedallion Taxi Industry," in *City Almanac* (fall 1988). The full research report is on file at the Urban Planning Department, Columbia University. As described in Saskia Sassen, "The Informal Economy," in *Dual City: Restructuring New York*, edited by John Mollenkopf & Manuel Castells (1991), 101 n. 52:

    [Sclar, Grava, and Downs] found that virtually every black or white neighborhood had some form of "gypsy" and "livery" car service, and that these were typically run by members of the community: thus there are black, Puerto Rican, Haitian, Korean, and Hassidic Jewish "livery" car services. They estimated the current livery car service fleet at 22,000 vehicles. While many of these are in compliance, many are not. None of the estimated 8,000 gypsy cabs, on the other hand, are in compliance.

22 Franz S. Leichter, Banking on the Rich: Commercial Bank Branch Closings and Openings in the New York Metropolitan Area, 1978–1988 (1989) (unpublished manuscript, on file with Urban Planning Dep't, Columbia Univ.)

23 The earlier wave of closings left several poor and minority communities in the leading financial center of the country without any banking services.

24 From 1985 to 1987, fifty-five full-service commercial branches were closed, thirty-four in 1987 alone, the highest number of closings for any one year in the last decade. The previous peak was in 1983 with thirty-eight closings. See Leichter, *supra* note 22, at Part II.

25 During this period, only two new full-service branches opened: one Chinese-owned bank in Chinatown and a small black-owned bank (Freedom National Bank). The latter bank was the only branch opened in a New York City neighborhood with a black population greater than thirty percent. In all counties with black and Hispanic populations above the regional average, the ratio of residents to commercial bank branches increased. The Bronx, the borough with the highest black and Hispanic populations by percentage, suffered the most severe reduction in its commercial branch network, a twenty percent loss from 1978 to 1987. Forty full-service commercial branches were closed over the period. The residents-to-branch ratio in the Bronx increased by thirty percent from 1980 to 1987. Brooklyn, the borough with the second highest population of blacks and Hispanics by percentage, saw a fourteen percent increase in its resident-to-branch ratio from 1980 to 1987. Today, Brooklyn has the highest such ratio: 15,000 residents per branch. *Id.*

26 The seven percent increase in bank branch openings cannot simply be explained as a function of suburban population growth. In 1987, the resident-to-branch ratio was 12,000 to one in the outer boroughs and 3,000 to one in the suburbs. *Id.*

27 On the basis of secondary data analysis, fieldwork, and interviews, I have found the following profile of the informal economy in the New York City area: 1) informal work is present in a wide range of industrial sectors including, with varying incidence: apparel, accessories, general construction contractors, special trade contractors, footwear, toys and sporting goods, furniture and woodwork, electronic components, packaging, and transportation; 2) such operations also take place to a lesser degree in activities such as packaging notions; making lampshades, artificial flowers, and jewelry; distributing; photo engraving; and manufacturing of explosives (mostly firecrackers); 3) such operations tend to be located in densely populated, predominantly immigrant areas; 4) there is an emergent tendency for areas undergoing partial residential and commercial gentrification to displace "traditional" sweatshop activity (notably in the garment industry); and 5) there is a growing tendency for new forms of unregistered work catering to a new clientele to locate in gentrifying areas. *See* Sassen, The Global City, *supra* note 2, at ch. 9; The Informal Economy in Low-Income Communities in New York City, *supra* note 4; Sassen and Wendy Grover, Unregistered Work in the New York Metropolitan Area (1986) (research report on file with Urban Planning Dep't, Columbia Univ.); Sassen & Smith, *Postindustrial Growth and Economic Reorganization, supra* note 4.

28 National household surveys reveal that in the mid1990's, eighty-three percent of U.S. households used informally produced or delivered goods and services. Most of this consumption constituted home repairs ($21.4 billion) and food sold informally ($10.3 billion), U.S. Dep'T of Labor, the Underground Economy in the United States, Occasional Paper Series on the Informal Sector, No. 2, at 11 (1992).

29 *See* New Jersey Dep't of Labor, Study of Industrial Homework (1988).

30 The New York City Tax and Finance Commission developed and implemented this policy, the goal of which was to insure compliance with the City's tax laws by punishing evasion. Many of the targets were informal operations. *See New York State's Underground Economy: Untaxed and Growing,* Report, Comm. on Oversight, Analysis, and Investigation, N.Y. State Legislature (1982); New York City Dep't. of Finance, *Unearthing the Underground Economy,* Report (1986); Deborah Sontag, "Unlicensed Peddlers, Unfettered Dreams," *N.Y. Times,* June 14, 1993, et al.

31 See Columbia Univ., Program in Urban Planning, Development and Preservation in Manhattan's Chelsea (1986) (on file at Urban Planning Dep't, Columbia Univ.).

32 See Edgar S. Cahn, "Reinventing Poverty Law," 103 *Yale L.J.* 2133 (1994).

SECTION IV

OUT OF SPACE

9

ELECTRONIC SPACE AND POWER[1]

——————

Electronic space is easily read as a purely technological event and in that sense as self-contained and neutral. But this is a partial account. I will argue here that what is left out of this technological reading is that electronic space is embedded in the larger dynamics organizing society. Whether in the geography of its infrastructure or in the structure of cyberspace itself, electronic space is inscribed, and to some extent shaped, by power, concentration, and contestation, as well as by openness and decentralization. Thus, it is by now well known that the particular features of the Internet (or Net) are in part a function of the early computer hacker culture which designed software that strengthened the openness and decentralization of the Net and which sought to make it universally available. It is also clear that since 1994 when business "discovered" the Net, we have been seeing attempts to commercialize it through the development of software that can capitalize on the Net's properties through the imposition of copyrights—in other words, the opposite of the early hacker culture.

In this regard, it seems to me that we need to re-theorize electronic space and uncouple it analytically from the properties of the Internet which have shaped our thinking about electronic space. We tend to think of this space as one that is characterized by distributed power, by the absence of hierarchy. The Internet is probably the best known and most noted electronic space. Its particular attributes have engendered the notion of distributed power: decentralization, openness, possibility of expansion, no hierarchy, no center, no conditions for authoritarian or monopoly control.

Yet the networks are also making possible other forms of power. The financial markets, operating largely through private electronic networks, are a good instance of an alternative form of power. The three properties of electronic networks: speed, simultaneity, and interconnectivity have produced strikingly different outcomes in this case from those of the Internet. These properties have made possible orders of magnitude and concentration far surpassing anything we had ever seen in financial markets. The consequence has been that the global capital market now has the power to discipline national governments, as became evident with the Mexico "crisis" of December 1994. We are seeing the formation of new power structures in electronic space, perhaps most clearly in the private networks of finance but also in other cases.

The concern here is to elaborate the proposition that electronic space is embedded and to do so through the examination of what I think of as cyber-segmentations. The focus here is particularly on economic electronic space and the digitalization of a growing component of the economy. This focus provides a particular set of analytic pathways to the broader notion that electronic space is embedded. These are pathways grounded in realms of practice rather than in ideas about electronic space. It is the beginning of a research inquiry and presents only elements of a new theoretical perspective. Whether this analysis can be used for other types of electronic space and realms of practice is a question for research..

Here I examine three ways in which the embeddedness of electronic space can be captured:

1. There is no fully virtualized enterprise nor fully digitalized industry. Leading economic sectors that are highly digitalized require strategic sites with vast concentrations of infrastructure, the requisite labor resources, talent, and buildings. This holds for finance but also for the multimedia industries, which use digital production processes and produce digitalized products.

2. The sharpening inequalities in the distribution of the infrastructure for electronic space, whether private computer networks or the Net, in the conditions for access to electronic space, and, within electronic space, in the conditions for access to high-powered segments and features, are all contributing to new geographies of centrality both on the ground and in electronic space.

3. Commercialization of public networks and hierarchical concen-

trations of power in private networks are producing what I think of as cyber-segmentations – manifestations of the dynamics of inequality and power.

After an examination of these three subjects, the final section incorporates these issues in a larger discussion about space and power.

THE TOPOI OF E-SPACE:
GLOBAL CITIES AND GLOBAL VALUE CHAINS

The vast new economic topography that is being implemented through electronic space is one moment, one fragment, of an even vaster economic chain that is in good part embedded in nonelectronic spaces. There is no fully virtualized firm and no fully digitalized industry. Even the most advanced information industries such as finance are installed only partly in electronic space. And so are industries that produce digital products, such as software design. The growing digitalization of economic activities has not eliminated the need for major international business and financial centers and all the material resources they concentrate, from state-of-the-art telematics infrastructure to intellectual talent (Sassen 1994; Pillon and Querrien Rotzer).

Nonetheless, telematics and globalization have emerged as fundamental forces reshaping the organization of economic space. This reshaping ranges from the spatial virtualization of a growing number of economic activities to the reconfiguration of the geography of the built environment *for* economic activity. Whether in electronic space or in the geography of the built environment, this reshaping involves organizational and structural changes. Telematics maximizes the potential for geographic dispersal, and globalization entails an economic logic that maximizes the attractions/profitability of such dispersal.

One outcome of these transformations has been captured in images of geographic dispersal at the global scale and the neutralization of place and distance through telematics in a growing number of economic activities. Yet it is precisely the combination of the spatial dispersal of numerous economic activities *and* telematic global integration which has contributed to a strategic role for major cities in the current phase of the world economy.

Cities are production sites for the leading service industries of our time, and they contain the infrastructure of activities, firms, and jobs necessary to run the advanced corporate economy (Castells 1989; Chen Le Debat 1994; Friedman 1995). Specialized services are usually understood in terms of specialized outputs rather than the production process involved. A focus on the production process in these service industries allows us to capture some of their locational characteristics and to examine the proposition that there is a new dynamic for agglomeration in the advanced corporate services because they function as a production complex, a complex which serves corporate headquarters, yet has distinct locational and production characteristics. It is this producer services complex, more so than the headquarters of firms generally, that benefits from and often needs a city location.

This dynamic for agglomeration operates at different levels of the urban hierarchy, from the global to the regional At the global level, some cities concentrate the infrastructure and the servicing that produce a capability for global control. The latter is essential if geographic dispersal of economic activity – whether factories, offices, or financial markets – is to take place under continued concentration of ownership and profit appropriation. This capability for global control cannot simply be subsumed under the structural aspects of the globalization of economic activity. It needs to be produced. It is insufficient to posit, or take for granted, the awesome power of large corporations or the existence of some "international economic system."

Beyond their sometimes long history as centers for world trade and banking, these cities now function as:

• command points in the organization of the world economy

• key locations and marketplaces for the leading industries of this period (finance and specialized services for firms)

• sites for the production of innovations in those industries.

The continued and often growing concentration and specialization of financial and corporate service functions in major cities in highly developed countries is, in large part, a strategic development. It is precisely because of the territorial dispersal facilitated by telecommunications advances that agglomeration of centralizing activities has expanded immensely.

This is well illustrated by the case of the leading telecommunications firms in the world. The combination of a global scope of operations and the lack of a seamless communications network at the global scale has meant that it is becoming cheaper and easier for multinational firms to outsource the management of their communications networks. For example, J.P. Morgan, one of the largest U.S. financial services firms, has contracted with British Telecom (BT) North America to handle its overseas terminal-to-host networks. And BT North America has contracted with Gillette to manage its telecommunications operations in 180 countries. AT&T provides the network linkages for General Electric in sixteen countries. This expanding network of services has significantly raised the complexity and importance of central functions in all these major telecommunications firms.

Here we have, not a continuation of old patterns of agglomeration, but a new logic for agglomeration. The formation and continuity of an economic center in the types of cities that I call global rests on the intersection of two major processes: 1) the growing service intensity in the organization of all industries and 2) the globalization of economic activity. Both growing service intensity and globalization rely on and are shaped by the new information technologies and both have had and will continue to have pronounced impacts on urban space. The growing service intensity in economic organization generally and the specific conditions under which information technologies are available combine to make cities once again strategic "production" sites, a role they had lost when large-scale mass manufacturing became the dominant economic sector. It is through these information-based production processes that centrality is constituted. Nevertheless, a majority of firms and economic activities do not inhabit these major centers; the latter are strategic sites.

Centrality remains a key property of the economic system, but the spatial correlates of centrality have been profoundly altered by the new technologies and by globalization. This raises the question of what constitutes centrality today in an economic system where 1) a share of transactions occurs through technologies that neutralize distance and place, and do so on a global scale, and 2) centrality has historically been embodied in certain types of built environment and urban form. Economic globalization and the new information technologies have not only reconfigured centrality and its spatial correlates, they have also created new spaces *for* centrality. We are seeing the formation of a transterritorial "center" constituted via telematics and intense economic transactions. The most powerful of these new geographies of centrality at the inter-urban level binds the major international financial and business centers: New York, London, Tokyo, Paris, Frankfurt, Zurich, Amsterdam, Los Angeles, Sydney, and Hong Kong, among others. But this geography now also includes cities such as São Paulo and Mexico City. The intensity of transactions among these cities, particularly through the financial markets, trade in services, and investment, has increased sharply, and so have the orders of magnitude involved.

As a political economist interested in the spatial organization of the economy and in the spatial correlates of economic power, I see that a focus on place and infrastructure in the new global information economy creates a conceptual and practical opening for questions about the embeddedness of electronic space. It allows us to elaborate that point where the materiality of place/infrastructure intersects with those technologies and organizational forms that neutralize place and materiality. And it entails an elaboration of electronic space, a space that is not simply defined by transmission capacities but is one where new structures for economic activity and economic power are being constituted.

A NEW GEOGRAPHY OF CENTRALITY

We are seeing a spatialization of inequality evident both in the geography of the communications infrastructure and in the emergent geographies in electronic space itself. Global cities are hyper-concentrations of infrastructure and attendant resources while vast areas in less developed regions are poorly served. But also within global cities we see a geography of centrality and one of marginality. For instance, New York City has the largest concentration of fiber optic cable-served buildings in the world, but they are mostly in the center of the city, while Harlem, a low-income African-American community a mere two miles north of Manhattan's center, has only one such building. And South Central Los Angeles, the site of the 1993 uprisings, has none. This does not *have* to be so.

There are many instances of this new unequal geography of access. Infrastructure requires enormous amounts of money. For example, it is estimated that it will cost US$120 billion for the next ten years just to bring the Central and East European countries' communications networks up to date. The European Union will spend US$25 billion a year to develop a broadband telecommunications infrastructure. The levels of technical development to be achieved by different regions and countries, and indeed, whole continents, depend on the public and private resources available and on the logic guiding the development. This is evident even with very basic technologies such as the telephone and fax: in very rich countries there are fifty telephone lines per person; in poor countries, fewer than ten. In the United States, there are 4.5 million fax machines and in Japan, 4.3 million, but only 90,000 in Brazil, 30,000 each in Turkey and Portugal, and 40,000 in Greece.

The enormous growth in the worldwide trade in communications services and products has occurred against this background of sharp inequalities in infrastructure. Insofar as much of the growth has been enjoyed by the technological "haves," these inequalities have worsened. For example, in 1990 the market for international telephone calls was US$50 billion, but that for telecommunications equipment and services was US$370 billion, and rose to US$400 billion in 1992. Business demand has increasingly become more important than consumer demand in some of these industrial sectors.

And then there are the finer points. The worldwide deployment of integrated services digital networks (ISDN) depends on interoperability and on a technology base. Both of these conditions severely restrict where ISDN will actually be available. For example, even in Europe where there is a common communications policy calling for harmonization, ISDN deployment varies greatly: in France it has reached 100 percent; in Greece it is virtually nonexistent (Garcia 1993). Another instance is the establishment of the General European Network, providing eight channels of two megabits per second each by the early 1990s, but only among nodes in Frankfurt, Paris, London, Madrid, and Rome—a select geography. The availability of leased two-mbps circuits in Europe is highly uneven—from 40,000 circuits in Great Britain to 17 in Ireland (as of the early 1990s). The case of frame-relay technology is of interest here as well: many transnational corporations would use it as a networking technology, but it is only available in a few major cities (see Garcia 1993; Graham).

The growing economic value and hence potential profitability of communications are creating enormous pressures toward deregulation and privatization. The fact that the top players need state-of-the-art communications systems further creates pressure for immense amounts of capital and high-level expertise. This has meant that public telecommunications companies all over the world are finding themselves between the pressure to privatize coming from the private sector and the insufficiency of public funds to develop state-of-the-art systems – systems which may well largely benefit top players. Even in countries such as France and Germany, with long-held preferences for state control, we are now seeing partial privatization. Similar developments are taking place in countries as diverse as Japan, Australia, New Zealand, Singapore, Indonesia, and Malaysia. The notion, particularly in less developed countries, is that privatization will help a nation gain access to the foreign capital and expertise needed to develop a national infrastructure. Thus Mexico, Argentina, Venezuela, India, and even the People's Republic of China are considering such initiatives.

There is also a trend toward the privatization of international agencies. This is well illustrated by the case of INMARSAT, an international treaty organization established in 1979 to provide communications services to ships, especially those from poor countries. As INMARSAT has expanded into increasingly profitable activities (services to media, portable satellites, and airlines) there have come pressures to privatize it; this particular agency has been growing at twenty percent a year since the mid 1980s.

Deregulation and privatization are facilitating the formation of mega-firms and global alliances. Further, new technological developments are facilitating convergence between telecommunications, computers, and TV, leading to the formation of a mega multimedia sector. This is supported and made possible through a range of innovations and technical developments: digitalization, optical fibers, compression, navigation software, PCs' new capacities, networks such as the Internet, and other internets. Further, global corporations need seamless worldwide networking technologies that can support applications such as electronic data interchange, computer-integrated manufacturing, databases for information management, video conferencing, etc. This will require enormous investment and expertise and will favor global players. Globalization is a key feature of the new multimedia sector. And all developments signal that this will only grow. These global players and the state-of-the-art infrastructure and technologies they will have access to, can only increase the distance between the technological "haves" and "have nots" among firms and among households.

Meanwhile, the leading telecommunications firms are positioning themselves to become part of the lucrative out-sourcing market to provide seamless global communications networks to the world's 500 largest multinational corporations. This market is estimated at US$10 billion a year and is growing rapidly. AT&T has established WorldPartners, a one-step shopping consortium and joint venture, with Japan's largest international provider, KDD, and with Singapore Telecom. (What I find interesting and politically significant, though rarely noted, is that to provide telecommunications services that neutralize distance, telecommunications companies need access to very material land, because the main technology is still fiber optic cable, which is also very material. Here lies a possibility for governments to exercise regulatory power, but this point is lost in the ascendant rhetoric of dematerialization.)

Finally, once in cyberspace users will also encounter an unequal geography of access. Those who can pay for it will have fast service, and those who cannot will increasingly find themselves in very "slow lanes." For instance, Time Warner ran a pilot project in a medium-sized community in the United States to learn whether customers would be willing to pay rather high fees for fast services; they found that customers would, that is, those customers who could pay would pay. The next section examines some of these issues.

EMERGENT CYBER-SEGMENTATIONS

One way to begin conceptualizing the possible structures of electronic space is to specify the emerging forms of segmentation. There are at least three distinct forms of cyber-segmentation today. One is the commercializing of access, a familiar subject. A second is the emergence of intermediaries to sort, choose, and evaluate information for paying customers. A third is the formation of privatized "firewalled" corporate networks on the Web.

Regarding commercialization of access, what matters is not the current forms assumed by paid services, but what lies ahead. Current commercial forms of access are undergoing change. Microsoft, after being an Internet laggard, is now offering free Internet access and browser programs. And AT&T, the world's largest telephone company, recently announced it will offer free access to the Internet to its customers. All this free access offered by giants in the industry is tactical. There is now an enormous battle among the major players to gain strategic advantages in what remains a fairly unknown, under-specified market. Microsoft's strategy in the past has been to set the standard, which it did for operating systems. The issue today, it seems, is once again to set standards, and to do this by providing the software for free in order, eventually, to control access and browsing standards and thus be able to charge.

Twenty European companies recently joined to form the European arm of an Internet research group. The group includes major tele-communications and computer firms from both the public and private sectors. It will be based at the French national computer research institute, Inria. The WWW Consortium's European branch will work with the U.S. Web Consortium on such global issues as electronic commerce. It will also work on the use of languages other than English on the Web. The French business and government establishment now shows a remarkable interest in the Web, when only two years ago it had dismissed the whole Internet as a version of the French Minitel. Inria has taken over some of the Web research from CERN, the nuclear research organization where the Web was created by Tim Berners-Lee in 1989; he, now at MIT, heads both the U.S. and European research consortia. One of the concerns of the newly formed European consortium is that improvements made by such rivals as Netscape and Microsoft (both members of the U.S. consortium) do not create separate parts of the Internet that can only be read by Microsoft or Netscape software.

We cannot underestimate the extent of the search for ways to control, privatize, and commercialize the Internet. According to *Business Week* revenues from Internet-related products and services will go from US$300 million in 1995 to a projected US$10 billion by 2000. About US$4.2 billion of that will be spent by consumers and businesses for access fees to get on line and for time spent there. Three major global alliance have been formed that aim at delivering a whole range of services to clients. Deutsche Telekom and France Telecom, the two latest operators in Europe, together will invest US$4.2 billion in the third partner, Sprint, the third largest long distance operator in the United States. The forecast is for sales of US$5 billion by 2000. The alliance is to be called Global One and will offer clients a single global network reached through single point of contact, with state-of-the-art technology and a range of new services. It will focus on three segments of the international telecom market: worldwide voice, data, and video services for corporate clients; international consumer services such as calling cards; and international transmission and support to other international carriers.

While the mechanisms for commercialization may not be available now, there is enormous effort to invent the appropriate billing systems. It is worth remembering that in the United States the telephone system started in the late 1800s as a decentralized, multiple-owner network of networks: there were farmers telephone networks, mutual aid societies telephone networks, etc. This went on for decades. But then in 1934 the Communications Act was passed, defining the communications systems as a "natural monopoly situation" and granting AT&T the monopoly. AT&T is up to 60 percent a billing company: it has invented and implemented billing systems. And much effort today addresses the questions of a billing system for access to and use of what is now public electronic space.

Worldwide it is mostly small companies that have till now offered access to the Internet. The total number of personal computers worldwide was estimated at fifty-seven million in 1995, and is projected to be 100 million by 1999. The large telecom and computing companies are well positioned to take advantage because Internet travels over the fiber optic backbone owned by the world's long distance carriers. These are now developing Internet services for business. For instance, the share of revenues from business clients has been rising for AT&T; over half of its profits from telephone services today come from business rather than consumers.

If corporations are to gain control of the Internet, they will do so through strategic partnership. Growth strategies and global alliances are not only geared to provide computer services and telephone calls, but also data transmission, video conferencing, home shopping, television, news, and entertainment. Mergers and acquisitions have risen sharply in the global IT industries, as companies are seeking the size and technology to compete in global markets. In 1995 these transactions reached record numbers with 2,913 deals, a fifty-seven percent increase over the 1,861 recorded in 1994. The total value of these deals was US$134 billion, a forty-seven percent increase over the US$90.5

billion in 1994 (see *Business Week,* various issues throughout 1996).
There was rapid growth in activity across all sectors in 1995. The largest deals were in the telecommunications sector, with ninety-eight
transactions worth US$20 billion. The most active sector was software
and services, with 356 deals valued at US$4.4 billion. In Europe we
increasingly see acquisitions of national brand-name firms by foreign
companies. Companies with expertise in the Internet were favored
targets, as were those with expertise in ISDN (the data transmission
technology). U.S. firms acquired eleven European ISDN specialists.
Two-thirds of Europe's top twenty transactions involved a buyer from
abroad.

Deregulation is a key step toward the expansion in service cover-
age and the formation of global alliances. But experts are forecasting
that after a period of sharp global competition, a few major global
players will monopolize the business. In the United States AT&T already has the nationwide infrastructure and a billing system in place
to provide the charge for services.

Intranets: Toward "Firewalled" Citadels on the Web?

Perhaps one of the most significant new developments is the use of
the Web and "firewalls" by firms to set up their own internal computer networks. Rather than using costly computer systems that need
expert staffing and employee training, firms can use the Web to do
what those systems do at almost no cost and with little need for expert
staffing. Firms can save enormous amounts of money by using the
Web for their own internal corporate purposes.

Is this a private appropriation of a public good? It seems to me there
are definite elements of that, especially in view of the millions of dollars firms can save. Are the "firewalled" intranets the citadels of electronic space? The formation of private intranets on the Web is
probably one of the more disturbing instances of cyber-segmentation.
I would like to give some details about it here since it is a very recent
development, but one that is growing very rapidly.

In 1995, businesses discovered that the WWW was a great medium
to communicate with customers, partners, and investors. Perhaps one
of the first and best-known cases is that of Federal Express, the international courier service. FedEx first set up a Web site in November
1994 so customers could track their packages worldwide by accessing

directly FedEx's own package tracking database. It was an enormous success (and a lot of fun for those with the time to track their packages). About 12,000 customers clicked on per day, clicking their way through Web pages to track their very own package instead of having an operator do it for them. FedEx saved up to US$2 million. FedEx has now also set up an intranet; today it has sixty web sites running inside the company.

Many companies are using the WWW to set up internal networks, surrounded by "firewalls." Beyond very elementary uses such as information about new developments and directories that can be updated easily, these intranets create access to firm's various databases and make these easy to use for everyone in the firm, no matter in what computer system, software, or time zone those databases reside. By using intranets, companies can now use databases that previously had been, *de facto*, of little use in decision-making. These intranets contrast to systems such as Lotus Notes (the leading internal computer network technology), which often have far more complexity than is necessary, are quite expensive, and require expert staffing.

Private intranets use the infrastructure and standards of the Internet and WWW. This is cheap and astoundingly efficient compared to other forms of internal communications systems. These intranets are also threats to software companies that produce network systems now being replaced by the far simpler device of using the Web. Intracompany communications systems used to require immense amounts of complex codes and specialized programs (e.g., Lotus Notes). The Web is far cheaper and simpler. Germany's SAP, a US$1.9 billion software maker, rose to the top of the industry with its complicated programs to override the differences among computer systems in a firm. Now the Web can do much of this faster and far cheaper. Also Lotus or SAP's programs require paying programmers to customize and maintain these systems. Further, using the Web reduces training costs. According to the analysts at *Business Week*, the Web's HTML (Hypertext Markup Language) standard has emerged as a universal electronic communications medium, and it serves as a standard user interface with which millions of PC users have become familiar. Because the same basic programming can be used on many different kinds of hardware, corporations will need fewer programmers to write and maintain software.

Because Web browsers run on any type of computer, the same electronic information can be viewed by any employee. Intranets using the Web can pull all the computers, software, and databases of a corporation into a single system that allows employees to find information wherever it is in the system. Computer and software makers have been working at producing such a feature but have not yet delivered it. Now firms have found that the Web *is* such a feature.

Intranets will not replace the complex business programs that have been refined over many years (e.g., in finance); further, security and confidentiality concerns may limit the use of intranets, which are at this time less secure than conventional programs. But more sophisticated intranets are being developed. One company, Silicon Graphics, for instance, began using the Web internally almost as soon as Mosaic, the original Web browser, had been developed. Today the company's 7,200 employees have access to 144,000 Web pages stored on 800 internal Web sites. Simply by clicking on hyperlinks, employees can traverse almost two dozen corporate databases. This feature of intranets sounds very attractive because it offers democratic access to a firm's information. However, what is troubling is the private appropriation of a public good to raise a firm's profits.

This corporate use of the Net has changed the software industry. At first software makers focused on Web browsers and other programs aimed at making the Web a consumer medium. Now it is increasingly aimed at building intranets for firms using the Web. *Business Week* forecasts that sales of software to run intranet servers will jump to US$4 billion in 1997, from less than half a billion in 1995. By 1998 it could be at US$8 billion, which is four times larger than the Internet server business. These figures exclude all the application packages, programming tools, and other requirements of intranets. All the big software makers (Netscape, Microsoft, Sun Microsystems, IBM, Oracle, Computer Associates) and just about all others are producing and launching intranet products. Thus, the "firewalling" of sites on the Web is only going to continue to expand at growing speed.

CONCLUSION: SPACE AND POWER

Electronic space has emerged not simply as a means for transmitting information, but as a major new theater for capital accumulation and the operations of global capital. This is one way of saying that electronic space is embedded in the larger dynamics organizing society, particularly the economy.

There is no doubt that the Internet is a space of distributed power that limits the possibilities of authoritarian and monopoly control. But it has become evident since 1994 that it is also a space for contestation and segmentation. Further, when it comes to the broader subject of the power of the networks, most computer networks are private. That leaves a lot of network power that may not necessarily have the properties/attributes of the Internet. Indeed, much of this is concentrated power that results in hierarchy rather than the distribution of power.

The Internet and private computer networks have coexisted for many years. But recent technological changes make it necessary to re-theorize the Net and to address the issue of electronic space in general rather than just the Net, or public electronic space. The three subjects discussed – global cities and value chains, centrality, and cyber-segmentation – can be read as empirical specifications of major new conditions:

- the growing digitalization and globalization of leading economic sectors has further contributed to the hyper-concentration of resources, infrastructure, and central functions, with global cities as one strategic site in the new global economic network

- the growing economic importance of electronic space has furthered global alliances and massive concentrations of capital and corporate power

- the above have contributed to new forms of segmentation in electronic space.

These developments have made electronic space one of the sites for the operations of global capital and the formation of new power structures.

This means that suddenly the two major actors in electronic space – the corporate sector and civil society – which until recently had little to do with one another in electronic space, are running into each other. In the past, corporate actors largely operated on private computer networks. As recently as 1993, businesses had not yet discovered the Internet in any significant fashion; the World Wide Web–the multimedia portion of the Net with all its potential for commercialization–had not yet been invented; and the digitalization of the entertainment industry and of business services had not exploded on the scene.

This is also the context within which we need to read the recent and sharp trends toward deregulation and privatization that have made it possible for the telecommunications industry to operate globally and in a growing number of economic sectors. It has profoundly altered the role of government in the industry, and, as a consequence, has further raised the importance of civil society as a site where a multiplicity of public interests can, wittingly or not, resist the overwhelming influence of the new corporate global actors. Civil society, from individuals to nongovernmental organizations, has engaged in a very energetic use of cyberspace from the bottom up.

To the extent that national communications systems are increasingly integrated into global networks, national governments will have less control. Further, national governments will feel sharp pressure to help firms avoid being excluded from the global electronic network because that would mean being excluded from the global economic network–an increasingly electronic system. If foreign capital is necessary to develop the IT infrastructure in developing countries, the goals of these investors may well rule and shape the design of that infrastructure. This is, of course, reminiscent of the development of railroads in colonial empires, which were clearly geared toward facilitating imperial trade rather than promoting the internal territorial integration of the colony. Such dependence on foreign investors is also likely to minimize concerns with public applications, from public access to uses in education and health.

There are today few public institutions at the national or global level that can deal with these various issues. It is in the private sector where this capacity lies, and then only among the major players. We are at risk of being ruled by multinational corporations, accountable only to the global market. Most governmental, nonprofit, and supranational organizations are not ready to enter the digital age. The political system, even in the most highly developed countries, is operating in a pre-digital era.

The overwhelming influence that global firms and markets have gained since 1994 in the production, shaping, and use of electronic space along with the shrinking role of governments, has created a political vacuum. But it does not have to.

Because the ascendance of digitalization is a new source of major transformations in society, we need to develop it as one of the driving forces of sustainable and equitable development in the world. It should be a key issue in political debates about society, particularly equity and development. We should not let business and the market shape "development" and dominate the policy debate. The good side of the new technology, from participation to telemedicine, is not necessarily going to come out of market dynamics.

Further, these technologies can be destabilizing even in the sites of concentrated power. The properties of electronic networks have created elements of a crisis of control within the institutions of the financial industry itself. There are a number of instances that illustrate this: the stock market crash of 1987 brought on by program trading and the collapse of Barings Bank brought on by a young trader who managed to mobilize enormous amounts of capital in several markets over a period of six weeks.

Electronic networks have produced conditions that cannot always be controlled by those who meant to profit the most from these new electronic capacities. Existing regulatory mechanisms cannot always cope with the properties of electronic markets. Precisely because they are deeply embedded in telematics, advanced information industries also shed light on questions of control in the global economy that not only go beyond the state but also beyond the notions of non-state-centered systems of coordination prevalent in the literature on governance.

Finally, the Net as a space of distributed power can thrive even against growing commercialization. But we may have to reinvent its representation as being impervious to such commercialization and being universally accessible. It may continue to be a space for *de facto* (i.e., not necessarily self-conscious) democratic practices. But it will be so partly as a form of resistance against overarching powers of the economy and of hierarchical power rather than the space of unlimited freedom which is part of its representation today. There have been enough changes since 1994 to suggest that the representation of the Internet needs to be subjected to critical examination. Perhaps the images we need to bring into this representation increasingly need to deal with contestation and resistance, rather than simply the romance of freedom and interconnectivity. Further, one of the very important features of the Internet is that civil society has been an energetic user, but this also means that the full range of social forces will use it, from environmentalist to fundamentalists such as the Christian Coalition in the United States. It becomes a democratic space for many opposing views and drives, and for a range of criminal uses – often referred to as the "blacknet."

We are at a particular moment in the history of electronic space, one when powerful corporate actors and high-performance networks are strengthening the role of private electronic space and altering the structure of public electronic space. But it is also a moment when we are seeing the emergence of a fairly broad-based – though as yet a demographic minority – civil society in electronic space. This sets the stage for contestation.

NOTES

1   This chapter originally appeared in the *Journal of Urban Technology*, vol. 4, no. 1 (1997): 1–17.

10

THE STATE AND THE GLOBAL CITY: NOTES TOWARD A CONCEPTION OF PLACE-CENTERED GOVERNANCE

This chapter reexamines the proposition of a declining significance of the state in the global economy. I argue that this proposition has been fed by an overemphasis on the hypermobility of capital and a conceptual background that posits a mutually exclusive relation between the national and the global. The chapter shows that 1) the state itself has been transformed by its participation in the design and implementation of global economic systems; and 2) even the most global and hypermobile industries, such as finance and the advanced corporate services, are ultimately embedded in a global grid of linkages and national territorial sites with great concentrations of material facilities and work processes, many of them strategic to the operation of hypermobile capital. Because of its strategic character and the density of resources and linkages it concentrates, this global grid could be a space for focused regulatory activity by an interstate system that has itself become more internationalized. But it would require considerable innovation in the framework for and objects of regulation.

Globalization has transformed the meaning of, and the sites for, the governance of economies. One of the key properties of the current phase in the long history of the world economy is the ascendance of information technologies, the associated increase in the mobility and liquidity of capital, and the resulting decline in the regulatory capacities of nation–states over key sectors of their economies. This is well illustrated by the case of the leading information industries, finance, and the advanced corporate services, the focus of this essay. These tend to have a space economy that is transnational and is partly embedded in electronic spaces that override conventional jurisdictions and boundaries. Yet, this is also a space economy which reveals the need for strategic sites with vast concentrations of resources and infrastructure, sites that are situated in national territories and are far less mobile than much of the general commentary on the global economy suggests. This signals possibilities for governance and a role for nation–states not typically foreseen in propositions about the declining significance of the state in the global economy.

Here I want to examine the underside of globalization in order to show that the dominant line of theorization with its emphasis on the hypermobility and liquidity of capital is a partial account; further, it is partial in a way that carries significant implications for questions of state and nonstate-centered regulatory capacities and, more generally, questions of governance and accountability in a global economy. The organizing focus here is the space economy of information industries at a time when the development of telematics maximizes the potential for geographic dispersal and mobility. I will seek to show how the space economy for major new transnational economic processes diverges in significant ways from the duality of global/national presupposed in much analysis of the global economy. The substantive rationality for this inquiry is to add to our understanding of questions of governance and accountability in the global economy.

Two propositions organize my analysis (for more extensive accounts, see Sassen 1991; 1994; 1996). One is that to a large extent the global economy materializes in concrete processes situated in specific places, and that this holds for the most advanced information industries as well. We need to distinguish between the capacity for global transmission/communication and the material conditions that make this possible.

The second proposition is that the spatial dispersal of economic activity made possible by telematics contributes to an expansion of central functions if this dispersal is to take place under the continuing concentration in control, ownership, and profit appropriation that characterizes the current economic system. More conceptually, we can ask whether an economic system with strong tendencies toward such concentration can have a space economy that lacks points of physical agglomeration.

From these two propositions I have derived a series of analytic pathways into questions of place and production and thereby into the placeboundedness of key processes of economic globalization. Recovering this placeboundedness illuminates certain aspects about the role of the state in today's global information economy which are easily lost in discussions of the hypermobility of information outputs.

But precisely because they are deeply embedded in telematics, advanced information industries also shed light on questions of control in the global economy that not only go beyond the state but also beyond the notions of nonstate-centered systems of coordination prevalent in the literature on governance. They are questions of control that have to do with the orders of magnitude that can be achieved in the financial markets thanks to the speed in transactions made possible by the new technologies. Among the best examples are the foreign currency markets: they operate largely in electronic space and have achieved volumes that have left the central banks incapable of exercising the influence on exchange rates they are expected to have. Here are questions of control that arise out of the properties of the new information technologies, notably the immense speed-up of transactions, rather than out of the extension of the economy beyond the state.

REGULATORY CAPACITIES AND SPACE ECONOMIES: PRELIMINARY NOTES

Current forms of economic transnationalism have a number of characteristics that matter for an examination of questions of governance. Two are particularly important (see Sassen, 1996 for a more extensive discussion). One of these is that many key components of economic globalization today do not strengthen the interstate system, in contrast to the situation during the three decades after World War II. A second one is that the state remains as the ultimate guarantor of the "rights" of global capital, that is, the protection of contracts and property rights.

There follows a brief discussion of each of these in order to set a context for the ensuing examination of global cities and the emergent transnational urban system as potentially significant sites for the implementation of mechanisms for governance and accountability in the global economy.

Globalization and the Interstate System

During the Pax Americana, economic internationalization had the effect of strengthening the interstate system. Leading economic sectors, especially manufacturing and raw materials extraction, were subject to international trade regimes that contributed to build the interstate system. Individual states adjusted national economic policies to further this type of international economic system, doubtless often pressured by the hegemonic power of the United States. (Even though already then certain sectors did not fit comfortably under this largely trade-dominated interstate regime: out of their escape emerged the euro-markets and offshore tax havens of the 1960s.)

The breakdown of the Bretton Woods system produced an international governance void rapidly filled by multinationals and global financial markets. This has fed the notion of the shrinking role of the state and the debate about nonstate-centered systems of governance (Jessop 1990; Rosenau 1992; Young 1989; Kooiman and van Vliet 1993; Leftwich 1994). According to some (see Panitch 1996; Mittelman 1996; Drache and Gertler 1991), the neoliberalism of the 1980s has redefined the role of states in national economies and in the interstate system. Further, the structure of the state itself in developed countries has undergone a shift away from those agencies most clearly tied to domestic social forces, as was the case in the United States during the Pax Americana, and toward those closest to the transnational process of consensus formation.

A focus on international finance and corporate services brings to the fore the extent to which the forms of economic globalization evident in the last two decades have not necessarily had the effect of strengthening the interstate system. Further, the ascendance of international finance has produced regulatory voids that lie beyond not only states but also the interstate system. In this regard, an analysis of these industries can help bring to the fore the differences between the role of the state in earlier forms of internationalization and the current globalization of economic activity evident in some (but by no means all) economic sectors.

One way of illustrating this weakened articulation of the growth dynamic of finance and corporate services to the state and interstate system is by examining what we could think of as the new valorization dynamic embedded in the ascendance of these industries – that is, a new set of criteria for valuing or pricing various economic activities and outcomes. (For more detail, see Sassen 1994, chapters 4 and 6.) We are seeing the formation of an economic complex with properties clearly distinguishing it from other economic complexes in that the articulation of its valorization dynamic with the public economic functions of the state is quite weak compared with Fordist manufacturing, for example.

Guaranteeing the Global Rights of Capital

Even though transnationalism and deregulation have reduced the role of the state in the governance of economic processes, the state remains as the ultimate guarantor of the rights of capital whether national or foreign. Firms operating transnationally want to ensure the functions traditionally exercised by the state in the national realm of the economy, notably guaranteeing property rights and contracts. The state here can be conceived of as representing a technical administrative capacity which cannot be replicated at this time by any other institutional arrangement (Sassen 1996); further, this is a capacity backed by military power.

But this guarantee of the rights of capital is embedded in a certain type of state, a certain conception of the rights of capital, and a certain type of international legal regime: It is largely the state of the most developed and most powerful countries in the world, Western notions of contract and property rights, and a new legal regime aimed at furthering economic globalization.[1]

Deregulation has been widely recognized as a crucial mechanism to facilitate the globalization of various markets and industries because it reduces the role of the state. But deregulation can also be seen as negotiating on the one hand the fact of globalization, and, on the other, the ongoing need for guarantees of contracts and property rights for which the state remains as the guarantor of last instance (Panitch 1996; Sassen 1996; see also Negri 1995). The deregulation of key operations and markets in the financial industry can be seen as a negotiation between nation-based legal regimes and the formation of a consensus among a growing number of states about furthering the world economy (Mittelman 1996; Trubek et al. 1993). In other words, it is not simply a matter of a space economy extending beyond a national realm. It also has to do with the formation and legitimation of transnational legal regimes that are operative in national territories. National legal fields are becoming more internationalized in some of the major developed economies and transnational legal regimes become more important and begin to penetrate national fields hitherto closed (e.g., Trubek et al., 1993; Aman, 1995).[2] The state continues to play a crucial role in the production of legality around new forms of economic activity.[3]

Transnational economic processes inevitably interact with systems for the governance of national economies. There are few industries where deregulation and transnationalization have been as important to growth as in international finance and advanced corporate services. What deregulation in finance makes clear is that it has had the effect of partly denationalizing national territory: for example, the International Banking Facilities in the United States can be seen as such an instance. Yet another, more familiar instance, can be found in various forms through which manufacturing production has been internationalized: for example, export-processing zones which fall under special regimes that reduce the obligations of firms to the state, notably regarding taxes and labor legislation (see, e.g., Bonacich et al., 1994; Gereffi 1996; Morales 1994; Mittelman 1996). Insofar as global processes materialize in concrete places, they continue to operate under sovereign regulatory umbrellas, but they do so under new emergent transnational regimes and, often, under circumstances of a denationalizing of national territory.

It is through the formation of such transnational regimes and the denationalizing of national territory that the state guarantees a far broader range of rights of national and foreign capital. These rights are often in addition to those guaranteed through strictly national regimes. In this regard, deregulation and other policies furthering economic globalization cannot simply be considered as an instance of a declining significance of the state. Deregulation is a vehicle through which a growing number of states are furthering economic globalization and guaranteeing the rights of global capital, an essential ingredient of the former. Deregulation and kindred policies constitute the elements of a new legal regime dependent on consensus among states to further globalization.

Elements for New Policy Frameworks

A focus on the space economy of information industries elaborates and specifies the meaning of deregulation insofar as important components of these industries are embedded in particular sites within national territories and others are located in electronic spaces that escape all conventional jurisdictions or borders.

To help situate my particular question here in the broader governance debate let me refer to one of the working argumentations that organize the larger project on which this brief essay is based: A focus on leading information industries in a strategic subnational unit such as the global city illuminates two conditions that are at opposite ends of the governance challenge posed by globalization and are not captured in the more conventional duality of national–global. These two contrasting conditions are placeboundedness and the virtualization of economic space. (See also chap. 9.)

Regarding the first, a focus on leading information industries in global cities introduces into the discussion of governance the possibility of capacities for regulation derived from the concentration of significant resources, including fixed capital, in strategic places, resources that are essential for participation in the global economy. The considerable placeboundedness of many of these resources contrasts with the hypermobility of information outputs. The regulatory capacity of the state stands in a different relation to hypermobile outputs than to the infrastructure of facilities, from fiber optic cable served office buildings to specialized workforces, present in global cities.

At the other extreme, the fact that many of these industries operate partly in electronic spaces raises questions of control that derive from key properties of the new information technologies, notably the orders of magnitude in trading volumes made possible by speed and the fact that electronic space is not bound by conventional jurisdictions. Here it is no longer just a question of the capacity of the state to govern these processes, but also of the capacity to do so on the part of the private sector, that is, of the major actors involved in setting up and operating in these electronic markets. Elementary and well-known illustrations of this issue of control are stock market crashes attributed to electronic program trading, and globally implemented decisions to invest or disinvest in a currency, or an emerging market which resemble a sort of worldwide stampede, all facilitated by the fact of global integration and instantaneous execution worldwide. Mexico's recent crisis and its aftermath are an illustration of this; so is the fall of the U.K. bank Barings.

The specific issues raised by these two variables, that is, placeboundedness and speed/virtualization, are quite distinct from those typically raised in the context of the national–global duality. As I argued in the Introduction here–and I will repeat–a focus on this duality leads to rather straightforward propositions about the declining significance of the state vis-à-vis global economic actors. This is partly a result of the overarching tendency in economic analyses of globalization and information industries to emphasize certain aspects: industry outputs rather than the production process involved, the capacity for instantaneous transmission around the world rather than the infrastructure necessary for this capacity, the inability of the state to regulate those outputs and that capacity insofar as they extend beyond the nation–state. And all of this is by itself quite correct; but it is a partial account of the implications of globalization for governance.

A focus on key properties of the new information technologies, such as speed, and their implications for questions of governance illuminates the extent to which we may be confronting a whole new configuration, one that cannot be addressed along the lines dominating much of the thinking about governance in a global economy. It is not just a question of coordination and order in a space economy that transcends a single state, but a qualitatively new variable: technologies that produce outcomes which the existing apparatus both private and governmental cannot handle because they are processes embedded in a speed that has made current mechanisms for management and control obsolete. It is impossible to address this subject here in depth (see Sassen 1996 for a more detailed analysis; see also chap. 9 here).

A focus on place, and particularly the type of place I call global cities, on the other hand, brings to the fore the fact that many of the resources necessary for global economic activities are not hypermobile and could, in principle be brought under effective regulation. But this would be a type of regulation focused not on the outputs of information industries–which are indeed hypermobile and circulate in electronic spaces–but on the material and socioeconomic infrastructure. Essential to this proposition in an understanding of the extent to which key components of the leading information industries are placebound and conversely, the extent to which key components of what we call the global economy actually materialize in places.

A refocusing of regulation onto infrastructures and production complexes in the context of globalization contributes to an analysis of the regulatory capacities of states that diverges in significant ways from understandings centered on hypermobile outputs and global telecommunications. One crucial piece of such an analysis is a detailed examination of the importance of place and placeboundedness in global economic processes. This is the subject in the remainder of this paper.

PLACE AND PRODUCTION-COMPLEX IN THE GLOBAL ECONOMY

The analysis of the space economy developed here is centered in the notion that we cannot take the existence of a global economic system as given, but rather need to examine the particular ways in which the conditions for economic globalization are produced. This entails examining not only communication capacities and the power of multinationals, but also the underside of the global economy.

The capabilities for global operation, coordination and control contained in the new information technologies and in the power of the multinationals need to be produced. By focusing on the production of these capabilities we add a neglected dimension to the familiar issue of the power of large corporations and the new technologies. The emphasis shifts to the *practice* of global control: the work of producing and reproducing the organization and management of a global production system and a global marketplace for finance, both under conditions of economic concentration.

I see the producer services, and most especially finance and advanced corporate services, as industries producing the organizational commodities necessary for the implementation and management of global economic systems (Sassen 1991, chapters 2–5).[4] Over the last few years we have seen the growth of a rich literature on the producer services, including major information industries such as international finance and advanced corporate services (e.g., Daniels 1985; Delaunay and Gadrey 1987; Noyelle and Dutka 1988; Daniels and Moulaert 1991). With a few exceptions (e.g., Castells 1989; Sassen 1991; Knox and Taylor 1995; Drennan 1992; Mitchelson and Wheeler 1994; Fainstein 1994; Stimson 1993; Corbridge et al., forthcoming) the literature on producer services and cities has not necessarily been concerned with the operation of the global economy as such, nor has it been seen as part of the literature on globalization.[5]

Introducing the research on producer services into our analysis of the global economy helps us explore how the categories of place and production process are involved in economic globalization. These are two categories that are easily overlooked in analyses of the hypermobility of capital and the power of multinationals. Developing categories such as place and production process does not negate the centrality of hypermobility and power. It adds other dimensions and in so doing intersects with the regulatory role of the state in a distinct way and one that diverges from much international political economy.

Specialized services are usually understood in terms of specialized outputs rather than the production process involved. A focus on the production process in these service industries allows us 1) to capture some of their locational characteristics and 2) to examine the proposition that there is a new dynamic for agglomeration in the advanced corporate services because they function as a production complex, a complex which serves corporate headquarters yet has distinct locational and production characteristics. It is this producer services complex, more so than headquarters of firms generally, that benefits and often needs a city location. We see this dynamic for agglomeration operating at different levels of the urban hierarchy, from the global to the regional. Some cities concentrate the infrastructure and the servicing that produce a capability for global control and servicing.

In brief, with the potential for global control capability, certain cities are becoming nodal points in a vast communications and market system. Advances in electronics and telecommunication have transformed geographically distant cities into centers for global communication and long-distance management. But centralized control and management over a geographically dispersed array of plants, offices, and service outlets does not come about inevitably as part of a "world system." It requires the development of a vast range of highly specialized services and of top-level management and control functions.

The next three sections develop these subjects in greater detail.

Globalization and Service Intensity

The globalization of economic activity has raised the scale and the complexity of transactions, thereby feeding the demand for top-level multinational headquarter functions and for advanced corporate services. This demand for specialized services is further fed by a second major process, the growing service intensity in the organization of all industries (Sassen 1991, chapter 5; 1994, chapter 4). This has contributed to a massive growth in the demand for services by firms in all industries, from mining and manufacturing to finance and consumer services. To this we should add the growing demand by firms for nonspecialized services, notably industrial services.

Two of the key variables that make these processes relevant to cities and to the argument in this paper are: 1) the rapid growth in the last fifteen years in the share of services that firms buy rather than produce in-house; and 2) the existence of agglomeration economies in the production of specialized services. If firms continued to produce most of their services in-house as used to be the case, particularly with the large vertically integrated firms, cities might have been less significant production sites for services. Service activities would have moved out of cities as part of the moves by the larger firms of which they were but one component; there could conceivably have been far more geographic dispersal of specialized service jobs than there is now, though these jobs would of course have been included in the industrial classification of the larger firms, which were not necessarily service firms.

I discuss these two variables next.

THE GROWING DEMAND FOR CORPORATE SERVICES

The increase in the share of bought services can be seen in the figures on growth in producer services jobs, in the numbers of producer services firms, and, perhaps most sharply, in the figures from the national input-output tables for the United States. Figures on employment and numbers of firms in producer services have by now become familiar and have been published widely. That cannot be said for the figures from the national input-output tables; I analyzed these figures for several years and several industries within major sectors and found a clear trend of growth in the value of bought service inputs for the industries examined.[6]

The sharp rise in the use of producer services has been fed by a variety of processes.[7] Among these are the territorial dispersal, whether at the regional, national, or global level, of multi-establishment firms. Firms operating many plants, offices, and service outlets must coordinate planning, internal administration and distribution, marketing, and other central headquarters activities. Formally, the development of the modern corporation and its massive participation in world markets and foreign countries has made planning, internal administration, product development, and research increasingly important and complex. Diversification of product lines, mergers, and transnationalization of economic activities all require highly specialized services.

For all firms, whether they operate globally or regionally, the rise of litigation, the growing importance of insurance, advertising, and outside financing, have all contributed to a growing need for specialized services. Further, as large corporations move into the production and sale of final consumer services, a wide range of activities, previously performed by free-standing, independent consumer service firms, are shifted to the central headquarters of the new corporate owners. Regional, national, or global chains of motels, food outlets, flower shops, require vast centralized administrative and servicing structures. The complexity of these will in turn generate a demand for specialized corporate services bought from specialized firms, something far less likely in the small independently owned consumer service firm. A parallel pattern of expansion of central high-level planning and control operations takes place in governments, brought about partly by the technical developments that make this possible and partly by the growing complexity of regulatory and administrative tasks. All of these trends have fed the growth of producer services in cities large and small.

A brief examination of the territorial dispersal entailed by transnational operations of large enterprises can serve to illustrate some of the points raised here. For instance, the numbers of workers employed abroad by the largest one hundred nonfinancial transnational corporations worldwide are rather large. (For detailed figures on this and the following items, see UNCTC 1993; Sassen 1994, chap. 4.) Thus about half of Exxon's and IBM's and about a third of Ford Motors' and GM's total workforce is employed outside the United States. We know furthermore that large transnationals have very high numbers of affiliates. Thus in 1990 German firms had over 19,000 affiliates in foreign countries, up from 14,000 in 1984; and the United States had almost 19,000. Finally, we know that the top transnationals have very high shares of foreign operations: the top ten largest transnational corporations in the world had sixty-one percent of their sales abroad. The average for the 100 largest corporations was almost fifty percent.

What these figures show is a vast operation dispersed over a multiplicity of locations. This generates a large demand for producer services, from international accounting to advertising. Operations as vast as these feed the expansion of central management, coordination, control, and servicing functions. Some of these functions are performed in headquarters, some are bought or contracted for therewith feeding the growth of the producer services complex.

THE FORMATION OF A NEW PRODUCTION COMPLEX

As for the second variable, agglomeration economies, the issue here is why has there not been more dispersal of specialized service firms, particularly since these are among the most advanced and intensive users of telematics and hence could supposedly locate anywhere. In order to understand why such a large share of these firms is concentrated in cities, and often in dense spatial concentrations reminiscent of industrial districts, we need to focus on the actual production process in these services.

The evidence on the locational patterns of the leading information industries shows sharp economic concentration in major cities. For instance, New York City accounts for thirty-five percent of earnings in producer services, compared to little over three percent of the national population, and between a fourth and a fifth of all producer services exports in the United States, which total about US$40 billion annually (Drennan 1992). London accounts for about forty percent of producer services exports in the United Kingdom, and Paris accounts for forty percent of all producer services employment in France and over eighty percent of the advanced corporate services (Cordier 1992; *Le Debat* 1994). There are many other such examples.

According to standard conceptions about information industries, the rapid growth and disproportionate concentration of producer services in major cities should not have happened. Because many of these services are thoroughly embedded in the most advanced information technologies, producer services could be expected to have locational options that by-pass the high costs and congestion typical of major cities. It is my argument that in order to understand their sharp concentration in large cities, we need to focus on the actual production process in these industries.

The production process in these services benefits from proximity to other specialized services. This is the case especially in the leading and most innovative sectors of these industries. Complexity and innovation often require multiple highly specialized inputs from several industries. The production of a financial instrument, for example, requires inputs from accounting, advertising, law, economic consulting, public relations, design, and printing. The particular characteristics of production of these services, especially those involved in complex and innovative operations, explain their pronounced concentration in major cities. The commonly heard explanation that high-level professionals require face-to-face interactions, needs to be refined in several ways. Producer services, unlike other types of services, are not necessarily dependent on spatial proximity to the consumers – firms – served. Rather, economies occur in such specialized firms when they locate close to others that produce key inputs or whose proximity makes possible joint production of certain service offerings. The top-of-the-line accounting firm can service its clients at a distance, but the nature of its service depends on proximity to other specialists, from lawyers to programmers. Moreover, it is well known that many of the new high-income professionals tend to be attracted to the amenities and lifestyles that large urban centers can offer. Frequently, what is thought of as face-to-face communication is actually a production process that requires multiple simultaneous inputs and feedbacks. At the current stage of technical development, immediate and simultaneous access to the pertinent experts is still the most effective way, especially when dealing with a highly complex product. The concentration of the most advanced telecommunications and computer network facilities in major cities is a key factor in what I refer to as the production process of these industries.[8]

Further, time replaces weight in these sectors as a force for agglomeration. In the past, the pressure of the weight of inputs from iron ore to unprocessed agricultural products, was a major constraint pushing toward agglomeration in sites where the heaviest inputs were located. Today, the acceleration of economic transactions and the premium put on time, have created new forces for agglomeration. This is increasingly not the case in routine operations. But where time is of the essence, as it is today in many of the leading sectors of these industries, the benefits of agglomeration are still extremely high–to the point where it is not simply a cost advantage, but an indispensable arrangement. This is further underlined by the centrality of the market in many of the most speculative and innovative branches of finance. Speculation and innovation in the context of deregulation and globalization have profoundly altered market operation in the industry, promoting far greater instability. Under these conditions, agglomeration carries additional advantages insofar as the market becomes a key site for new opportunities for profit and speed is of the essence. (Sassen 1991, chapters 2–4; Mitchelson and Wheeler 1994; but see also Lyons and Salmon 1995).

This combination of constraints suggests that the agglomeration of producer services in major cities actually constitutes a production complex. This producer services complex is intimately connected to the world of corporate headquarters; they are often thought of as forming a joint headquarters-corporate services complex. But in my reading, we need to distinguish the two.[9] Although it is true that headquarters still tend to be disproportionately concentrated in cities, over the last two decades many have moved out. Headquarters can indeed locate outside cities, but they need a producer services complex somewhere in order to buy or contract for the needed specialized services and financing. Further, headquarters of firms with very high overseas activity or in highly innovative and complex lines of business tend to locate in major cities. In brief, firms in more routinized lines of activity, with predominantly regional or national markets, appear to be increasingly free to move or install their headquarters outside cities. Firms in highly competitive and innovative lines of activity and/or with a strong world market orientation appear to benefit from being located at the center of major international business centers, no matter how high the costs.

Both types of firms, however, need a corporate services complex to be located somewhere.[10] Where this complex is located is probably increasingly unimportant from the perspective of many, though not all, headquarters. From the perspective of producer services firms, such a specialized complex is most likely to be in a city rather than, for example, a suburban office park. The latter will be the site for producer services firms but not for a services complex. And only such a complex is capable of handling the most advanced and complicated corporate demands.

Elsewhere (Sassen 1994, chapter 5), a somewhat detailed empirical examination of several cities served to explore different aspects of this trend toward spatial concentration.[11] Here there is space only for a few observations (see also Abu-Lughod 1995). The case of Miami, for instance, allows us to see, almost in laboratory-like fashion, how a new international corporate sector can become implanted in a site. It allows us to understand something about the dynamic of globalization in the current period and how it is embedded in place. Miami has emerged as a significant regional site for global city functions though it lacks a long history as an international banking and business center as is the case for such global cities as New York or London.

The case of Toronto, a city whose financial district was built up only in recent years, allows us to see to what extent the pressure toward spatial concentration of financial firms is embedded in an economic dynamic rather than simply being the consequence of having inherited a built infrastructure from the past, as one could think was the case in older centers such as London or New York.[12] But the case also shows that it is particularly certain industries which are subject to the pressure toward spatial concentration, notably finance and its sister industries (Gad 1991; Todd 1995).

The case of Sydney illuminates the interaction of a vast, continental economic scale and pressures toward spatial concentration. Rather than strengthening the multipolarity of the Australian urban system, the developments of the 1980s–increased internationalization of the Australian economy, sharp increases in foreign investment, a strong shift toward finance, real estate and producer services–contributed to a greater concentration of major economic activities and actors in Sydney. This included a loss of share of such activities and actors by Melbourne, long the center of commercial activity and wealth in Australia (Daly and Stimson 1992).

Finally, the case of the leading financial centers in the world today is of continued interest because one might have expected that the growing number of financial centers now integrated into the global markets would have reduced the extent of concentration of financial activity in the top centers.[13] One would further expect this given the immense increases in the global volume of transactions. Yet the levels of concentration remain unchanged in the face of massive transformations in the financial industry and in the technological infrastructure this industry depends on.[14]

For example, international bank lending grew from US$1.89 trillion in 1980 to US$6.24 trillion in 1991 – a fivefold increase in a mere ten years. New York, London, and Tokyo accounted for forty-two percent of all such international lending in 1980 and for forty-one percent in 1991 according to data from the Bank of International Settlements, the leading institution worldwide in charge of overseeing banking activity. There were compositional changes: Japan's share rose from 6.2 percent to 15.1 percent and Britain's fell from 26.2 percent to 16.3 percent; the U.S. share remained constant. All increased in absolute terms. Beyond these three, Switzerland, France, Germany, and Luxemburg bring the total share of the top centers to 64 in 1991, which is just about the same share these countries had in 1980. One city, Chicago dominates the world's trading in futures, accounting for sixty percent of worldwide contracts in options and futures in 1991.

This concentration in the top centers is partly a function of the concentration of the most advanced technical financial capabilities in these centers. And it is partly a function of various macroeconomic conjunctures, notably the perceived high risk of new markets in combination with the ease with which money can be shifted back and forth, as is illustrated by the current flight from the so-called emergent markets after the December 1994 Mexican devaluation of the peso and the ensuing financial crisis for foreign investors.

The Global Grid of Strategic Sites

The global integration of financial markets depends on and contributes to the implementation of a variety of linkages among the financial centers involved.[15] Prime examples of such linkages are the multinational networks of affiliates and subsidiaries typical of major firms in manufacturing and specialized services. Corporate service firms have developed vast multinational networks containing special geographic and institutional linkages that make it possible for client firms – transnational firms and banks – to use a growing array of service offerings from the same supplier (Marshall et al., 1986; Noyelle and Dutka 1988; Daniels and Moulaert 1991; Fainstein 1993, chap. 2).[16] There is also a growing number of less directly economic linkages, notable among which are a variety of initiatives launched by urban governments which amount to a type of foreign policy by and for cities. For example, New York State has opened business offices in several major cities overseas.

Whether these linkages have engendered transnational urban systems is less clear. It is partly a question of theory and conceptualization. So much of social science is profoundly rooted in the nation–state as the ultimate unit for analysis, that conceptualizing processes and systems as transnational is bound to engender much controversy. Even much of the literature on world or global cities does not necessarily posit the existence of a transnational urban system: in its narrowest form it posits that global cities perform central place functions at a transnational level. But that leaves open the question as to the nature of the articulation among global cities. If one posits that they merely compete with each other for global business, then they do not constitute a transnational system; in this case, studying several global cities becomes an instance of traditional comparative analyses.

If one posits that besides competing they are also the sites for transnational processes with multiple locations, then one can begin to posit the possibility of a systemic dynamic binding these cities. Elsewhere (1991, chapters 1 and 7) I have argued that in addition to the central place functions performed by these cities at the global level, as posited by Hall (1966), Friedmann and Wolff (1982) and Sassen (1982), these cities relate to one another in distinct systemic ways. For example, the interaction among New York, London, and Tokyo, particularly in terms of finance and investment, consists partly of a series of processes that can be thought of as the chain of production in finance. Thus, in the mid-1980s Tokyo was the main exporter of the raw material we call money while New York was the leading processing center in the world. It was in New York that many of the new financial instruments were invented, and where money either in its raw form or in the form of debt was transformed into instruments that aimed at maximizing the returns on that money. London, on the other hand, was a major entrepôt which had the network to centralize and concentrate small amounts of capital available in a large number of smaller financial markets around the world, partly a function of its older network for the administration of the British empire. This is just one example suggesting that these cities do not simply compete with each other for the same business. There is, it seems to me, an economic system that rests on the three distinct types of locations these cities represent.[17] In my view, there is no such thing as a single global city, unlike what was the case with earlier imperial capitals – a single world city at the top of a system. The global city is a function of the global grid of transactions, one site for processes which are global because they have multiple locations in multiple countries (see also Abu-Lughod 1995; Smith and Timberlake 1995).

If finance and the advanced corporate services are in fact embedded in such transnational systems then this might be a rather significant factor in examinations of the possibilities on deregulation and globalization but also on a complex and dense grid of linkages and sites. The hypermobility of these industries and the associated difficulties for regulation are only part of the picture, albeit the most intensely studied and debated one; the global grid of linkages and sites within which this hypermobility is embedded and through which it flows is potentially another part of the picture, and one that will require more research to elucidate.

CONCLUSION:
REGULATING THE GLOBAL GRID OF PLACES

Including cities in the analysis of economic globalization and the ascendance of information industries adds three important dimensions to the study of economic globalization. First, it decomposes the nation – state into a variety of components that may be significant in understanding international economic activity and regulatory capacities. Second, it displaces the focus from the power of large corporations over governments and economies to the range of activities and organizational arrangements necessary for the implementation and maintenance of a global network of factories, service operations, and markets; these are all processes only partly encompassed by the activities of transnational corporations and banks. Third, it contributes to a focus on place and on the strategic concentrations of infrastructure and production complexes necessary for global economic activity. Processes of economic globalization are thereby reconstituted as concrete production complexes situated in specific places containing a multiplicity of activities. Focusing on cities allows us to specify a global geography of strategic places as well as the microgeographies and politics unfolding within these places.

The transformation in the composition of the world economy, especially the rise of finance and advanced services as leading industries, is contributing to a new international economic order, one dominated by financial centers, global markets, and transnational firms. Correspondingly, we may see a growing significance of other political categories both sub- and supranational. Cities that function as international business and financial centers are sites for direct transactions with world markets.

These cities and the globally oriented markets and firms they contain mediate in the relation of the world economy to nation–states and in the relations among nation–states. Transnational economic processes inevitably interact with systems for the governance of national economies. Further, the material conditions necessary for many global economic processes–from the infrastructure for telematics to the producer services production complex–need to be incorporated in examinations of questions of governance and accountability in the global economy. They signal the possibility of novel forms of regulation and conditions for accountability.

In sum, an analysis focused on place and production has the effect of decoding globalization; the latter is conceptually reconstituted in terms of a transnational geography of centrality consisting of multiple linkages and strategic concentrations of material infrastructure. Globalization can then be seen as embedded and dependent on these linkages and material infrastructure. To a considerable extent, global processes are this grid of sites and linkages.

The existence of such a transnational grid of places and linkages that constitute the infrastructure for the globalization of finance and other specialized services points to regulatory possibilities. Precisely because of its strategic character and because of the density of resources and linkages it concentrates, this new geography of centrality could in turn be a space for concentrated regulatory activity. But the type of regulatory frameworks and operations it would entail need to be discovered and invented, as does the meaning of accountability and democratization of the new global information economy.

NOTES

1   For instance, France, which ranks among the top providers of information services and industrial engineering services in Europe and has a strong, though not outstanding, position in financial and insurance services, has found itself at an increasing disadvantage in legal and accounting services. French law firms are at a particular disadvantage because Anglo-Saxon law dominates the international transactions. Foreign firms with offices in Paris dominate the

servicing of the legal needs of firms operating internationally, for both French and foreign firms operating out of France.

2 The hegemony of neoliberal concepts of economic relations with its strong emphasis on markets, deregulation, free international trade has influenced policy in the 1980s in United States and United Kingdom and now increasingly also in continental Europe. This has contributed to the formation of transnational legal regimes that are centered in Western economic concepts. Through the IMF and IBRD as well as GATT this vision has spread to the developing world. An issue that is emerging as significant in view of the spread of Western legal concepts is the critical examination of the philosophical premises about authorship and property that define the legal arena in the West (e.g., Coombe 1993). Similarly, Anglo American law is increasingly dominant in international commercial arbitration, an institution grounded in continental traditions of jurisprudence, particularly French and Swiss (Dezalay and Garth 1995).

3 Many of these changes, of course, required explicit government action. Pastor's study [*Congress and the Politics of U.S. Foreign Economic Policy, 1929–1976*] on the United States about the arduous legislative road to open up the country to foreign investment is a good case in point.

4 Producer services are intermediate outputs, that is, services bought by firms. They cover financial, legal, and general management matters, innovation, development, design, administration, personnel, production technology, maintenance, transport, communications, wholesale distribution, advertising, cleaning services for firms, security, and storage. Central components of the producer services category are a range of industries with mixed business and consumer markets. They are insurance, banking, financial services, real estate, legal services, accounting, and professional associations.

5 There is, however, a rapidly growing literature on the impact of globalization on cities, which in various ways incorporates examinations of producer services, including, besides the ones already listed above, Friedmann 1986; Fainstein et al. 1993; Hitz et al. 1995; von Petz and Schmals 1992, Machimura 1992; Frost and Spence 1992; Rodriguez and Feagin 1986; Knox and Taylor 1995; Levine 1993; *Le Debat* 1994.

6 Using input-output tables from 1972 to 1987 we examined the use of service-based commodities in eleven four-digit SIC industries (ranging from wholesale trade to mining). The service-based industries examined as the intermediate commodity input, down to the four-digit SIC code, included among others, finance and insurance, and business services. For the sake of simplicity, the following figures cover the 1972 to 1982 period only because after this date the comparison becomes too complicated to describe in a footnote. Of all the industry combinations studied, the level of service inputs from the finance industry was most prominent, tripling from 1972 to 1982, in banking, wholesale trade, and insurance. The use of business services increased sharpest in the following industry groups: motor vehicles and equipment, insurance carriers, wholesale trade, and banking. The use of business services in banking more than tripled from 1972 to 1982. (See Sassen and Orlow 1995 for a full description.)

7 For a discussion of the literature and the broader trends lying behind the possibility of the formation of a free-standing producer services sector (Sassen 1991, chap. 5).

8 The telecommunications infrastructure also contributes to concentration of leading sectors in major cities. Long-distance communications systems increasingly use fiber optic wires. These have several advantages over traditional copper wire: large carrying capacity, high speed, more security, and higher signal strength. Fiber systems tend to connect major communications hubs because they are not easily spliced and hence not desirable for connecting multiple lateral sites. Fiber systems tend to be installed along existing rights of way, whether rail, water or highways (Moss 1991). The growing use of fiber optic systems thus tends to strengthen the major existing telecommunication concentrations and therefore the existing hierarchies. (See also chap. 9.)

9   It is common in the general literature and in some more scholarly accounts to use headquarters concentration as an indication of whether a city is an international business center. The loss of headquarters is then interpreted as a decline in a city's status. The use of headquarters concentration as an index is actually a problematic measure given the way in which corporations are classified. Which headquarters concentrate in major international financial and business centers depends on a number of variables. First, how we measure or simply count headquarters makes a difference. Frequently, the key measure is size of firm in terms of employment and overall revenue. In this case, some of the largest firms in the world are still manufacturing firms and many of these have their main headquarters in proximity to their major factory complex, which is unlikely to be in a large city due to space constraints. Such firms are likely, however, to have secondary headquarters for highly specialized functions in major cities. Further, many manufacturing firms are oriented to the national market and do not need to be located in an international business center. Thus, the much publicized departure of major headquarters from New York City in the 1960s and 1970s involved these types of firms. If we look at the Fortune 500 largest firms in the United States (cf. "*Fortune* Magazine 500 list") many have left New York City and other large cities. If instead of size we use share of total firm revenue coming from international sales, a large number of firms that are not part of the Fortune 500 list come into play. For instance, in the case of New York City, the results change dramatically: forty percent of U.S. firms with half their revenue from international sales have their headquarters in New York City and its environs.

    Second, the nature of the urban system in a country is a factor. Sharp urban primacy will tend to entail a disproportionate concentration of headquarters no matter what measure one uses. Third, different economic histories and business traditions may combine to produce different results. Further, headquarters concentration may be linked with a specific economic phase. For instance, unlike New York's loss of top Fortune 500 headquarters, Tokyo has been gaining such headquarters. Osaka and Nagoya, the two other major economic centers in Japan are losing headquarters to Tokyo. This is in good part linked to the increasing internationalization of the Japanese economy and the corresponding increase in central command and servicing functions in major international business centers. In the case of Japan, extensive government regulation over the economy is an added factor contributing to headquarter location in Tokyo insofar as all international activities have to go through various government approvals.

10 For example, Wheeler (1986) examined the spatial linkages between major U.S. corporations and financial institutions and found that corporations do not necessarily use the firms available in their location but rather tend to work with firms located higher up in the metropolitan hierarchy, a trend that is particularly strong for large corporations. Schwartz (1992) found that large firms located in the New York metropolitan area continued to use Manhattan firms for most of their service needs.

11 A very different category through which some of these issues can be examined is that of "centrality." The spatial correlates of centrality today can assume a multiplicity of forms, ranging from the traditional central business district (CBC) as well as a metropolitan grid of economic nodes intensely connected via telematics (see chap. 9 here). Examining the evidence for a number of major cities I found a clear trend toward centrality, but with a far broader range of spatial correlates than the traditional CBD. Telematics and the growth of a global economy, both inextricably linked, have contributed to a new geography of centrality (and marginality). To simplify an analysis made elsewhere (Sassen 1994), there are four forms of centrality today. First, the CBD remains a key form of centrality although there is no longer a simple straightforward relation between centrality and such geographic entities as the downtown, or the central business district, as was the case in the past. But the CBD in major international business centers is one profoundly reconfigured by technological and economic change.

    Second, the center can extend into a metropolitan area in the form of a grid of nodes of intense business activity. This regional grid of nodes represents, in my analysis, a reconstitution of the concept of region. Far from neutralizing geography, the regional grid is likely to be embedded in conventional forms of communications infrastructure, notably rapid rail and highways connecting to airports. Ironically perhaps, conventional infrastructure is likely to maximize the economic benefits derived from telematics. I think this is an important issue that has been lost somewhat in discussions about the neutralization of geography through telematics. Third, we are seeing the formation of a transterritorial "center" constituted via telematics and intense economic transactions. The most powerful of these new geographies of centrality at the interurban level binds the major international financial and business centers: New York, London, Tokyo, Paris, Frankfurt, Zurich, Amsterdam, Los Angeles, Sydney, Hong Kong, among others. But this geography now also includes cities such as São Paulo and Bombay. The intensity of transactions among these cities, particularly through the financial markets, trade in services, and investment, has increased sharply, and so have the orders of magnitude involved. Fourth, new forms of centrality are being constituted in electronically generated spaces (see chap. 9 here). The city is a strategic site in the first three of these forms of centrality.

12 In his study of the financial district in Manhattan, Longcore found that the use of advanced information and telecommunication technologies has a strong impact on the spatial organization of the district because of the added spatial requirements of "intelligent" buildings (see also Moss 1991). A ring of new office buildings meeting these requirements was built over the last decade immediately around the old Wall Street core, where the narrow streets and lots made this difficult; further, renovating old buildings in the Wall Street core is extremely expensive and often not possible. The occupants of the new buildings in the district were mostly corporate headquarters and the financial services industry. These firms tend to be extremely intensive users of telematics and availability of the most advanced forms typically is a major factor in their real estate and locational decisions. They need complete redundancy of telecommunications systems, high carrying capacity, often their own private branch exchange, etc. With this often goes a need for large spaces. For instance, the technical installation backing a firm's trading floor is likely to require additional space the size of the trading floor itself.

13 Further, this unchanged level of concentration has happened at a time when financial services are more mobile than ever before: globalization, deregulation (an essential ingredient for globalization), and securitization have been the key to this mobility – in the context of massive advances in telecommunications and electronic networks. One result is growing competition among centers for hypermobile financial activity. In my view there has been an overemphasis on competition in general and in specialized accounts on this subject. As I have argued elsewhere (Sassen 1991, chap. 7), there is also a functional division of labor among various major financial centers. In that sense we can think of a transnational system with multiple locations (see also Abu-Lughod 1995).

14 Much of the discussion around the formation of a single European market and financial system has raised the possibility, and even the need if it is to be competitive, of centralizing financial functions and capital in a limited number of cities rather than maintaining the current structure in which each country has a financial center.

15 There is a rapidly growing and highly specialized literature focused on different types of economic linkages that bind cities across national borders (Castells 1989; Noyelle and Dutka 1988; Daniels and Moulaert 1991; Leyshon, Daniels and Thrift 1987; Sassen 1991).

16 There is good evidence that the development of multinational corporate service firms was associated with the needs of transnational firms. The multinational advertising firm can offer global advertising to a specific segment of potential customers worldwide. Further, global integration of affiliates and markets requires making use of advanced information and telecommunications technology which can come to account for a significant share of costs – not only operational costs but also, and perhaps most important, research and development costs for new products or advances on existing products. The need for scale economies on all these

fronts contributes to explain the recent increase in mergers and acquisitions, which has consolidated the position of a few very large firms in many of these industries, and further strengthened cross-border linkages among the key locations which concentrate the needed telecommunications facilities. They have emerged as firms that can control a significant share of national and international markets. The rapid increase in direct foreign investments in services is strongly linked with the growing tendency among leading service firms to operate transnationally. Subcontracting by larger firms and the multiplicity of specialized markets has meant that small independent firms can also thrive in major centers (Sassen 1991; Noyelle and Dutka 1988; Leyhson, Daniels and Thrift 1987).

17 The possibility of such a transnational urban system raises a question as to the articulation of such cities with their national urban systems. It is quite possible that the strengthening of cross-national ties among the leading financial and business centers is likely to be accomplished by a weakening of the linkages between each of these cities and their hinterlands and national urban systems (Sassen 1991). Cities such as Detroit, Liverpool, Manchester, Marseille, the cities of the Ruhr, and now increasingly Nagoya and Osaka, have been affected by the territorial decentralization of many of their key manufacturing industries at the domestic and international level. This process of decentralization has contributed to the growth of service industries that produce the specialized inputs to run spatially dispersed processes and global markets for inputs and outputs. These specialized inputs – international legal and accounting services, management consulting, financial services – are heavily concentrated in business and financial centers rather than in these manufacturing cities themselves.

Abbott, Kenneth W. 1992. "Gatt as a Public Institution: The Uruguay Round and Beyond." *Brooklyn Journal of International Law*, vol. 18, nr.: 31–85.

Abu-Lughod, Janet Lippman. 1995. "Comparing Chicago, New York and Los Angeles: Testing Some World Cities Hypotheses." In *World Cities in a World-System,* eds. Paul L. Knox and Peter J. Taylor, 171–91. Cambridge, U.K.: Cambridge University Press.

Acuerdo de Cartagena, Junta. 1991a. *Acta Final de la lra. Reunión de Autoridades Migratorias del Grupo Andino.* Lima: JUNAC.

——. 1991b. *Bases de Propuesta para la Integración Fronteriza Andina.* Lima: JUNAC.

——. 1991c. *La Migración Internacional en los Procesos Regionales de Integración en América del Sur.* Lima: JUNAC.

Aksen, Gerald. 1990. "Arbitration and Other Means of Dispute Settlement." In *International Joint Ventures: A Practical Approach to Working with Foreign Investors in the U.S. and Abroad,* eds. D. Goldsweig and R. Cummings. Chicago: American Bar Association.

Aman, Alfred C., Jr. 1995. "A Global Perspective on Current Regulatory Reform: Rejection, Relocation, or Reinvention?" *Indiana Journal of Global Legal Studies,* vol. 2: 429–64.

AMPO. 1988. "Japan's Human Imports: As Capitol Flows Out, Foreign Labor Flows In." *Japan Asia Quarterly Review* 19: 4.

Appelbaum, Eileen, and Peter Albin. 1990. "Shifts in Employment, Occupational Structure, and Educational Attainment." In *Skills,*

Wages, and Productivity in the Service Sector, ed. T. Noyelle, 31–66. Boulder, Colo.: Westview Press.

Arrighi, Giovanni. 1994. *The Long Twentieth Century: Money, Power, and the Origins of Our Times.* London: Verso.

Asian Women's Association. 1988. *Women from Across the Seas: Migrant Workers in Japan.* Asian Women's Association.

Balmori, D. 1983. "Hispanic Immigrants in the Construction Industry: New York City, 1960–1982." *Occasional Papers* no. 38. Center for Latin American and Caribbean Studies, New York University.

Banco Interamericano de Desarrollo/JUNAC. 1993. *Política de Integración Fronteriza de los Paises Miembros del Grupo Andino. Cooperación Técnica.* Lima: JUNAC.

Basch, Linda, Nina Glick Schiller, and Cristina Szanton-Blanc. 1994. *Nations Unbound: Transnationalized Projects and the Deterritorialized Nation-State.* New York: Gordon and Breach.

Baubock, Rainer. 1994. *Transnational Citizenship: Membership and Rights in International Migration.* Aldershot, U.K.: Edward Elgar.

Bednarzik, Robert. 1990. "A Special Focus on Employment Growth in Business Services and Retail Trade." In T. Noyelle, op. cit., 67–80.

Benamou, C. 1985. "'La Aguja': Labor Union Participation among Hispanic Immigrant Women in the New York Garment Industry." *Occasional Papers.* Center for Latin American and Caribbean Studies, New York University.

Beneria, Lourdes, and Catherine Stimpson, eds. 1987. *Women, Households and the Economy.* New Brunswick, N.J.: Rutgers University Press.

Berman, Nathaniel. 1995. "Economic Consequences, Nationalist Passions: Keynes, Crisis, Culture, and Policy." *The American University Journal of International Law and Policy,* vol. 10, nr. 2 (winter): 619–70.

Berner, Erhard, and Rudiger Korff. 1955. "Globalization and Local Resistance: The Creation of Localities in Manila and Bangkok." *International Journal of Urban and Regional Research,* vol. 19, no. 2: 208–22.

Bluestone, B., B. Harrison, and L. Gorham. 1984. "Imperialist Initiatives and the Puerto Rican Worker: From Foraker to Reagan." *Contemporary Marxism* 5:1–18.

Blumberg, P. 1980. *Inequality in an Age of Decline.* New York: Oxford University Press.

Body-Gendrot, Sophie. 1993. *Ville et violence: L'irruption de nouveaux acteurs.* Paris: PUF (Presses Universitaires de France).

Bohning, W. R., and M. L. Schloeter-Paredes, eds. 1994. *Aid in Place of Migration.* Geneva: International Labor Office.

Bonacich, Edna, et al., eds. 1994. *Global Production: The Apparel Industry in the Pacific Rim.* Philadelphia: Temple University Press.

Bose, Christine E., and Edna Acosta-Belen, eds. 1995. *Women in the Latin American Development Process.* Philadelphia: Temple University Press.

Boserup, E. 1970. *Women's Role in Economic Development.* New York: St. Martin's Press.

Bosniak, Linda S. 1992. "Human Rights, State Sovereignty and the Protection of Undocumented Migrants Under the International Migrant Workers Convention." *International Migration Review* xxv, no. 4: 737–70.

Boulding, E. 1980. *Women: The Fifth World.* Washington, D.C.: Foreign Policy Association, Headline Series 248. (February.)

Boyd, Monica. 1989. "Family and Personal Networks in International Migration: Recent Developments and New Agendas." *International Migration Review* 3: 638–70.

Brigg, P. 1973. "Some Economic Interpretations of Case Studies of Urban Migration in Developing Countries." Washington, D.C.: International Bank for Reconstruction and Development, Staff Working Paper 10.151. (March.)

Briggs, Vernon M., Jr. 1992. *Mass Immigration and the National Interest.* Armonk, N.Y.: M. E. Sharpe.

Burbach, G., and S. Flynn. 1980. *Agribusiness in the Americas.* New York: Monthly Review Press and NACLA.

Byerlee, D. 1972. "Research on Migration in Africa: Past, Present and Future." Department of Agricultural Economics, African Rural Employment Paper No. 2. Michigan State University. (September.)

Carbonneau, Thomas, ed. 1990. *Lex Mercatoria and Arbitration.* Dobbs Ferry, N.Y.: Transnational Juris Publications.

Castells, Manuel. 1989. *The Informational City.* London: Blackwell.

Castells, Manuel, and Yuko, Aoyama. 1994. "Paths Towards the Informational Society: Employment Structure in G-7 Countries, 1920–90." *International Labor Review* 133, 1: 5–33.

Castro, M. G. 1982. "Mary and Eve's Reproduction in the Big Apple: Colombian Voices." *Occasional Papers* no. 35. Center for Latin American and Caribbean Studies, New York University.

Caughman, S., and M. N'diaye Thiam. 1980. "Soap-making: The Experiences of a Woman's Co-operative in Mali," *Appropriate Technology* 7(3) (Dec.): 4–6.

CEPAL. 1992. "Consideraciones sobre la formación de recursos humanos en Centroamérica." (Mimeo.) Mexico: CEPAL.

——. 1994. *Desarrollo reciente de los procesos de integración en América Latina y el Caribe.* Santiago, Chile: CEPAL.

Chaney, E. M. 1984. *Women of the World: Latin America and the Caribbean.* Washington, D.C.: Office for Women for Development, U.S. Agency for International Development. (May.)

Chaney, E. M., and M. W. Lewis. 1980. "Women, Migration and the Decline of Small Holder Agriculture." Washington, D.C.: United States Agency for International Development, Office of Women in Development. (Oct.)

Chant, Sylvia, ed. 1992. *Gender and Migration in Developing Countries.* London and New York: Belhaven Press.

Charlesworth, Hilary, et al. 1991. *Feminist Approaches to International Law. American Journal of International Law* 85: 613.

——. 1992. "The Public/Private Distinction and the Right to Development in International Law." *Austrl. Y.B. Intl. Law* 12: 190.

Chen, Xiangming. 1995. "Chicago as a Global City." *Chicago Office* 5 (1995).

Chinkin, Christine. 1992. "A Gendered Perspective to the International Use of Force." *Austl. Y.B. Int'l. L.* 12: 279.

Cho, S. K. 1984. "The Feminization of the Labor Movement in South Korea." Department of Sociology, University of California, Berkeley. Unpublished.

Clark, Gracia. 1996. "Implications of Global Polarization for Feminist Work." A Discussion of Saskia Sassen's presentation at the Conference on Feminism and Globalization, Ind. Univ. Law School, March 22.

Clark, Rebecca L., et al. 1994. *Fiscal Impacts of Undocumented Aliens: Selected Estimates for Seven States.* Report to the Office of Management and Budget and the Department of Justice. September. Washington, D.C.: The Urban Institute.

Cohen, Michael A., Blair A. Ruble, Joseph S. Tulchin, and Allison M. Garland, eds. 1996. *Preparing for the Urban Future: Global Pressures and Local Forces.* Washington, D.C.: Woodrow Wilson Center Press.

Cohen, S. M., and S. Sassen-Koob. 1982. *Survey of Six Immigrant Groups in Queens, New York City.* Queens College, City University of New York.

Cohen, Stephen S., and John Zysman. 1987. *Manufacturing Matters: The Myth of the Post-Industrial Economy.* New York: Basic Books.

Comisión Migraciones, Seguridad e Informática. 1992. ACTA. Montevideo, 17–20 November.

Competition and Change: The Journal of Global Business and Political Economy. vol. 1, no. 1. Harwood Academic Publishers.

Coombe, Rosemary J. 1993. "The Properties of Culture and the Politics of Possessing Identity: Native Claims in the Cultural Appropriation Controversy." *The Canadian Journal of Law and Jurisprudence,* vol. 6, no. 2, (July): 249–85.

Corbridge, S., R. Martin, and N. Thrift, eds. *Money, Power and Space.* Forthcoming.

Cordier, Jean. 1992. "Paris, place financière et bancaire." In *L'Ille de France et la recherche urbaine,* eds. M. Berger and C. Rhein. STRAITES-CNRS Univ. Paris 1, et Plan Urbain-DATAR.

Cornelius, Wayne A., Philip L. Martin, and James F. Hollifield, eds. 1994. *Controlling Immigration: A Global Perspective.* Stanford, Calif.: Stanford University Press.

Cox, Robert. 1987. *Production, Power, and World Order: Social Forces in the Making of History.* New York: Columbia University Press.

Daes, Erica-Irene A. 1993. "Explanatory Note Concerning the Draft Declaration on the Rights of Indigenous Peoples" 20–23. UN Doc. E/CN.4/Sub. 2/1993.

Daly, M. T., and R. Stimson. 1992. "Sydney: Australia's Gateway and Financial Capital." In *New Cities of the Pacific Rim,* eds. E. Blakely and T. J. Stimpson, chap. 18. Institute for Urban & Regional Development, University of California, Berkeley.

Daniels, Peter W. 1985. *Service Industries: A Geographical Appraisal.* London and New York: Methuen.

Daniels, Peter W., and Frank Moulaert, eds. 1991. *The Changing Geography of Advanced Producer Services.* London and New York: Belhaven Press.

Dauber, R., and M. L. Cain, eds. 1981. *Women and Technological Change in Developing Countries.* Boulder, Colo.: Westview Press.

Deere, C. D. 1976. "Rural Women's Subsistence Production in the Capitalist Periphery." *Review of Radical Political Economy* 8, 1: 9-17.

Delaunoy, I. V. 1975. Formación, Empleo y Seguridad Social de la Mujer en América Latina y el Caribe." In *Participación de la Mujer en el Desarollo de América Latina y el Caribe,* eds. Henriques de Paredes, P. Izaguirre, and I. V. Delaunoy, 59-114. Santiago, Chile: UNICEF Regional Office.

Delauney, Jean Claude, and Jean Gadrey. 1987. *Les Enjeux de la societé de service.* Paris: Presses de la Fondation des Sciences Politiques.

Dezalay, Yves, and Garth Bryant. 1995. "Merchants of Law as Moral Entrepreneurs: Constructing International Justice from the Competition for Transnational Business Disputes." *Law and Society Review* 29, no. 1: 27-64.

Directores Generales de Migraciones, Centroamérica. 1992. "Políticas de control sobre las corrientes migratorias en Centroamérica." *La migración internacional: Su impacto en Centroamérica.* San Jose, Costa Rica.

Drache, D., and M. Gertler, eds. 1991. *The New Era of Global Competition: State Policy and Market Power.* Montreal: McGill-Queen's University Press.

Drennan, Mathew P. 1992. "Gateway Cities: The Metropolitan Sources of U.S. Producer Service Exports." *Urban Studies* 28, 2: 217-35.

Dunlap, Jonathan C., and Ann Morse. 1995. "States Sue Feds to Recover Immigration Costs." NCSL *Legisbrief* 3, no. 1 (January). Washington, D.C.: National Conference of State Legislatures.

Dunn, Seamus, ed. 1994. *Managing Divided Cities.* Staffs, U.K.: Keele University Press.

Eisenstein, Zillah. 1996. "Stop Stomping on the Rest of Us: Retrieving Publicness from the Privatization of the Globe." Paper presented at the Conference on Feminism and Globalization, Ind. Law School.

Elshtain, Jean Bethke. 1991. "Sovereign God, Sovereign State, Sovereign Self." *Notre Dame Law Review* 66: 1355.

Engle, Karen. 1994. "After the Collapse of the Public/Private Distinction: Strategizing Women's Rights." In *Reconceiving Reality: Women and International Law*, eds. Dorinda G. Dallmeyer et al. Am. Soc'y Int'l. Series Studies in Transnational Legal Policy, No. 25.

Espenshade, Thomas J., and Vanessa E. King. 1994. "State and Local Fiscal Impacts of U.S. Immigrants: Evidence from New Jersey." *Population Research and Policy Review* 13: 225–56.

Fagen, Patricia Weiss, and Joseph Eldridge. 1991. "Salvadorean Repatriation from Honduras." In *Repatriation Under Conflict: The Central American Case*, ed. Mary Ann Larkin. Washington, D.C.: HMP, CIPRA, Georgetown University.

Fainstein, Susan. 1994. *The City Builders: Property, Politics, and Planning in London and New York.* Cambridge, Mass.: Blackwell.

Fainstein, S., I. Gordon, and M. Harloe. 1993. *Divided Cities: Economic Restructuring and Social Change in London and New York.* Cambridge, Mass.: Blackwell.

Falk, Richard. 1989. "A New Paradigm for International Legal Studies: Prospects and Proposals." In *Revitalizing International Law* 3, 38.

Fernandez-Kelly, M. P. 1983. *For We Are Sold, I and My People: Women and Industrialization in Mexico's Frontier.* Albany: SUNY Press.

——and Ana Garcia. 1990. "Power Surrendered Power Restored: The Politics of Home and Work among Hispanic Women in Southern California and Southern Florida." In *Women and Politics in America*, eds. Louise Tilly and P. Guerin, 130–49. New York: The Russell Sage Foundation.

Foner, Nancy. 1986. "Sex Roles and Sensibilities: Jamaican Women in New York and London." In *International Migration: The Female Experience*, eds. Rita Simon and C. Brettell, 133–49. Totowa, N.J.: Rowman and Allanheld.

Franck, Thomas M. 1992. "The Emerging Right to Democratic Governance." *American Journal of International Law*, vol. 86, no. 1: 46–91.

Friedmann, John. 1995. "Where We Stand: A Decade of World City Research." In Knox and Taylor, eds., op. cit., 21–47.

——. 1986. "The World City Hypothesis." *Development and Change* 17: 69–84.

Frost, Martin, and Nigel Spence. 1992. "Global City Characteristics and Central London's Employment." *Urban Studies* 30, 3: 547–58.

Gad, Gunter, 1991. "Toronto's Financial District." *Canadian Urban Landscapes* 1. 203–07.

Garcia, Linda. 1995. "The Globalization of Telecommunications and Information." In *The New Information Infrastructure: Strategies for U.S. Policy,* ed. William J. Drake. New York: Twentieth Century Fund Press.

Gardam, Judith G. 1993. "The Law of Armed Conflict: A Feminist Perspective." In *Human Rights in the Twenty-First Century: A Global Challenge,* eds. Kathleen E. Mahoney and Paul Mahoney.

General Accounting Office. 1994. *Illegal Aliens: Assessing Estimates of Financial Burden on California.* November, GAO/HEHS-95-22. Washington D.C.: U.S. GAO.

——. 1995. *Illegal Aliens: National Net Cost Estimates Vary Widely.* July, GAO/HEHS-95-133. Washington D.C.: U.S. GAO.

George, S. 1977. *How the Other Half Dies: The Real Reasons for World Hunger.* Montclair, N.J.: Allanheld, Osmun.

Georges, Eugenia. 1990. *The Making of a Transnational Community: Migration, Development, and Cultural Change in the Dominican Republic.* New York: Columbia University Press.

Gereffi, Gary. 1996. "The Elusive Last Lap in the Quest for Developed Country Status." In *Globalization: Critical Reflections. International Political Economy Yearbook,* vol. 9, ed. by James H. Mittelman. Boulder, Colo.: Lynne Reinner Publishers.

Gershuny, Jonathan, and Ian Miles. 1983. *The New Service Economy: The Transformation of Employment in Industrial Societies.* New York: Praeger.

Giddens, Anthony. 1987. *The Nation-State and Violence.* Berkeley: University of California Press.

Glenn, Evelyn Nakano. 1986. *Issei, Nisei, War Bride: Three Generations of Japanese-American Women in Domestic Service.* Philadelphia: Temple University Press.

Goldstein, Judith, and Robert O. Keohane, eds. 1993. *Ideas and Foreign Policy: Beliefs, Institutions and Political Change.* Ithaca, N.Y.: Cornell University Press.

Goodwin-Gill, G. S. 1989. "Nonrefoulement and the New Asylum Seekers." In *The New Asylum Seekers: Refugee Policy in the 1980s,* ed. D. A. Martin. Dordrecht, Netherlands: Martinus Nijhoff.

Grasmuck, S. 1982. "The Impact of Emigration on National Development: Three Sending Communities in the Dominican Republic." *Occasional Papers*, No. 32. Center for Latin American and Caribbean Studies, New York University.

Grasmuck, Sherri, and Patricia Pessar. 1991. *Between Two Islands: Dominican International Migration.* Berkeley: University of California Press.

Gross, R. 1979. "Women's Place in the Integrated Circuit," *Southeast Asia Chronicle* 66: 2–17.

Hall, S. 1991. "The Local and the Global: Globalization and Ethnicity." In Anthony D. King, ed., *Culture, Globalization and the World-System: Contemporary Conditions for the Representation of Identity. Current Debates in Art History 3.* Department of Art and Art History, State University of New York at Binghamton.

Harris, J., and M. Todaro. 1970. "Migration, Unemployment, and Development: A Two-Sector Analysis," *American Economic Review* 60, 1 (March): 126–42.

Hartmann, Heidi. 1987. "Changes in Women's Economic and Family Roles in Post-World War II United States." In Beneria and Stimpson, op. cit.

Hassan, Farooq. 1983. "The Doctrine of Incorporation." *Human Rights Quarterly* 5: 68–86.

Haus, Leah. 1995. "Openings in the Wall: Transnational Migrants, Labor Unions, and U.S. Immigration Policy." *International Organization* 49, no. 2 (spring): 285–313.

Heisler, Martin. 1986. "Transnational Migration as a Small Window on the Diminished Autonomy of the Modern Democratic State." *Annals* (American Academy of Political And Social Science) 485 (May): 153–66.

Henkin, Louis. 1990. *The Age of Rights.* New York: Columbia University Press.

Herrick, B. 1971. "Urbanization and Urban Migration in Latin America: An Economist's View." In *Latin American Urban Research*, vol. 1, eds. F. Rabinovitz and F. Trueblood. Beverly Hills, Calif.: Sage Publications.

Hitz, Hansruedi, et al., eds. 1995. *Financial Metropoles in Restructuring: Zurich and Frankfurt En Route to Postfordism.* Zurich: Rootpunkt.

Hollifield, James F. 1992. *Immigrants, Markets, and States.* Cambridge, Mass.: Harvard University Press.

Holston, James, ed. 1996. "Cities and Citizenship." A Special Issue of *Public Culture,* vol. 8, no. 2 (winter).

Hobsbawm, Eric. 1991. *Nations and Nationalism since 1780: Programme, Myth, Reality.* Cambridge: Cambridge University Press.

Hondagneu-Sotelo, Pierrette. 1994. *Gendered Transitions.* Berkeley: University of California Press.

Hugo, Graeme, 1995. "Indonesia's Migration Transition." *Journal für Entwicklungspolitik* 11, 3:285–309.

Information Technologies and Inner-City Communities. Special issue of the *Journal of Urban Technology* 3 (fall 1995).

International Labor Office. 1982. *Yearbook of Labor Statistics, 1981.* Geneva: ILO.

——. 1981. *Employment Effects of Multinational Enterprises in Developing Countries.* Geneva: ILO.

Institute of Social Studies, New Delhi. 1979. "A Case Study on the Modernization of the Traditional Handloom Weaving Industry in the Kashmir Valley: The Integrated Development Project for the Woolen Handloom Weaving Industry in Jammu and Kashmir." Bangkok: Asian and Pacific Centre for Women and Development. (May.)

Institute for Social Research. 1987. "Measurement of Selected Income Flows in Informal Markets 1981 and 1985–1986." University of Michigan, Ann Arbor.

Ibister, John. 1996. *The Immigration Debate: Remaking America.* West Hartford, Conn.: Kumarian Books.

Iyotani, T., and T. Naito. 1989. "Tokyo no Kokusaika de Tenkan Semarareru Chusho Kigyo" (Medium- and small-sized corporations under pressure of change by Tokyo's internationalization), *Ekonomisuto,* (Sept. 5): 44–49.

Jelin, E. 1979. "Women and the Urban Labor Market." International Labor Office, World Employment Programme Research. Working Papers No. 77 of the Population and Labor Policies Programme. (Sept.)

Jessop, Robert. 1990. *State Theory: Putting Capitalist States in Their Place.* University Park: Pennsylvania State University Press.

Johnston, Douglas M. 1988. "Functionalism in the Theory of International Law." 26 *Can. Y.B. Int'l L.* 3.

Journal für Entwicklungspolitik. Schwerpunkt: Migration. 1995. Special Issue on Migration. vol. 11, no. 3. Frankfurt: Brandes & Apsel Verlag.

JUNAC-OIM. 1993. *Integración, migración y desarrollo sostenible en el grupo Andino.* Lima: JUNAC-OIM.

Kabria, Nazli. 1993. *Family Tightrope.* Princeton, N.J.: Princeton University Press.

Kelly, D. 1984. "Hard Work, Hard Choices: A Survey of Women in St. Lucia's Export Oriented Electronics Factories." Unpublished Research Report.

Kennedy, David. 1992. "Some Reflections on 'The Role of Sovereignty in the New International Order.'" In *State Sovereignty: The Challenge of a Changing World: New Approaches and Thinking on International Law,* 237 (Proceedings of the 21st Annual Conference of the Canadian Council on International Law, Ottawa, October 1992).

Kessler-Harris, Alice, and Karen Brodkin Sacks. 1987. "The Demise of Domesticity in America." In Beneria and Stimpson, op. cit. pp. 65–84.

King, Anthony, ed. 1996. *Representing the City: Ethnicity, Capital and Culture in the 21st Century.* London: Macmillan.

——. 1990. *Urbanism, Colonialism, and the World Economy: Culture and Spatial Foundations of the World Urban System.* The International Library of Sociology. London and New York: Routledge.

Knop, Karen. "Re/Statements: Feminism and State Sovereignty in International Law." *Transnational Law and Contemporary Problems,* vol. 3, Fall 1993: 293–344.

——1992. "The 'Righting' of Recognition: Recognition of States in Eastern Europe and the Soviet Union." in *State Sovereignty,* op. cit. pp. 36–43.

Knox, Paul, and Peter J. Taylor, eds. 1995. *World Cities in a World-System.* Cambridge, U.K.: Cambridge University Press.

Komai, H. 1992. "Are Foreign Trainees in Japan Disguised Cheap Laborers?" *Migration World* 20: 13–17.

Kooiman, Jan, and Martin van Vliet 1993. "Governance and Public Management." In *Managing Public Organizations: Lessons from Contemporary European Experience,* eds. K. A. Eliassen and J. Kooiman, 58–72. London: Sage.

Kratochwil, Friedrich. 1986. "Of Systems, Boundaries and Territoriality." *World Politics*, vol. 34 (October): 27–52.

Kratochwill, K. Herman. 1995. "Movilidad transfronteriza de personas y procesos de integración regional en América Latina." *Revista de la OIM sobre Migraciones en América Latina*, vol. 13, no. 2: 3–12.

Kunzmann, K. R., and M. Wegener. 1991. "The Pattern of Urbanisation in Western Europe, 1960–1990." Report for the Directorate General XVI of the Commission of the European Communities, as part of the study "Urbanisation and the Function of Cities in the European Community." Dortmund, Germany: Institut for Raumplanung. (March 15.)

Lamphere, Louise. 1987. *From Working Daughter to Working Mother: Immigrant Women in a New England Community*. Ithaca, N.Y.: Cornell University Press.

Land, K. 1969. "Duration of Residence and Prospective Migration: Further Evidence." *Demography* 6, 2:133–40.

Lawrence, R. Z. 1984. "Sectoral Shifts and the Size of the Middle Class," *Brookings Review*.

Le Débat. Le Nouveau Paris. Special Issue of *Le Débat*. Summer 1994.

Leftwich, A. 1994. "Governance, the State, and the Politics of Development." *Development and Change*, 24, 4: 363–86.

Leon, Ramon, and K. Herman Kratochwil. 1993. "Integración, migraciones y desarrollo sostenido en el Grupo Andino." *Revista de la OIM sobre Migraciones en América Latina*, vol. 11, no. 1 (April): 5–28.

Levine, Marc. 1993. *Montreal.* Philadelphia: Temple University Press.

Lim, L.Y.C. 1980. "Women Workers in Multinational Corporations: The Case of the Electronics Industry in Malaysia and Singapore." In *Transnational Enterprises: Their Impact on Third World Societies and Cultures*, ed. Krishna Kumar.

Longcore, T. R. 1993. "Information Technology and World City Restructuring: The Case of New York City's Financial District." Unpublished thesis, Department of Geography, University of Delaware.

Lyons, Donald, and Scott Salmon. 1995. "World Cities, Multinational Corporations and Urban Hierarchy: The Case of the United States." In P. Knox & P. J. Taylor, eds., *World Cities*, 98–114.

Machimura, Takashi. 1992. "The Urban Restructuring Process in the

1980s: Transforming Tokyo into a World City." *International Journal of Urban and Regional Research* 16, 1: 114–28.

MacKinnon, Catherine A. 1989. *Towards a Feminist Theory of the State.*

Mahler, Sarah. 1995. *American Dreaming: Immigrant Life on the Margins.* Princeton, N.J.: Princeton University Press.

Markusen, A., and V. Giwasda. 1994. "Multipolarity and the Layering of Functions in the World Cities: New York City's Struggle to Stay on Top." *International Journal of Urban and Regional Research* 18: 167–93.

Marmora, Lelio. 1994. "Desarrollo sostenido y políticas migratorias: su tratamiento en los espacios latinoamericanos de integración." *Revista de la OIM sobre Migraciones en América Latina,* vol. 12. no. 1/3 (April–December): 5–50.

——. 1985a. *Las migraciones laborales en Colombia.* Washington: OEA.

——. 1985b. *Las migraciones laborales en Venezuela.* Washington: OEA.

Marshall, A. 1983. "Immigration in a Surplus-Worker Labor Market: The Case of New York." *Occasional Papers,* No. 39. Center for Latin American and Caribbean Studies, New York University.

——. 1976. *Inmigración, demanda de fuerza de trabajo y estructura occupacional en el área metropolitana.* Buenos Aires: Facultad Latinoamericana de Ciencias Sociales.

Marshall, J. N., et al. 1986. *Uneven Development in the Service Economy: Understanding the Location of Producer Services.* Report of the Producer Services Working Party, Institute of British Geographers and the ESRC. August.

Martin, Philip L. 1993. *Trade and Migration: NAFTA and Agriculture.* Washington D.C.: Institute for International Economics. (October.)

Martinotti, Guido. 1993. *Metropoli: La nuova morfologìa sociale della città.* Bologna: Il Mulino.

Massey, Douglas S., et al. 1993. "Theories of International Migration: A Review and Appraisal." *Population and Development Review* 19, 3: 431–66.

Mazlish, Bruce, and Ralph Buultjens, eds. 1993. *Conceptualizing Global History.* Boulder, Colo.: Westview Press.

McDougal, Myres S., and W. Michael Reisman. 1983. "International Law in Policy Oriented Perspective." In *The Structure and Pro-*

cess of International Law: Essays in Legal Philosophy, Doctrine and Theory, eds. R. St. J. Macdonald and Douglas M. Johnston.

Minnow, Martha. 1990. *Making All the Difference: Inclusion, Exclusion, and American Law.*

Mitchell, Christopher. "International Migration, International Relations and Foreign Policy." *International Migration Review* (fall 1989).

Mitchelson, Ronald L., and James O. Wheeler. 1994 "The Flow of Information in a Global Economy: The Role of the American Urban System in 1990." *Annals of the Association of American Geographers* 84, 1: 87–107.

Mittelman, James, ed. 1996. *Globalization: Critical Reflections. International Political Economy Yearbook*, vol. 9. Boulder, Colo.: Lynne Reinner.

Miyajima, T. 1989. *The Logic of Receiving Foreign Workers: Amongst Dilemmas of Advanced Societies* (Gaikokujin Rodosha Mukaeire no Ronri: Senshin shakai no Jirenma no make de). Tokyo: Akashi Shoten.

Morales, Rebecca. 1994. *Flexible Production: Restructuring of the International Automobile Industry.* Cambridge, U.K.: Polity Press.

——. 1983. "Undocumented Workers in a Changing Automobile Industry: Case Studies in Wheels, Headers and Batteries." *Proceedings of the Conference on Contemporary Production: Capital Mobility and Labor Migration.* Center for U.S.-Mexican Studies, University of California, San Diego.

Morita, K. 1992. "Japan and the Problem of Foreign Workers." Research Institute for the Japanese Economy, Faculty of Economics, University of Tokyo-Hongo.

Morokvasic, Mirjana. 1984. Special Issue on Women Immigrants, *International Migration Review* 18, no. 4.

Morrison, P. 1967. "Duration of Residence and Prospective Migration: The Evaluation of a Stochastic Model." *Demography* 4:553–61.

Moss, Mitchell. 1991. "New Fibers of Urban Economic Development." *Portifolio: A Quarterly Review of Trade and Transportation* 4, 1: 11–18.

Multinational Monitor. 1982. "Focus: Women and Multinationals." Washington, D.C. (Summer.)

Nanami, T., and Y. Kuwabara, eds. 1989. *Tomorrow's Neighbors: For-*

eign Workers (Asu no Rinjin: Gaikokujin Rodosha). Tokyo: Toyo Keizai Shimposha.

Nash, June, and Helen Sefa, eds. 1986. *Women and Change in Latin America.* Op. cit.

Nedelsky, Jennifer. 1989. "Reconceiving Autonomy." 1 *Yale J.L. & Feminism* 7.

Negri, Toni 1995. "A quoi sert encore l'Etat." *Pouvoirs Pouvoir,* vol. 25–26 of *Futur Anterieur,* 135–52. Paris: L'Harmattan.

Nelson, J. 1974. "Sojourners vs. New Urbanities: Causes and Consequences of Temporary vs. Permanent Cityward Migration in Developing Countries." Center for International Affairs, Harvard University.

New York State Department of Labor. 1982a. *Report to the Governor and the Legislature on the Garment Manufacturing Industry and Industrial Homework.* Albany: New York State Department of Labor.

——. 1980. *Occupational Employment Statistics: Services, New York State, April-June 1978.* Albany: New York State Department of Labor.

——. 1979. *Occupational Employment Statistics: Finance, Insurance and Real Estate, New York State, May-June 1978.* Albany: New York State Department of Labor.

North American Congress on Latin America. 1978. "Capital's Flight: The Apparel Industry Moves South." *Latin America and Empire Report* 11, 3.

——. 1977. "Electronics: The Global Industry." *Latin America and Empire Report* 11, 4.

Noyelle, T., and A. B. Dutka. 1988. *International Trade in Business Services: Accounting, Advertising, Law and Management Consulting.* Cambridge, Mass.: Ballinger Publishing.

OIM. 1991a. *Proyecto Regional de la Organización Centroamericana de Migración. Políticas e Instrumentos Migratorios para la Integración de América Central.* Costa Rica: PROCAM/OIM.

——. 1991b. *Programa de Integración y Migraciones para el Cono Sur.* Buenos Aires: PRIMCOS/OIM.

——. 1991c. *Aspectos Jurídicos e Institucionales de las Migraciones: Peru, Colombia, Bolivia, Venezuela.* Geneva: OIM.

——. 1991d. *Aspectos Jurídicos e Institucionales de las Migraciones:*

Costa Rica, El Salvador, Honduras, Nicaragua y Panama. Geneva: OIM.

Ong, Aihwa. 1996. "Globalization and Women's Rights: The Asian Debate on Citizenship and Communitarianism." Paper presented at the conference on Feminism and Globalization, Ind. Law School.

Organization for Economic Co-operation and Development. 1981. *International Investment and Multinational Enterprises: Recent International Direct Investment Trends*. Paris: OECD.

——. 1980. "International Subcontracting: A New Form of Investment." Paris: OECD, Development Center. 136.

Orlansky, D., and S. Dubrovsky. 1978. "The Effects of Rural-Urban Migration on Women's Role and Status in Latin America." *Reports and Papers in the Social Sciences*, no. 41. Paris: UNICEF.

Panitch, Leo. 1996. "Rethinking the Role of the State in an Era of Globalization." In Mittelman, ed., op. cit.

Parra Sandorval, R. 1981. "The Impact of Industrialization on Women's Traditional Fields of Economic Activity in Developing Countries." New York: UNIDO.

Pateman, Carole. 1983. "Feminist Critiques of the Public/Private Dichotomy." In *Public and Private in Social Life*, eds. Stanley I. Benn and Gerald F. Gaus.

Paul, Joel R. 1994/95. "Free Trade, Regulatory Competition and the Autonomous Market Fallacy." *The Columbia Journal of European Law*, vol. 1, no. 1 (fall/winter): 29–62.

Peraldi, Michel, and Evelyne Perrin, eds. 1996. *Reseaux Productifs et Territories Urbains*. Toulouse: Presses Universitaires du Mirail.

Pessar, Patricia. 1995. "On the Homefront and in the Workplace: Integrating Immigrant Women into Feminist Discourse." *Anthropological Quarterly* 68, no. 1: 37–47.

Peterson, V. Spike, ed. 1992. *Gendered States: Feminist (Re)Visions of International Relations Theory.*

von Petz, Ursula, and Klaus M. Schmals, eds. *Metropole, Weltstadt, Global City: Neue Formen der Urbanisierung*, vol. 60, Dortmund: Dortmunder Beitrage zur Raumplanung, Universitat Dortmund.

Pillon, Thierry, and Anne Querrien, eds. 1995. *La Ville-Monde Aujourd'hui: Entre Virtualité et Ancrage*. Special issue of *Futur Anterieur* 30–32.

Pineda-Ofreneo, R. 1982. "Philippine Domestic Outwork: Subcontracting for Export Oriented Industries." *Journal of Contemporary Asia* 12, 3:281–93.

Plender, R. 1988. *International Migration Law.* Dordrecht, Netherlands: Martinus Nijhoff.

Port Authority of New York and New Jersey. 1982. *Regional Perspective: The Regional Economy, 1982 Review, 1982 Outlook.* New York: Planning and Development Department, Regional Research Section.

Portes, Alejandro, ed. 1995. *The Economic Sociology of Immigration.* New York: The Russell Sage Foundation.

——. 1979. "Illegal Immigration and the International System: Lessons from Recent Legal Mexican Immigrants to the United States." *Social Problems* 26 (April).

Prieto, Yolanda. 1992. "Cuban Women in New Jersey: Gender Relations and Change." In *Seeking Common Ground,* ed. Donna Gabaccia, 185–201. Westport, Conn.: Greenwood Press.

Reaume, Denise G. 1992. "The Social Construction of Women and the Possibility of Change: Unmodified Feminism Revisited." (Book Review.) *Canadian Journal of Women and Law,* vol. 5, no. 2: 463–83.

Recchini de Lattes, Z., and C. H. Wainerman. 1979. "Data from Household Surveys for the Analysis of Female Labor in Latin America and the Caribbean: Appraisal of Deficiencies and Recommendations for Dealing with Them." Santiago: CEPAL.

Reding, Andrew A. 1995. *Democracy and Human Rights in Mexico.* New York: World Policy Institute, World Policy Papers.

Reimers, David M. 1983. "An Unintended Reform: The 1965 Immigration Act and Third World Immigration to the U.S." *Journal of American Ethnic History* 3 (fall): 9–28.

Rodriguez, Nestor P., and J. R. Feagin. 1986. "Urban Specialization in the World System." *Urban Affairs Quarterly* 22, 2: 187–220.

Rosen, Fred, and Deidre McFayden, eds. 1995. *Free Trade and Economic Restructuring in Latin America.* A NACLA Reader. New York: Monthly Review Press.

Rosenau, J. N. 1992. "Governance, Order, and Change in World Politics." In *Governance without Government: Order and Change in World Politics,* eds. Rosenau and E. O. Czempiel, 1–29. Cambridge, U.K.: Cambridge University Press.

Rotzer, Florian. 1995. *Die Telepolis: Urbanität im digitalen Zeitalter.* Mannheim: Bollmann.

Ruggie, John Gerard. 1993. "Territoriality and Beyond: Problematizing Modernity in International Relations." *International Organization* 47, 1 (winter): 139–74.

Salacuse, Jeswald. 1991. *Making Global Deals: Negotiating in the International Marketplace.* Boston: Houghton Mifflin.

Salaff, J. 1981. *Working Daughters of Hong Kong.* New York: Cambridge University Press, ASA Rose Monograph Series.

Safa, Helan. 1995. *The Myth of the Male Breadwinner: Women and Industrialization in the Caribbean.*

Safa, H. I. 1981. "Sunway Shops and Female Employment: The Search for Cheap Labor," *Signs* 7, 2 (winter): 418–33.

Sandercock, L. and A. Forsyth. 1992. "A Gender Agenda: New Directions for Planning Theory." *APA Journal* 58: 49–59.

Sassen, Saskia. 1996. *Losing Control? Sovereignty in an Age of Globalization.* New York: Columbia University Press.

——. 1995. "Immigration and Local Labor Markets." In *The Economic Sociology of Immigration,* ed. A. Portes, op. cit.

——. 1995. "The State and the Global City: Notes Toward a Conception of Place-Centered Governance." *Competition and Change* 1:1.

——. 1994. *Cities in a World Economy.* Thousand Oaks, Calif.: Pine Forge/Sage Press.

——. 1994a. "The Informal Economy: Between New Developments and Old Regulations." *Yale Law Journal,* vol. 103, no. 8 (June): 2289–2304.

——. 1991. *The Global City: New York, London, Tokyo.* Princeton, N.J.: Princeton University Press.

——. 1988. *The Mobility of Labor and Capital: A Study in International Investment and Labor Flow.* Cambridge, U.K.: Cambridge University Press.

——. 1984a. "The New Labor Demand in Global Cities." In *Cities in Transformation,* ed. M.P. Smith. Beverly Hills, Calif.: Sage.

——. 1984b. "Foreign Investment: A Migration Push Factor?" In *Government and Policy* 2 (Nov.): 399–416. Special Issue on International Migration. Edited by Bennett and Muller. London: Pion.

——. 1982. "Recomposition and Peripheralization at the Core." In *Immigration and Changes in the New International Division of Labor,* 88–100, San Francisco: Synthesis Publications.

——. 1981a. "Toward a Conceptualization of Immigrant Labor." *Social Problems* 29 (Oct.).

——. 1981b. "Exporting Capital and Importing Labor." *Occasional Papers* No. 28. Center for Latin American and Caribbean Studies, New York University.

——. In progress. *Immigration Policy in a Global Economy: From National Crisis to Multilateral Management.* Under preparation for 20th Century Fund.

Sassen, Saskia, and B. Orloff. Forthcoming. "Trends in Purchases of Services in Multiple Industries over the last Twenty Years." Department of Urban Planning, Columbia University.

Sassen, Saskia, and Bradley J. Orlow. 1995. "The Growing Service Intensity in Economic Organization: Evidence from the Input-Output Tables." Department of Urban Planning, Columbia University, New York City.

Schmink, M. 1982. "La mujer en la economía en América Latina." Working Papers No. 11. Mexico: The Population Council, Latin America and Caribbean Regional Office. (June.)

Schwartz, Alex. 1992. "The Geography of Corporate Services: A Case Study of the New York Urban Region." *Urban Geography* 13, 1: 1–24.

Shah, N. M., and P. C. Smith. 1981. "Issues in the Labor Force Participation of Migrant Women in Five Asian Countries." Working Papers No. 19. East-West Population Institute, East-West Center. (Sept.)

Shank, G., ed. 1994. Japan Enters the 21st Century: A Special Issue of *Social Justice,* vol. 21, no. 2 (summer).

SIECA. 1991a. *III Reunión de la Organización Centroamericana de Migración.* Managua, Nicaragua: SIECA.

——. 1991b. *Antecedentes y Acuerdos de la Comisión Centroamericana de Migración.* Guatemala: OCAM.

Sikkink, Kathryn. 1993. "Human Rights, Principled Issue-Networks, and Sovereignty in Latin America." *International Organization* 47 (summer): 411–41.

Sinclair, Timothy J. 1994. "Passing Judgment: Credit Rating Processes as Regulatory Mechanisms of Governance in the Emerging World Order." *Review of International Political Economy* 1, 1 (spring): 133–58.

Singer, P. 1974. "Migraciones internas: consideraciones teóricas sobre

su estudio." *Las migraciones internas en América Latina.* Fichas
N. 38, Nueva Visión. Argentina.

Smith, David A., and Michael Timberlake. 1995. "Cities in Global Matrices: Toward Mapping the World System's City System." In
World Cities, op. cit., 79–97.

Smith, Joan, and Immanuel Wallerstein, eds. 1992. *Creating and
Transforming Households: The Constraints of the World-
Economy.* Cambridge and Paris: Cambridge University Press and
Maison des Sciences de l'Homme.

Social Justice. 1993. "Global Crisis, Local Struggles." Special Issue, vol.
20, no. 3–4 (fall–winter).

Solorzano Torres, R. 1983. "Female Mexican Immigrants in San Diego
County." Center for U.S.-Mexican Studies, University of California, San Diego. Research in progress.

Soysal, Yasmin Nuhoglu. 1994. *Limits of Citizenship.* Chicago: University of Chicago Press.

Spain, Daphne. 1992. *Gendered Spaces.* Chapel Hill: University of
North Carolina Press.

Spelman, Elizabeth V. 1988. *Inessential Woman: Problems of Exclusion
in Feminist Thought.*

Stanback, T. M., Jr., and T. J. Noyelle. 1982. *Cities in Transition: Changing Job Structures in Atlanta, Denver, Buffalo, Phoenix, Columbus
(Ohio), Nashville, Charlotte.* New Jersey: Allanheld, Osmun.

Standing, G. 1975. "Aspiration Wages, Migration and Female Employment." ILO: World Employment Programme, Working Paper No.
23 of the Population and Employment Project (Nov.).

Stein, Eduardo, 1993. "Las dinámicas migratorias en el Istmo Cen-
troamericano en la perspectiva de la integración y el imperativo
de la sostenibilidad." *Revista de la OIM sobre Migraciones en
América Latina*, vol. 11, no. 2 (Aug.): 5–51.

Steiner, Henry J. 1988. "Political Participation as a Human Right." *Harvard Human Rights Yearbook*, vol. 1 (spring): 77–134.

Stimson, Robert J. "Process of Globalisation and Economic Restructuring and the Emergence of a New Space Economy of Cities and
Regions in Australia." Presented at the Fourth International
Workshop on Technological Change and Urban Forum: Productive and Sustainable Cities, Berkeley, California, April 14–16,
1993.

Stoewsand, Corinne. 1996. "Women Building Cities." Ph.D. dissertation, Department of Urban Planning, Columbia University.

Storper, Michael, and Richard Walker. 1989. *The Capitalist Imperative: Territory, Technology, and Industrial Growth.* Oxford, U.K.: Blackwell.

Susser, Ida. 1982. *Norman Street.* New York: Oxford University Press.

Thranhardt, Dietrich, ed. 1992. *Europe: A New Immigration Continent.* Hamburg: Lit Verlag.

Tilly, Charles, ed. 1975. *The Formation of National States in Western Europe.* Princeton, N.J.: Princeton University Press.

Tinker, I., and M. Bramsen, eds. 1976. *Women Patterns of Trade in World Industry: An Empirical Study on Revealed Comparison Advantage.* (ID/281.) Vienna: UNIDO.

Todd, Graham. 1995. "'Going Global' in the Semi-Periphery: World Cities as Political Projects. The Case of Toronto." In *World Cities*, op. cit., 192–214.

Torales, Ponciano. 1993. *Migración e integración en el Cono Sur. La Experiencia del Mercosur.* Buenos Aires: OIM.

Trachtman, Joel. 1993. "International Regulatory Competition, Externalization, and Jurisdiction." *Harvard International Law Journal* 47.

Trubek, David M., et al. "Global Restructuring and the Law: The Internationalization of Legal Fields and Creation of Transnational Arenas." Working Paper Series on the Political Economy of Legal Change no. 1. Madison, Wis.: Global Studies Reseach Program, University of Wisconsin.

UNIDO. 1980. *Export Processing Zones in Developing Countries.* New York: UNIDO.

——. 1979. *World Industry Since 1960: Progress and Prospects.* (ID/229.) Vienna: UNIDO.

United Nations. 1996. *World Population Monitoring 1993. With a Special Report on Refugees.* New York: UN Department for Economic and Social Information and Policy Analysis, Population Division.

United Nations Conference on Trade and Development, University of Transnational Corporations. 1993. *World Investment Report 1993: Transnational Corporations and Integrated International Production.* New York: United Nations.

——. 1992. *World Investment Report 1992: Transnational Corporations as Engines of Growth.* New York.

U.S. Department of Commerce, Bureau of the Census. 1983. Census of Population 1980. *Characteristics of the Population. General and Social Characteristics. U.S. Summary.* Washington, D.C.

Waldinger, Roger, and Greta Gilbertson. 1994. "Immigrants' Progress: Ethnic and Gender Differences Among U.S. Immigrants in the 1980s." *Sociological Perspectives* 37, 3: 431–44.

Wallerstein, Immanuel. 1990. "Culture as the Ideological Battleground of the Modern World-System." In *Global Culture: Nationalism, Globalization and Modernity,* ed. Mike Featherstone. London: Sage.

——. 1974. *The Modern World System,* vol. 1. New York: Academic Press.

Ward, Kathyrn B., ed. 1990. *Women Workers and Global Restructuring.* Ithaca, N.Y.: ILR Press.

Weil, Patrick. 1991. *La France et ses étrangers.* Paris: Calmann-Levy.

Weiner, Myron. 1995. *The Global Migration Crisis.* New York: Harper Collins.

Wheeler, James O. 1986. "Corporate Spatial Links with Financial Institutions: The Role of the Metropolitan Hierarchy." *Annals of the Association of American Geographers* 76, 2: 262–74.

Wong, A. K. 1980. *Economic Development and Women's Place: Women in Singapore. International Reports: Women and Society.* London: Change.

World Bank Staff. 1975. "Internal Migration in Less Developed Countries." Washington, D.C.: International Bank for Reconstruction and Development, Bank Staff Working Paper No. 215. Prepared by L. Y. L. Yap. (Sept.)

Yamanaka, K. 1991. *Asian and Latin American Workers in Japan: Should Japan Open the Unskilled Labor Market?* Iowa: Department of Sociology, Grinnell College.

Young, Alma H., and Jyaphia Christos-Rodgers. 1995. "Resisting Racially Gendered Space: The Women of the St. Thomas Resident Council, New Orleans." In *Marginal Spaces,* ed. Michael Peter Smith, 95–112. Comparative Urban and Community Research, vol. 5.

Young, O. R. 1989. *International Cooperation: Building Regimes for Natural Resources and the Environment.* Ithaca, N.Y.: Cornell University Press.

Youssef, N. H. 1974. "Women and Work in Developing Societies." University of California, Berkeley, Institute of International Studies.

Zhou, Min. 1992. *Chinatown*. Philadelphia: Temple University Press.

Zolberg, Aristide R. 1990. "The Roots of U.S. Refugee Policy." In *Immigration and U.S. Foreign Policy*, eds. R. Tucker, Charles B. Keely, and L. Wrigley. Boulder, Colo.: Westview Press.

Index